Authentic
NORWEGIAN
Cooking

Astrid Karlsen Scott

Nordic Adventures

Olympia, Washington USA

First printed June 1995

10 9 8 7 6 5 4

Printed in the United States of America

Scott, Astrid Karlsen
Authentic Norwegian Cooking (Ekte Norsk Mat)
Includes bibliographical references and index.
ISBN 0-9634339-7-0

Other books by Astrid Karlsen Scott:

Ekte Norsk Mat (Authentic Norwegian Cooking) Out of print
Ekte Norsk Jul, Vol. I (Traditional Norwegian Christmas)
Ekte Norsk Jul, Vol. II (Traditional Norwegian Christmas Foods)
Ekte Norsk Jul, Vol. III (Traditional Norwegian Christmas Songs, Stories and Poems)
Norway's Fest Days
Norway's Best (Cheese and other Delicacies) Out of print

Disclaimer

This book is intended to be an informational resource, and should be used as a general guide and not an ultimate source of Norwegian cooking.

Every effort has been made to make this book as complete and factual as possible. The author and Nordic Adventures have neither responsibility nor liability to any person or entity with respect to any loss or damage caused, or alleged to be caused, directly or indirectly by the information in this book.

Any person not wishing to be bound by the above may return this book to the publisher for a full refund.

Published by:

Nordic Adventures
7602 Holiday Valley Dr. N.W.
Olympia, Wa. 98502-9513

Printed in the United States by:

Publishers Press
P.O. Box 27408
Salt Lake City, Utah 84127-0408

Dedicated to all those who
generously contributed to this work;
to preserve the traditional Norwegian Cuisine.

Contents

Acknowledgments

There are many people who contribute, often unaware and over a period of time, to the writing of a book. For instance, from childhood I grew up around women who were good cooks, who served nutritious and lovingly prepared food. They did not know then, nor did I, that they created memories for future generations.

Likewise, on my visits to Norway, opportunities to sample the best in traditional Norwegian food, created a curiosity within me which also contributed to this book. I wish to thank all the excellent Norwegian cooks, who, surely unwittingly, inspired me to keep Norwegian food traditions alive in America.

I deeply appreciate the assistance and liberal help of the following experts in Norway and USA, Anna-Karin Lindstad, Division Manager, Nutrition and Home Economics Department at Tine, Liv Gregersen Kongsten, Home Economics Consultant at Forma A/S, Britt Kåsen, Home Economic Consultant, Office of Information for Fruit and Vegetables, Guri Tveit, Home Economic Consultant, Office of Information for Egg and Poultry, Even Nordahl, Office of Information for Meat, Ingrid Espelid Hovig, Culinary Expert, TV Chef and Senior TV-Producer Norwegian Broadcasting Corporation, Bodil Bergan, Chief Guide, A/S Freia, Norwegian Seafood Export Council, King Oscar, USA, Inc., Norwegian Potato Industries, Eva Mælseter, Food Editor, Hjemmet, Ellen C. Daatland, Food Editor, Familien, Chr. Schibsteds Forlag, J.W. Cappelens Forlag A/S, Torunn Linneberg, Olympia Utvikling, Troll Park A/S.

I acknowledge the favorite recipes shared by Dr. Thor Heyerdahl, Eva Johannessen, Edith Jaques, Else Rønnevig, Sigrid Juul Røset, Marianne Lindboe, and Helga Jonassen.

My deep appreciation to award-winning artist Randy Clark for the book cover, and to my son John William Scott. For generous help with pictures of Norway I am thankful to Mittet Co., and Norwegian Seafood Export Council.

Many thanks to Marleigh (Martha Harrison), and my brother Steinar Bjarne Karlsen for illustrations, and to Laurie Burdett for typesetting at all hours day or night.

To my father-in-law, Melvin McCabe Scott, Sr. I am grateful for his generous support of, and editing this work, and to Edith Jaques for help with proofreading.

I greatly appreciate the profesionalism of Lyle Mumford, Publishers Press, Salt Lake City, Utah, whose experience and knowledge was a great help in the final stages of this work.

And always, to my husband Scotty, our children, their spouses, and my grandchildren, I am thankful and secure in your eternal love and reassurance.

Introduction

Norway is a winter-land where snow covers most of the country for more than half of the year. It also is a land of mountains where only 3% of the land can be cultivated.

Norway has a long rugged coast with many fjords, and half of the country lies north of the Arctic Circle. However the weather is milder than one would expect because of the Gulf Stream which crosses the Atlantic from America. People in the past subsisted on minuscule land because the sea provided an abundance of fish.

Nature and climatic conditions caused the Norwegians to adapt to the circumstances where they lived. Diverse food traditions developed through the centuries in north and south Norway, as well as in the East and the West.

Notwithstanding, mingled with these food traditions, a deep friendliness and sincere hospitality unfolded toward strangers. In the ancient Edda poems, *Håvamål,* it says, "... the man who has traveled in the mountains needs food and drink."

It is self-evident that people took advantage of the summers because of the long difficult winters. They needed time to till the ground, to plant and harvest crops, yet in many places the climate was such that the grain did not ripen. The people received their main nourishment from grain, meat, fish and milk. The fish-farmers along the coast always kept a cow and a few sheep. Inland they sowed barley and oats on the minuscule land available. They would say "Grain is borrowed from God", or often, "Grain is life."

The life-sustaining potato was not grown in Norway until the late 1700's. The so-called potato-priests from their pulpits encouraged people to cultivate potatoes. Today many Norwegians clearly remember the war years, 1940-1945. In many homes hunger would have been unbearable had we not been able to grow potatoes.

The Norwegian people learned early from experience to preserve food. They learned various conservation methods. Cattle and goats gave little milk during the winter months, but the summer-milk was churned to butter and made into cheese. Many Norwegian cheeses have a long history, and even today we think that *gammalosten* - a pungent sour milk cheese - and the goat cheese are among the best. Many new cheeses have a milder taste like the *gudbrandsdalosten* something many enjoy.

The old farmers attempted to be self-sufficient. However, no matter how remote some farms were, salt was necessary for all. Most meat was salted down. Fresh meat was provided only for certain days, like church holidays and other important celebrations. From the middle ages the grain was ground in water gristmills. Up to the 1800's grains were mostly used for flatbread and porridge. Porridge, a food for all, was often eaten with sour milk, a piece of cured meat or a few pieces of flatbread. Porridge was *vassgraut,* (a gruel usually made with barley), and *rømmegraut,* a sour cream porridge. *Vassgraut* has saved many a life. Sour cream porridge (served with sugar, cinnamon and currant juice) is enjoyed as a celebration food even today wherever people cherish Norwegian food traditions.

Fresh meat was available in the fall when the animals were slaughtered. Many claim that fårikål - lamb with cabbage - a typical dish served at that time is our national dish. One could discuss how many spices to use. It was not a problem for Norwegians who managed with whatever nature provided.

Lutefish and *rakørret* (cured trout) had a bad reputation in the old topographical writings, but, is today, a much enjoyed (and expensive) food served in restaurants and homes.

Notwithstanding, there was a marked difference between *hverdagsmat,* everyday food, and foods served on fest days. Heavy physical labor required nourishment first. However, at weddings and funerals, and other important social events, neighbors helped each other with what was called *sendings*, a beautiful expression of unity by people who out of necessity toiled heavily. They cherished the security and enjoyment of these gatherings.

Since World War II many foreign food traditions have been introduced to Norway, but simultaneously, there is a deeper appreciation for the old food traditions. We cling to the simple food of two open-face pieces of bread, in place of lunch. On 17th of May (Norway's Constitution Day), we are only too pleased to be invited for sour cream porridge and cured meat.[*]

With her thorough knowledge of cooking, and of Norwegian recipes and a background in tradition and popular food usage in Norway, Astrid Karlsen Scott has produced a book which rightly deserves the title of *Authentic Norwegian Cooking*.

The translated poems and her own youth and childhood memories from Norway add much to the charm and genuinity of her work, and also make it enjoyable reading apart from the recipes.

Dr. Olav Bø
Professor of Philosophy

---

[*] Professor Bø, is one of Norway's foremost folklorists, and has lectured at universities in several foreign lands. He has authored many books and has co-authored many works. His book *Skiing throughout History* was one of the quality books included in the Cultural Program of the XVII Olympic Winter Games at Lillehammer in 1994.

Traditional Norwegian Table Prayer

*This traditional Norwegian table prayer is
known throughout Norway. It is used in the
schools, at official gatherings, in the homes
and the royal castle. Quite often it is sung,
and most likely every Norwegian child
knows it by heart.*

<u>Norwegian</u>   <u>English</u>

Before the meal:

I Jesu navn går vi til bords   We go to the table in Jesus name
Å spise, drikke på ditt ord   To eat and drink by Your word
Deg Gud til ære, oss til gavn   To God the honor, ours the gain
Så får vi mat i Jesu navn.   We receive our food in Jesus name.

Amen   Amen

After the meal:

I Jesu navn til bords we satt   We sat at the table in Jesus name
Og fikk fra Herrens hånd vår mat   And received food from His hand
Til gavn for legem og for sjel   To nourish our body and our soul
Gud lat oss det bekomme vel.   God let it bless our lives we pray.

Amen   Amen

Appetizers

Appetizers, when shared in a friendship or family circle, brings relaxation and enjoyment. It affords people an opportunity to unwind before the main meal, and it shows a caring host or hostess. In lives crowded with responsibilities it enhances the dinner hour, and the time allocated for enjoyment. It does not require an immense effort of time, or means, only a little creativity.

There are numerous foods you can attach to toothpicks by themselves or in combinations and position into fruits or vegetables. You can use a combination of ingredients for example, Jarlsberg cheese and radishes, cocktail sausages broiled with a piece of bacon, or olives and cheese. Or thread separately, fresh small mushrooms, green or black olives, small pickles, berries or bits of fruit on to the toothpick. Attach all of one kind into a fruit or intermingle them so as to form a colorful pattern.

Walnuts and Cheese (Valnøtter og ost)

Walnut halves
Normanna cheese
  (Norwegian Roquefort)

Butter or light cream
Green grapes

Walnuts taste excellent with cheese. Normanna or Roquefort has a piquant taste, try mixing them with a little cream or butter. Or use cream cheese mixed with crushed, well drained pineapple.

Rub cheese through a sieve, or mash with a fork and blend with a little butter (room temperature) or cream. Place a small amount of cheese on whole walnut halves, press a grape into the cheese on one half and top with the other half. Attach a toothpick into the center and place into desired fruit. To give added color place fruit on bed of curly endive.

Meatball Snacks (Kjøttkakepinnemat)

Make bite-size Norwegian meatballs. Attach to a toothpick. Add a small piece of marinaded, drained well, cucumber or small piece of Boston lettuce (for marinade see Cucumber salad). Place into desired vegetable.

Cheese Trays (Ostebretter)

Make some great cheese platters with fruit for an evening snack, a light supper, or desserts after a light buffet, or dinner.

Serve cheese with *kjeks*, a dry cookie-like cracker, hardtack, or any kind of bread that does not clash with the cheese flavors. Vegetables such as celery, radishes, tomatoes, or cucumbers taste delicious with cheese. Or add fruit such as sliced apples, orange or tangerine wedges, kiwi fruit, pears or grapes. If you use apple slices or bananas, use a little lemon juice to prevent the fruit from darkening.

You need a minimum of two to three different kinds of cheese for just the two of you, or for several people you might want up to five or six different kinds of cheese. For example, Ridder, Brie, Jarlsberg, Norzola, and a typical dessert cheese like Ridder. And among Norwegian-Americans, no matter what the occasion, there will be someone on the lookout for the brown, sweet goat cheese. Choose cheese with different flavors and textures, something for everyone to enjoy.

Some soft cheeses come in their own little containers and look best in these, place them directly on the cheese tray. The hard cheese may be left in a whole piece or partly pre-sliced. Cut into logs and stack crisscross, or cube some of the cheeses and place in small clear glass bowls with toothpicks nearby.

When arranging a tray, take color and flavor into consideration. Strategically place the fruit or vegetables to be used in between the cheeses. Depending on the size of your platter you may add crackers, hardtack, or bread sticks directly to the platter. If you have several types place on a separate platter or in a breadbasket with a colorful doily.

Marinated Edam Cheese (Marinért edamerost)

I shall always be appreciative to Anna-Karin Lindstad of Tine for sharing this recipe with me. It is a marvelous delicacy to give as a gift at Christmas, serve guests or when you yearn for a little godbit for yourself. Serve with crackers or dark bread.

11 oz., scant (300 g) Edam cheese	1 tbsp. oregano
1 red paprika, cut in strips	1 tbsp. thyme
1¼ cups (3 dl) olive oil	1 tbsp. green peppercorns
⅞ cup (2 dl) white vinegar	2 garlic cloves
1 tbsp. red pepper, finely chopped	

Dice cheese the size of sugar cubes. Prick with a fork to allow the marinade to be absorbed. Mix all ingredients for marinade in a heavy-bottomed casserole and bring to a boil. Cool. Layer cheese and paprika in a jar and pour marinade over all. Cover and chill. Keeps 2-3 weeks in refrigerator. Let come to room temperature before serving, allowing cheese to come to full-flavor.

Ridder Appetizer (Ridder appetittvekker)

A beautiful, tasty, nutritious and simple appetizer made with Ridder *ost*, the distinctive dessert cheese.

Ridder cheese	Lemon juice	Mint leaves
Honeydew melon, ripe	Strawberries	

Cut a long strip of Ridder cheese with cheese slicer while cheese is still chilled. Fold it up like a rose. Slice 5 small wedges of honeydew melon, about 1 inch (2½ cm) thick, and cut in half. Sprinkle with lemon juice and place like a pin wheel on a clear glass plate. Place your cheese flower in the center, and garnish with mint leaves and strawberries.

Open-Face Sandwich Tidbits (Appetittbiter)

A tray of bite-size sandwiches will get any meal off to a good start. They should be made just before your guests arrive so they will be fresh, crisp and tasty. Use firm bread and cut out desired shapes, rectangles, rounds, diamonds, etc. Because they are small, use toothpicks to hold the toppings in place. Any of the sandwich fillings printed in this book can be used, but in bite-size portions. Decorate with cocktail onions, small olives, slices of cucumbers, cocktail tomato wedges, chopped green onions, chives, parsley and dill sprigs. Whichever combination you choose, make it colorful. And always top bread with a small piece of crisp lettuce before adding sandwich ingredients. Display your appetizers on a serving platter covered with an attractive doily. Figure on 3 to 4 cocktail sandwiches per person. Here are a few samples;

Brie (Brie): Add small pie shaped piece with grapes or walnut half.
Cucumber (Slangeagurk): Slice thin, top with fresh small shrimp, wedge of liver paté with piece of tomato, or shell-fish salad. Garnish.
Edam cheese (Edamerost): Add sliced olives or radishes.
Eggs (Egg): To hard boiled egg slices, add lox rolled in chopped chives and fastened with a toothpick, or use anchovies and add some dill.
Eggs, scrambled (Eggerøre): Add ham and chives or bacon and tomato.
Roquefort cheese (Roquefort): Add small seedless grape clusters, or fresh cherries with stem.
Salami (Salamipølse): Fold a slice of salami and hold together with two cocktail onions speared on a toothpick.
Sardines in tomato sauce: Need no addition but a piece of Boston lettuce tucked under in one corner.

Sardine Spread (Sardinpålegg)

2 cans 3¾ oz. (106 g) each Norway sardines in oil, drained	3 tbsp. fresh dill, chopped or 1 tbsp. dill weed, dry	*Horseradish and mustard blended with*
4 oz. (115 g) light cream cheese, softened	3 tbsp. horseradish, prepared	*delicate sardines from*
½ cup (60 g) celery, chopped	2 tbsp. yellow mustard, prepared	*Norway give this*
¼ cup (35 g) red onion, chopped	Assorted crackers or bite-size firm bread	*creamy spread its snappy flavor.*

Combine all ingredients, except crackers or bread, with a fork, blend thoroughly. Serve mounded in a bowl or in red and/or green bell pepper halves. Surround with crackers. Can be prepared and refrigerated up to two days ahead. **Makes 2 cups (5 dl).**

Open-Face Sandwiches (Smørbrød)

Few foods are as adaptable to ones various moods or time of day as open-face sandwiches. They are nourishing and inviting, and quickly and easily prepared for drop in guests. They are just as suitable for a luncheon as for a light supper or an evening snack. The latter is traditionally enjoyed, accompanied by a hot cup of coffee, cocoa, a cake or cookies. You can serve bite-size sandwiches as appetizers, or fruit sandwiches as a special treat. Or salad sandwiches and hot scrumptious sandwiches as a whole meal. *Smørbrød*, literally translated, means buttered bread. The bread must be of firm consistency and thinly sliced. *Smørbrød* are served in Norwegian restaurants in a staggering variety and even the most experienced *smørbrød* fan, at times, must take a moment to meditate before making a choice. Daily, families leave for school or work with their lunch boxes packed with their favorite *smørbrød*, or with a surprise creation. Though, like in America, regrettably, more people are finding "fast foods" are becoming a part of their daily routine. When Norwegians *drar på tur,* go on picnics to the woods or mountains, or *drar på stranda,* go to the beach, a tasty variety of *smørbrød*, carefully packed, is usually included.

Certain rules must be followed to insure success of this delicacy:

- ♥ **Organize. This will ensure the enjoyment of the entire project.**
- ♥ **Prepare a working area large enough to accommodate all necessary ingredients which have been assembled in advance.**
- ♥ **Use soft, flavored or unflavored butter. Arrange the bread slices in a row on a work area and butter all bread at once, unless, you are preparing a tremendous amount.**
- ♥ **Spread entire surface of each slice to the very edges.**
- ♥ **Keep uppermost in mind that the sandwich filling and the tidbits used for decoration should complement each other. Just as important as taste is the chosen color combination. Open-face sandwiches should tempt the eye as well as please the palate.**
- ♥ **When the *smørbrød* are completed, arrange them attractively on a large platter, making sure colors blend for maximum eye appeal. Cover immediately with plastic wrap to prevent them from drying out or flavor from escaping.**
- ♥ **There are numerous varieties of bread, and choosing the right one is important. Rye and pumpernickel are widely used as they are moist, yet firm in texture. Another good choice is hardtack, available in light, dark or rye. Keep in mind the flavor of the bread should blend with the sandwich toppings. Bread should be thinly sliced about $\frac{1}{8}$ inch (3 mm) thickness. Whichever type of bread is chosen, light or dark, it should be firm.**

Sandwiches with Shellfish (Smørbrød med skalldyr)

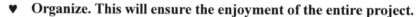

A discriminating guest will be pleased when served lobster, crab or shrimp sandwiches. These sandwiches are more expensive than other types, but worth it! Mayonnaise can be blended with the shellfish or added decoratively from a tube after the fish has been arranged on the bread. The use of mayonnaise is optional. Just a dab of mayonnaise topped with a lemon slice or wedge will suffice.

Be generous with the filling. Use 3-4 ounces (85-115 g), depending on the size of bread slice. When prepared thoughtfully these sandwiches will serve as a complete meal. Any *firm* bread will do, white or whole grain.

Shrimp Salad *(Rekesalat)*

White firm bread
Butter
Asst. lettuce, dark and
  light greens

3-4 oz. (85-115 g) shrimp, small
Cocktail tomato slices
Dill or parsley
Lemon slice and paprika

Lobster or crab sandwiches may be prepared in the same manner.

Place a crisp lettuce leaf on buttered bread. Heap the shrimp blended with mayonnaise or not, on top of lettuce. Mayonnaise may be added decoratively using a tube. Slit a thin lemon slice to the center, twist and place on sandwich. Place some fresh dill and tomato on the side. Sprinkle with paprika.

Italian Salad *(Italiensk salat)*

3 cups (7½ dl) cabbage, finely
  shredded and well packed
¾ cup (1¾ dl) mayonnaise
½ tsp. lemon juice
1 small carrot, barely cooked,
  and grated

Pinch of white pepper
½ apple, grated
2 slices of ham, diced
1 small sour pickle, chopped
Tomato & parsley
Lemon slice

The origin and name of this salad is a mystery, since cabbage is a staple food, and has been served continually for generations. Maybe it was a fancy name to add some excitement to dark, cold winter days. Nonetheless, it is as much a part of Norwegian food fare as sardines. It can be served on sandwiches or as a salad in a bowl.

Blend all ingredients using two forks. Arrange a lettuce leaf on buttered pumpernickel bread. Place on this a generous amount of Italian salad. Decorate with a tomato wedge, a lemon slice or a slice of cucumber slit to the center and twisted, plus a sprig of parsley. **Makes 3½-4 cups.**

Sardine Salad Sandwich *(Sardinsalat smørbrød)*

6 slices dark bread
½ tsp. grated lemon peel
6 Boston lettuce leaves
2 cups (5 dl) cottage cheese
Red onion rings

2 red-skinned apples, medium
1 can 3¾ oz. (106 g) Norwegian sardines,
  drained
Mustard, mayonnaise, optional
Lemon juice
Parsley

Mix cottage cheese with lemon peel. Place a lettuce leaf on top of buttered bread, and spread ⅓ cup of cheese on each slice. Slice apples, brush with lemon juice, and arrange in overlapping rows over cottage cheese. Top with onion rings and sardines. Serve with mustard-mayonnaise if desired.

Mustard Mayonnaise: Mix ⅔ cup (1½ dl) mayonnaise with 1 teaspoon Dijon mustard and 1 tablespoon lemon juice. **Makes 6 sandwiches.**

Simple Sardine Sandwich *(Enkelt sardinsmørbrød)*

There surely is nothing more Norwegian than sardines. By having a few cans of sardines on hand, you always have ready fare when you want a special treat or for unexpected guests. Serve on firm, dark or white bread, plain or buttered bread or with a little mayonnaise, or make up your own creations.

Sardines in tomato sauce or oil
Lettuce

Lemon slice
Paprika

Butter a firm slice of bread evenly. If only large slices are available, cut bread into rectangular shape. Place a crisp lettuce leaf on top. Add two or three sardines, decorate with a lemon slice cut to the center and twisted. Sprinkle with paprika.

Saturday Afternoon Sandwich (Lørdagens smørbrød)

Treat your taste buds to this perfect Saturday afternoon sandwich, using a medley of classic ingredients with delicious Norway Sardines.

4 slices rye bread
¼ cup (½ dl) cream cheese, softened
4 lettuce leaves
8 tomato slices, thick

1 can 3¾ oz. (106 g) Norway sardines in oil, drained
4 oz. (115 g) Jarlsberg cheese, sliced
2 dill pickles, small
Fresh herb sprigs

Spread each slice of bread with 1 tablespoon of the cream cheese, then top with a lettuce leaf, 2 tomato slices, several sardines and rolled-up cheese slice. Slice pickle lengthwise and garnish, and add herbs. **Makes 4 sandwiches.**

Pickled Herring (Sursild)

Always has and always will be a favorite among Norwegians.

Firm dark rye bread
Boston lettuce
Pickled herring
Apple slice
Dab of sour cream
Fresh dill

Or try:
Boston lettuce
4 slices of boiled potato
Pickled herring
Red onion slices, if needed
Fresh dill

Butter coarse, dark or pumpernickel bread lightly. Top with Boston lettuce leaf. Cover generously with herring and onion slices from the pickled herring. Add a dab of sour cream, an apple slice (sprinkled with lemon juice) and a sprig of dill or parsley.

Herring Salad Sandwich (Sildesalat)

2 herring fillets, soaked
1 Granny Smith apple, small
1 tbsp. onion, finely chopped
1 gherkin, chopped

2 eggs, hard boiled
1 tbsp. mustard, sweet
½ cup, scant (1¼ dl) sour cream

Heavily salted herring should be soaked a minimum of 12 hours. Soaking the herring in a mixture of milk and water assures a firm white flesh. Finely chop fillets, unpeeled apple, onion and gherkin. Divide eggs, remove egg yolk and save. Chop egg white finely and add to herring mixture. Mix mustard with sour cream and carefully blend with other ingredients. Refrigerate over night to develop flavor. Scoop salad on to a lettuce leaf on top of bread slice, top with chopped egg yolks, and dash of paprika.

Ham Sandwich (Skinkesmørbrød)

Adding a little mustard or horseradish to the butter gives a piquant flavor to this marvelous sandwich.

Boston lettuce
Boiled ham slice
Jarlsberg cheese, cut in strips

2 cucumber slices
Slices of hard boiled egg
Pickle and tomato wedge
Parsley

Butter bread, place lettuce on top. Fold ham slice in two, top with cheese in a criss-cross pattern (lots of it), and decorate as desired.

Liver Paté *(Leverpostei)*

Liver paté	**Beets, pickled or**
Bacon strips, fried crisp	**pickles of your choice**
Marinated mushrooms or	**Boston lettuce**

Butter bread. Place a lettuce leaf on a slice of dark bread, top with liver paté. Add 1 or 2 slices of crisp, drained bacon and a few mushroom pieces. Or instead of bacon and mushrooms, add pickles or beets and a small sprig of parsley. Yummy!

Use homemade paté or ready made liverwurst; but the liverwurst you buy will never have the flavor of homemade paté.

Head Cheese *(Sylte)*

Head cheese
Pickles of choice, or beets, pickled

Butter dark bread. Cover with slices of head cheese and decorate to taste.

Breakfasts during the Christmas week never were complete without this delicacy. Make your own or buy at your import delicatessen, but your homemade sylte will be best.

Egg Sandwiches *(Eggesmørbrød)*

Egg sandwiches with a variety of accompaniments are ever popular in Norway. Try some with sliced, hard boiled eggs. Or the many combinations used with scrambled eggs such as; sardines in tomato sauce, kippers, ham, gravlaks, smoked eel and many more.

Egg and tomato: Add lettuce, tomato, parsley, salt and pepper.
Egg and Anchovies or Herring Tidbits (Gaffelbiter): Use Scandinavian anchovies, as those from southern Europe are too salty. Add lettuce, anchovies or herring tidbits, a sprig of parsley, salt and pepper.

Scrambled Eggs with Bacon *(Eggerøre med flesk)*

Egg(s)	**Salt and pepper**
2 strips bacon	**Chives**
1 tbsp. milk	**Tomato and Boston lettuce**

Fry bacon until crisp and drain on paper towel. Butter bread. Beat egg, add milk, salt, pepper and chives. Remove all grease but two tablespoon. Pour egg mixture into hot pan, and over low heat, allow to congeal slightly. Then stir carefully making sure the eggs do not brown. But do not stir too much - the eggs should be firm and lumpy, but not dry. Place the eggs on bread, add the crisp bacon. Tuck a lettuce leaf under eggs in one corner. Sprinkle with more chives if desired, and add tomato wedges.

Smoked Eel *(Røket ål)*

Smoked eel is another delicacy with such a distinct, pleasing flavor that it is best to keep the sandwiches simple. Leave plain with just a touch of real mayonnaise, a lemon slice, and paprika, or add a spoonful of scrambled eggs.

Scrambled Eggs with Lox (Eggerøre med røkelaks)

1 tbsp. margarine
1 egg
1 tbsp. milk
½ tsp. chives, chopped

1 slice lox
Tomato wedge
Parsley or dill

Whisk egg, milk and chives together. Melt margarine in frying pan and add eggs. Stir to scramble. Butter bread, heap egg in the center and add lox. Add a tomato wedge and a tuft of dill or parsley.

Sumptuous Sandwich Cake (Luksuriøs smørbrødkake)

Smørbrødkake filled with shrimp, crab, lox and cheese is reserved for the most memorable occasions like 17th of May, (Norway's Independence Day), or other distinctive days when we desire to *fråsse*, revel in the occasion. It takes a little extra time to prepare, but there are occasions when we want the extraordinary.

Sandwich cake:

Prepare the *cake* the day before. It can be filled hours in advance of serving. Leaving just the garnish till the last minute.

1 pkg. yeast
2 cups (5 dl) water, lukewarm
4 ¾ cups (12 dl) flour, or more

1 tsp. salt
2 tsp. sugar
2 tsp. oil

Mix yeast with water. If dry yeast is used mix with flour. Add all other ingredients and work into a pliant dough, about 6-8 minutes. Cover and let rise until double in bulk. Remove to lightly floured board. Knead until smooth. Press it evenly into a large 12-inch (30 cm) greased and floured spring form pan. Cover and set to rise approx. 30 minutes. Place in preheated oven at 435°F (225°C) on the lowest rack for 25 minutes, or until done. Remove from oven, place on rack and cover with a damp cloth. Cool.
Makes 1 round loaf cake.

Filling 1:
3½ ounce (100 g) cream cheese with
   a little finely chopped crab
   or shrimp added
3 tbsp. butter, room temperature

¼ cup (½ dl) sour cream,
2 tbsp. fresh dill, chopped
1 tbsp. lemon juice

Filling 2:
1 6⅛ oz. (170 g) can tuna,
   drained
1 14 oz. (395 g) can asparagus
2 tbsp. butter, room temperature
1 tbsp. mayonnaise, light

½ cup, scant (1 dl) sour cream,
   light
2 tbsp. fresh dill, chopped
Touch of white pepper

Filling 3:
5½ oz. (165 g) mayonnaise, light
3½ oz. (100 g) crab, minced

2 tbsp. dill

Garnish:

1 head red leaf lettuce	10 radishes, medium
5 slices lox, approx.	½ to 1 lemon
18 oz. (500 g) small to medium shrimp	2 inches (5 cm) European
5 oz. (150 g) Jarlsberg cheese, cut	cucumber, sliced thin
in strips	Fresh dill

Cut crust from bread and slice in three layers. (It is easier to cut if partially frozen).

Filling 1:   Mix all ingredients and spread across bottom layer.

Filling 2:   Chop tuna and asparagus and mix with remaining ingredients. Add second layer on top of first and add the filling and spread to the edges. Place third layer on top.

Filling 3:   Mix the ingredients and spread on top and around the cake. Cover and chill until ready to garnish.

Garnish: Prepare by cutting lox into strips large enough to roll into "roses". Tear salad leaves apart, wash and dry on paper towel. Peel the shrimp. Make flowers from radishes by making deep cuts down towards the stem. Place in cold water awhile and they will spread apart. Slice cucumber and lemon.

To decorate: Gently press proper size salad leaves around the edge of the cake. Stick the cheese strips upright into center. Place other ingredients in groups, and decorate in between with thin cucumber, lemon slices and radish roses. If not served right away, cover carefully and refrigerate.

Hot Sandwiches (Varme smørbrød)

These sandwiches can be used as an appetizer with a light supper, first course, or a luncheon. The filling can be fried, baked or broiled. Use firm bread, preferably day old, or hard rolls hollowed out (save the inside for crumbs) and fill with a favorite tasty filling.

Hard Rolls with Shellfish (Rundstykker med skalldyr)

Hard rolls	Parsley
White sauce	Paprika
Lobster, shrimp, crab or clams	

Slice the hard rolls in two lengthwise. Scoop out and lightly butter inside of the rolls. Make thick white sauce. Leave out some of the milk substituting part of the clam juice if canned clams are being used. Exact portions of the shellfish is not important - add more or less of whichever fish happens to be your favorite. Add the chopped fish to the cream sauce.

Fill the hard roll shells with creamed mixture and place in oven until both bread and the filling is heated through. Decorate with parsley sprig and sprinkle with paprika.

Other fillings:

- ♥ Fried ground round or chuck (well drained) decorated with fried onion and sprinkled with Jarlsberg or other Norwegian cheeses.
- ♥ Creamed eggs with crumbled bacon and shredded cheese.
- ♥ Fried sausage, crumbled, decorated with stewed apples.
- ♥ Mushrooms, cooked, whole, and melted cheese.
- ♥ Scrambled eggs and chives, with herring tidbits, *gaffel-biter.*
- ♥ Fishpudding, chopped and blended with white sauce, with a touch of curry.

Fishpudding (Fiskepudding)

These sandwiches are always welcome and can be served hot or cold. You may use canned, fresh or frozen fishpudding.

Pumpernickel bread	Fish pudding
Butter	Onion, sliced
Boston lettuce	Parsley

Slice the pudding in even, medium thick slices. Brown in butter. Remove from pan and keep warm. Sauté onion until transparent. Butter pumpernickel bread and cover with slices of fishpudding topped with fried onion. Tuck a small lettuce leaf in on the side and sprinkle with parsley. Delicious served with sliced tomatoes and cucumber salad.

Pork with Sweet/Sour Cabbage (Svinestek med surkål)

The following two sandwiches may be served hot or cold. A dab of added lingonberries is a must.

Boston lettuce	Red apple wedges, unpeeled
Pork, cooked and sliced	Lemon juice
Sweet/sour cabbage	Prunes and parsley

Butter dark bread, add lettuce, and slices of pork. Add a tablespoon or two of well-drained sweet-sour cabbage. Top with a couple of apple wedges, brushed with lemon juice, and parsley.

Pork with Stewed Apples (Svinestek med epler)

Boston lettuce	Orange slice, thin
Pork, sliced	Lingonberries, optional
Stewed apples	Parsley

Butter dark bread. Place lettuce on top. Roll two large pork slices around a spoonful or two of stewed apples. Place on top of lettuce leaf. Slit orange slice to center, twist and add to sandwich with some fresh parsley.

Dinner Sandwich (Middagssmørbrød)

4 slices oatmeal bread, toasted
1 lb. (450 g) country sausage
1 onion, sliced

1 apple, cored and sliced into 4 rings
1 can 3¾ oz. (115 g) Norwegian sardines,
  drained

Shape sausage into four patties. Brown slowly in skillet; remove and keep warm. Sauté onion in 2 tablespoons of the drippings; add apple rings, cover and cook for 6 to 8 minutes. Butter toast lightly. Place sausage patty on toast; spoon apple and onion rings over all and top with sardines.

I do not know what the forest trolls eat besides porridge and the soups their hags stir with their 6 feet long noses. Notwithstanding, if they could get their hands on these sandwiches, no doubt they would be very pleased.

Sausage Mushroom Sandwich (Pølse og soppsmørbrød)

Bratwurst or small cocktail sausages
Butter
Flour
Cream, light

Mushrooms, canned, whole
Tomato
Parsley

Butter choice of bread. Whole grain homemade is fabulous. Slice bratwurst crosswise or lengthwise in desired size and fry in a little butter. Set aside. Prepare cream sauce from flour, butter, cream and liquid from mushrooms. Simmer 5 to 7 minutes. Add mushrooms. Place sausages around outer edges of bread and spoon the creamed mushrooms in the center. Bake briefly in medium hot oven. Decorate with tomato and parsley.

Ground Round Patties (Karbonadekaker)

1 onion, large
¾ lb. (340 g) ground round
2 tsp. potato flour
¾ tsp. salt

Black pepper
¼ tsp. nutmeg
3 tbsp. milk, cold
Pickled beets and parsley

Over medium heat brown the onion in a little butter until golden and glossy. Remove and keep warm. In food processor quickly mix meat with flour, salt, pepper, nutmeg and milk. Form 4 round patties, place in hot frying pan and flatten slightly with fork. Brown a couple of minutes on each side. Do not fry too long as you will end up with dry tasteless patties. They continue to cook with their internal heat after removed from the pan. Place lettuce on a slice of bread and top with meat patties. Decorate with fried onion, beets and parsley. **Serves 4.**

Tender ground round meat patties fried to perfection, and covered with golden fried onions. In Norway they can buy delicious, ready made patties. But with food processors we can have our own homemade karbonadekaker *ready in a short time.*

Ground Pork Patties (Medisterkaker)

Pork patties, hot (see recipe
  in meat section)
Butter, soft
Boston lettuce

Horseradish sauce
Thin orange slices or
  pickles
Stirred lingonberries

Butter bread, cut in half. Cover with a pork patty. Tuck a lettuce leaf under one corner of the patty. Top with a dollop of horseradish sauce, orange slices which have been slit to the center and twisted, or sliced pickles. Add stirred lingonberries on the side.

Serve on pumpernickel bread, with a spoonful of stirred lingonberries or lingonberry jam on the side.

Fruit Sandwiches (Fruktsmørbrød)

Children like fruit and berry sandwiches anytime. They make an exciting lunch or as a special treat at night. There are many types of fruit sandwiches, sometimes served as a finale to a *smørbrød* meal. You may use one type of fruit or a combination, but be sure that flavors and colors blend well. Fresh or canned fruit (drained well) may be used as well as fruit salad. Colorful jello with a little whipped cream makes an interesting creation. All fruit sandwiches must be made just prior to serving to be appetizingly good.

Raspberry Sandwich (Bringebærsmørbrød)

As a child, no sandwich tasted better to me than a sandwich of homemade bread with berries straight from the garden. Any kind of fresh berries may be used.

Bread	**Confectioners' sugar**
Butter	**Whipped cream, optional**
Raspberries	

Butter slice of light, firm bread. Pile with raspberries and sprinkle with confectioners' sugar. For an extra taste-treat the berries may be put on a bed of whipped cream.

Banana Sandwich (Banansmørbrød)

Bread	**Milk chocolate, grated**
Butter	**Nuts, finely chopped**
Bananas	**Confectioners' sugar**

Butter light, firm bread. Slice bananas crosswise and place in rows on bread. Sprinkle with chocolate, nuts and confectioners' sugar.

Fruit Salad Sandwich (Fruktsalat smørbrød)

5 slices firm white bread	**Boston lettuce**
⅔ cups (1 ½ dl) green small grapes, seedless	**½ cup (1 dl) whipping cream**
	½ tsp. confectioners' sugar
1 red apple, small	**2 tbsp. walnuts, ground**
1 celery stalk, sliced fine	**Lemon pepper**
¼ cup (½ dl) walnuts, chopped	

Lightly butter bread and slice rectangularly. Wash and dry grapes and place in bowl. Wash apple, dice small and sprinkle with a little lemon juice. Slice celery leaf-thin, and coarsely chop walnuts. Add all to the grapes. In a separate, small bowl whip cream into soft peaks. Add confectioners' sugar, and mix with fruit, celery and nuts. Place lettuce leaves on bread, scoop salad on top and sprinkle with lemon pepper. **Makes 10 sandwich halves.**

Soups

Cauliflower Soup (Blomkålsuppe)

1 cauliflower, large or
 2 small heads
Water and salt
2 tbsp. butter
1 tbsp. onion, minced
2 tbsp. flour

1 qt. (liter) meat broth
1 egg yolk
½ cup (1¼ dl) cream
Nutmeg to taste
White pepper

Today we buy cauliflower all year round. Yet this vegetable reminds me of summer. I can still feel the late summer breezes as they rustled mamma's pretty kitchen curtains while her delicious cauliflower soup simmered on the stove.

Remove green leaves from the cauliflower, wash and place the cauliflower in cold water, with a little salt added, for a few minutes. Add the cauliflower to a soup pot. Add 1 teaspoon salt to each quart water. When tender, about 10-15 minutes, remove one half and brake into florets. Continue to cook the remaining cauliflower until mushy. Cool slightly, place in food processor with some of the water, and run on high speed for 30 seconds or until it has turned to a smooth sauce. In a frying pan sauté onion until glossy, being careful not to brown. Stir in flour, and add the broth and the "sauce" all at once. Stir continually while bringing the soup to a boil. Let simmer 10 minutes. Remove from heat. Beat the egg yolk with the cream, a touch of grated nutmeg and white pepper and add to soup in a thin stream and under constant stirring. Add florets and place soup pot back on the burner. Heat through, but do not let it boil. Serve immediately. **Serves 6-8.**

Pollack Party Soup (Selskapssei i gryte)

5 oz. bacon
1 celery root, small
3 potatoes, medium
2 onions, small
2¾ cups (6¾ dl) water
⅞ cup (2¼ dl) whipping cream

1²/₃ cups (1¾ dl) leeks, sliced
1 lb. (450 g) pollack
5 oz. (140 g) lox
Salt and white pepper
Parsley

If you deprive the average person of his illusions, you deprive him of his happiness as well.
Ibsen

Dice bacon, celery root and potatoes. Peel and cut onions in wedges, and add all to heavy bottomed saucepan. Add water. Bring to a boil, lower heat and let simmer approximately 30 minutes. Pour off most of the water (save it) and place the remaining mixture in the pan in food processor or blender, and combine on high setting. Remove sauce to a casserole dish and add the saved water and cream. Bring to a boil. Add sliced leek (save some for decoration) and let simmer 3-4 minutes. Add pollack cut in chunks. Remove from heat and let fish steep 4 to 5 minutes. Thinly slice lox (save some for decoration), add to saucepan and steep for another 2-3 minutes. Add salt and pepper to taste. If soup is too thick, add a little more water or cream. Pour into soup bowls, decorate with parsley, leek rings and thin strips of lox. Serve with crisp bread.

Appetizing Fish Soup (Appetittvekkende fiskesuppe)

Fish broth:

Making the broth from salmon and trout heads is what gives this soup its superb flavor. Save your left-over salmon or trout heads, bones, tails etc. in the freezer until you have enough to make a broth. Your fishmonger may even have a few extra to give you.

2 tbsp. butter
4 tsp. potato starch flour
2¼ cups (5½ dl) salmon/trout broth
⅞ cup (2 dl) creme fraiche or
  sour cream

2 egg yolks
Salt
Pepper
¼ cup (½ dl) chives, chopped

In a saucepan add enough cold water to cover bones, skin, tails, and fish heads. To get a clear broth remove the eyes from the heads before cooking. Simmer no more than 30 minutes, and strain. Add 1 tbsp. salt to each quart (liter) of broth.

Melt the butter in a heavy-bottomed pan. Cool slightly. Stir in the potato flour, and add the broth a little at a time. Bring to a boil. Thoroughly whisk the egg yolks into the creme fraiche. Remove the pan from the heat and fully stir in the egg mixture. Salt and pepper to taste. Pour into soup bowls and sprinkle with chopped chives. Hard rolls or french bread makes a good accompaniment. **Serves 4 as a first course or 2 for dinner.**

Oxtail Soup (Oksehalesuppe)

3 lbs. oxtails
1½ tbsp. margarine
2 strips of bacon
1½ tsp. salt
1 tsp. peppercorns
1½ tsp. marjoram
1 leek, chopped
1 onion, chopped

1 parsnip
Half a celery stalk
Boiling water
1 carrot
2 tbsp. tomato purée (not paste)
2 tbsp. soy sauce
Cayenne pepper
Parsley, chopped

Ask your butcher to cut the tail apart in the joints. Wash. Brown the margarine and add the oxtails and bacon. Brown well. Transfer to a large soup pot. Add salt, peppercorns, marjoram, green tops of the leek and onion. Dice half of the parsnip and celery root. Pour boiling water over ingredients to cover, approximately 2 quarts. Bring to a boil, then lower heat and simmer about 2½ to 3 hours. The longer the oxtail simmers, the richer the flavor.

Strain. Pour the broth back in the soup pot. Julienne the carrot, the other half of the parsnip and celery root and the remainder of the leek. Let simmer 5 to 10 minutes. Remove the meat from the bones and add to broth. Flavor the soup with tomato purée, soy sauce and cayenne pepper to taste. Pour into a soup tureen, sprinkle with chopped parsley and enjoy the aroma. Serve with hot onion bread, some Jarlsberg or Gouda cheese, and a salad.

Beef Stew (Lapskaus)

1½ lbs. (675 g) meat*	1 leek, small
¾ lb. (340 g) carrots	1 onion, small
1 celery root	3 cups (7½ dl) broth
¾ cup (2 dl) rutabagas	Salt and pepper
4 potatoes	

Use leftover boiled or baked meat, fresh or salted, or a mixture. Cut meat into even, not too large pieces and set aside. Wash and peel carrots, celery root and rutabagas, and dice. In a soup pot bring broth to a boil and add vegetables. Cook 15 minutes. Peel and dice potatoes. Cut leek lengthwise and wash thoroughly and slice, add with peeled, sliced onion and potatoes to the soup pot. Cook until almost tender. Add meat. Any leftover gravy may be added to the stew. Add salt and pepper to taste. Meat, vegetables and potatoes should all be tender but not mushy. Stir as little as possible while cooking, but be careful that it does not burn.

   *If fresh meat is used, cook separately. When nearly tender remove meat. Skim, and
    add vegetables. Proceed as above.

Browned Beef Stew (Brun lapskaus)

2 onions, thinly sliced	4-5 potatoes. medium to large
Butter	3 carrots, diced
2 lbs. (900 g) beef stew meat	Salt

In a heated skillet fry onion in a little butter until glossy but not browned, transfer to a large saucepan. Cut meat into ½-1-inch (1¼-2½ cm) cubes, and potatoes into 1-inch (2½ cm) cubes. Dice the carrots. Brown meat quickly in the butter the onions were fried in, add more butter if necessary and get it nicely browned before adding meat. Add potatoes, carrots and water to cover. Cook slowly until it thickens, about two hours, stirring once in awhile to prevent sticking. Add more water if necessary, but it should be of a rather thick consistency. This is another dish that tastes even better warmed the next day. **Serves 6-8.**

Many like the vegetables and potatoes in a beef stew to be tender, not mushy. Others prefer the stew to be of a thick consistency. This recipe has the thick consistency.

Spinach Soup (Spinatsuppe)

¾ lb. (340 g) spinach, or	¼ tsp. nutmeg, grated fresh
use frozen spinach	¼ tsp. pepper
1 qt. (liter) chicken or beef stock	Salt
2 tbsp. butter	¼ cup (½ dl) whipping cream
2 tbsp. flour	3 hard-boiled eggs
1 tbsp. chives, chopped	

Wash the fresh spinach (thoroughly under running water and drain well). Defrost and drain frozen spinach if used. Bring stock to a boil. Chop spinach and add to the boiling stock. Simmer, uncovered 6 minutes. Remove from heat, cool slightly and place spinach and broth in food processor and process on high speed about 30 seconds. Do not add more than maximum capacity to your machine at a time, or it could froth over. Set aside. Melt the butter in a frying pan, stir in the flour; when well mixed pour in the spinach broth all at once, and stir continually while bringing the soup to a boil. Allow to simmer 6-8 minutes. Add chives, spices, salt and pepper and stir in whipping

Not too many people are nostalgic about spinach soup. But it is a great way to get this nourishing food into growing bodies. Even guests will enjoy it. Float a half of hard boiled egg in the center of the bowl, and sprinkle with paprika. You may also serve this soup with a deviled egg half in the center.

cream. Heat through. Place a half of a hard boiled egg in the center of each soup bowl, and sprinkle with paprika. **Serves 6.**

Yellow Pea Soup with Ham (Ertesuppe med flesk)

2 cups (5 dl) yellow peas, dried	**2 large leeks**
1 smoked picnic, or 1 smoked	**Small baking potatoes**
** butt plus ham bone**	**Rutabagas**
Salt	

Whenever I think of ertesuppe med flesk *nostalgia floods my mind. Our family spent many a Thursday evening around this hearty dish. It actually tastes even better the day after. It is an excellent cold-weather meal which can be prepared well in advance.*

Soak peas in water at least three hours or overnight. Put picnic (or butt and ham bone) in large pot with enough water to cover. Add sliced leeks and the peas. Cover and cook slowly until peas are tender and meat is done, 2-2½ hours. If the ham being used is small, do not add until the last hour or so, or it will overcook. Salt to taste. The size of the ham and the amount of water used determine the strength of the soup. If too thin, cook uncovered until it becomes more concentrated.

Following the soup, serve the sliced ham with a mild-type mustard, boiled/steamed potatoes, and sliced, cooked rutabaga..

Vegetable and Barley Soup (Grynsodd)

3 tbsp. barley	**2 cups (5 dl) cabbage**
2 cups (5 dl) water	**1 cup (2½ dl) carrots**
½ leek	**½ cup (1¼ dl) rutabagas**
2 celery tops with leaves	**3 potatoes**
3 cups (7½ dl) beef stock or	**Salt to taste**
** bouillon**	**Fresh parsley, chopped**

This inexpensive, nourishing soup is a well established winter-time soup in Norway.

Rinse barley and soak overnight in the cold water. Place barley in the soup pot with the soaking water. Cut the leek in half, wash and slice. Cut celery and add to the soup pot; simmer about 1 hour. Add beef stock, slice cabbage and add; simmer 20 minutes. Slice carrots, dice rutabagas and add, simmer 10 minutes. Dice and add potatoes. Continue to simmer 15 minutes more or until vegetables are done, but not mushy. Add salt. Serve piping hot sprinkled with fresh, chopped parsley. Serve with dark bread. **Serves 6.**

Leek Soup (Purresuppe)

3 tbsp. butter	**1 qt. (liter) beef broth**
3 leeks, sliced	**2 egg yolks, slightly beaten**
5 potatoes, medium	**1 tsp. salt**
2 carrots, medium	**¼ tsp. pepper**
¼ cup (½ dl) flour	**Fresh parsley, chopped**

Melt the butter in a large heavy bottomed saucepan. Cut the leeks in half lengthwise and wash thoroughly. Slice. Dice the potatoes and carrots and add with the leeks to the saucepan. Cook 5 minutes while stirring occasionally to prevent vegetables from browning. Add flour stirring constantly; remove from heat and add broth all at once, while continuing to stir. Reduce heat and let simmer until vegetables are tender. Beat egg yolks into a soup tureen. Pour soup over egg yolks, a little at the time, stirring constantly. Season with salt and pepper to taste. Sprinkle with fresh parsley. Serve at once. **Serves 6-8.**

Lamb and Vegetable Soup (Betasuppe)

Some cooks use lightly salted mutton or ham, others use fresh beef or mutton. A combination of salt and fresh meat is my favorite. Remember to soak salted meat in cold water overnight. (About parsley and celeriac see Vegetable chapter.)

A marvelous winter-treat which should be served piping hot. A classic loved by most. Recipe varies somewhat from district to district.

½ cup (1¼ dl) pearl barley
2 qts. (liters) water
1 lb. (450 g) lamb flank
4 carrots
1 small celeriac, diced
¼ leek, sliced thin

1 parsley root, diced
Chunk of cabbage sliced,
1 thick slice rutabaga, diced
1 cup (200 g) potatoes
1 cup (2½ dl) peas, frozen
2 slices lamb or ham, cured

Soak barley overnight. Simmer in the soaking water about 1 hour. In separate saucepan cook the lamb until tender, about 30 minutes. Skim thoroughly. Set meat aside, strain the meat broth and add to the barley. Add evenly diced vegetables, except peas and potatoes, and cook 15-30 minutes. Add potatoes cook another 15 minutes. Add diced, fresh and cured meat (preferably cured leg of lamb), and peas. Bring to a boil and let simmer until peas are tender. **Serves 8.**

Vegetable Soup with Tiny Lamb Balls (Sodd)

1½ qts. (liters) water
1 lb. (450 g) lamb, boneless
1 leek, sliced
½ tsp. salt
½ tsp. pepper

1 piece of ginger, small
1 carrot
1 parsnip
Tiny lamb balls
Parsley

In the county of Trøndelag sodd *has been served for generations and at all festive occasions, and especially at Christmas buffets. The tiny meatballs can be served in their broth with or without vegetable.*

Cover the meat with water and bring to a boil. Remove from heat and skim well. Add leek, salt, pepper, and ginger and simmer 40 minutes. Add remainder of vegetables whole and cook until meat and vegetables are tender. Remove meat and vegetables and dice separately. Strain the broth and pour back into the soup pot. Add lamb, *soddboller,* (recipe follows) and vegetables and bring to a quick boil. Pour into heated soup tureen and sprinkle with chopped parsley. Serve piping hot with boiled potatoes. **Serves 8-10.**

Tiny Lamb Balls (Soddboller)

Once when we sailed out of Trollfjord in the Lofoten Islands, on the express boat, we were served these tiny (and savory) lambballs in broth. They called it Trollbroth and played Edvard Grieg's music, "In the Hall of the Mountain King" but in reality they were *soddboller.*

Fit for guests, but often in times past they were served during the slaughtering season. You may serve them as an appetizer in the broth, or add to the vegetable soup in previous recipe. This recipe calls for 1 cup (2½ dl) cream and you want to use all of it, a tablespoon at a time. If the lamb balls are to be used for Vegetable Soup with Tiny Lamb Balls, cook them in the soup, and eliminate broth.

10 oz. (285 g) ground lamb
½ tbsp. potato starch flour
½ tbsp. flour
½ tbsp. salt

1 cup (2½ dl) coffee cream
Nutmeg
1 qt. (liter) lamb or beef broth

The old recipes called for meat to be ground with the spices and flour 10-12 times! In other words grind it well. Add coffee cream a spoonful or two at a time, and beat well after each addition. Add nutmeg to taste. Bring the broth to a boil. With a teaspoon make ½-¾-inch (1¼-1¾ cm) lamb balls and drop into the boiling broth. Reduce heat and simmer until done. Serve piping hot with flatbread, or homemade bread. **Serves 6.**

Salads

Cucumber Salad (Agurksalat)

English or European cucumbers are quite expensive, but there is no comparison in taste. Slice them thin for salads, a Norwegian cheese knife works well. This salad tastes good with either baked or fried foods.

1 European cucumber
²/₃ cup (1½ dl) vinegar, white
²/₃ cup (1½ dl) water
3½ tbsp. sugar

¼ tsp. salt
Dash of white pepper
Fresh parsley

Thinly slice a European cucumber. Mix dressing well and pour over cucumber slices in serving bowl. Make salad ready early enough to let dressing penetrate without making cucumbers soft (about one-half hour). Sprinkle with fine chopped fresh parsley.

Pickled Beets (Syltede rødbeter)

Beets, with their deep, red color, enhance many foods from vegetable plates to open-face sandwiches. They are also delicious as a side dish.

8-10 medium beets
¼ cup (½ dl) vinegar, white
¼ cup (½ dl) sugar
¾ tsp. caraway seeds
¾ tsp. salt

8-10 cloves, whole
Few drops of red food coloring
1¼ tbsp. cornstarch
¹/₃ cup (¾ dl) water

Drop well scrubbed beets into boiling water and simmer until barely tender. Drain and reserve liquid. Cool the beets quickly by placing under cold running water. Peel and slice thin. Boil 2 cups (5 dl) reserved liquid (add water if needed to equal 2 cups (5 dl), the vinegar, sugar, salt, caraway seeds, cloves and food coloring. Combine ¹/₃ cup (1¾ dl) water with cornstarch to form a smooth paste and add. Cook 3 minutes. Pour over beets. Serve hot or cold.

Lobster Salad (Hummersalat)

2 small lobsters
1 14-16 oz. can asparagus
1 jar artichokes, small
2 eggs, hard boiled
2 tomatoes

1 head Boston lettuce
1 lemon, thinly sliced
³/₈ cup (¾ dl) mayonnaise
½ cup (1¼ dl) whipping cream

Remove meat from prepared lobsters and cut into bite-size pieces. Drain liquid from vegetables. Cut tomato and eggs into wedges. Whip cream and blend with mayonnaise. Line a salad bowl or platter with lettuce and arrange all salad ingredients, reserving eggs, tomatoes and lobster claws for decoration. Pour dressing over all and decorate.

Herring and Ham Salad *(Sild og skinkesalat)*

3 salted herring fillets, soaked
3 potatoes, boiled and peeled
1 apple
Lemon
1 onion, small
1 pickle, sweet
3 slices of ham, boiled
6 slices pickled beets

Dressing:
6 tbsp. mayonnaise
2 tbsp. whipping cream
2 tbsp. chili sauce
Garnish:
Boston lettuce
1 or 2 eggs, hard boiled
Parsley

For herring lovers! Serve with dark bread as an appetizer, late evening snack or meal.

Drain beets well. Dice all ingredients. Sprinkle lemon juice over apple to prevent darkening. Mix dressing and blend with all diced ingredients. Line a salad bowl or platter with lettuce leaves and spoon mixture on top. Garnish with chopped egg and sprinkle with parsley.

Nordic Sardine Salad *(Nordisk sardin salat)*

Florets from 1 bunch broccoli
2 carrots, large, thickly sliced
  on the diagonal
2 leeks, medium
3 cups (7½ dl) shredded cabbage

2 cans 3¾ oz. (106 g) each, Norway
  sardines in oil, drained
Warm Dill Dressing (recipe follows)
Fresh dill sprigs

Leek, carrots, and red cabbage the traditional winter vegetables in Norway, are perfect partners in this salad topped with Norway sardines and a warm dill dressing.

Wash and peel vegetables as needed. Separately steam broccoli, carrots and leeks until crisp-tender; drain immediately. Cut leeks into quarters lengthwise, then cut into 2-inch (5 cm) lengths. Line platter with cabbage. Arrange broccoli, carrots, leeks and sardines on cabbage. Pour Warm Dill Dressing over salad. Garnish with dill sprigs. Serve immediately.

Warm Dill Dressing: In a saucepan combine ¼ cup (½ dl) each olive oil and water. 2½ tablespoons distilled vinegar, 1 large clove garlic, finely chopped, and ¼ teaspoon pepper. Whisk over low heat just to boiling. Remove from heat. Stir in 2 to 3 tablespoons chopped fresh dill or 2 to 3 teaspoons dried dill weed, and salt to taste. **Serves 4.**

Warm Sardine Salad *(Varm sardin salat)*

2 tbsp. vegetable oil
1 lb. (450 g) potatoes, cubed
½ cup (70 g) red onion, chopped
1 cup (225 g) ham, diced
8 mushrooms, sliced
1 avocado, ripe and sliced
Lemon juice

Salt and pepper to taste
1 qt. (liter) spinach leaves
1 can 3¾ oz. (106 g) Norway
  sardines in oil, drained
½ cup (85 g) cherry tomato halves
Fresh chives
(Dijon Vinaigrette Dressing recipe follow)

Hearty flavors of potatoes, mushrooms, ham and avocado combine with Norway sardines to make this delicious salad.

Heat oil in large, non-stick skillet. Add peeled and cubed potatoes; cook over medium heat until golden and tender, 15-20 minutes, stirring occasionally to brown all sides. Drain on toweling and reserve. Add onion, ham and mushrooms to skillet; saute until onions are soft. Peel and slice avocado and add a generous squeeze of lemon juice. Add with cooked potatoes to the skillet, salt and pepper. Toss gently to mix; remove from heat. Arrange spinach on serving plate; top with potato mixture, sardines and cherry tomatoes. Garnish with chives. Spoon dressing over all. Serve warm.

Dijon Vinaigrette Dressing;   Combine $^1/_3$ cup (¾ dl) vegetable oil, 2 tablespoons red wine vinegar, 2 teaspoons Dijon-style mustard and 1 teaspoon snipped fresh or ½ teaspoon dried chives. Whisk to blend. Season with salt and pepper. **Serves 4.**

Fisherman's Potato Salad (Fiskerens potetsalat)

Whether ocean-going or fly casting on a mountain stream, every fisherman will love this potato salad with its delicious combination of potatoes, crisp apples and hearty Norway sardines.

¼ cup (½ dl) olive oil
1½ tbsp. lemon juice
1 tsp. Dijon-style mustard
1 tsp. mustard seeds
1½ tsp. fresh dill, chopped
  or ½ tsp. dill weed, dried
½ tsp. lemon peel, grated
2 green onions, sliced
Pepper to taste

¾ lb. (340 g) red potatoes, small
  cooked and sliced ¼-inch (6 mm)
  thick
2 red apples, small, cored and
  thinly sliced
2 cans 3¾ oz. (106 g) each Norway
  sardines in oil, drained
Lettuce leaves
Fresh dill sprigs and lemon wedges

Whisk together oil, lemon juice, mustard, mustard seeds, dill, lemon peel, onions and pepper. Pour over potato and apple slices, tossing to coat. Chill. To serve: Arrange potatoes, apples and sardines on four lettuce-lined plates. Garnish with dill sprigs and lemon wedges. **Serves 4.**

Sauces

Nøkkelost Sauce (Nøkkelost saus)

Serve over fresh cooked vegetables sprinkled with cooked ham.

3 tbsp. butter
3 tbsp. flour
1½ cups (3 dl) milk
½ tsp. salt

½ tsp. Dijon mustard
3 cups (7½ dl) Nøkkelost, grated
Ham, chopped

Melt butter in saucepan. Stir in flour. Pour milk in all at once and stir until smooth and thick. Simmer 5 minutes. Season with salt and mustard. Add cheese, stirring until melted. **Makes 2¾ cups.**

Game Sauce (Tradisjonell viltsaus)

2 tbsp. butter
2 tbsp. flour
1 cup (2½ dl) bouillon
1 cup (2½ dl) sour cream

½ cup (1¼ dl) 100% goat cheese, diced
3 juniper berries
2 tsp. salt
1 tsp. pepper

Brown butter and flour in an iron frying pan. Add bouillon and sour cream all at once. Stir over medium heat until smooth and bubbly. Add diced cheese and spices. Let simmer 10 minutes. If a darker color is desired, add a little Maggi seasoning. **Makes 2¾ cups.**

Gravy for Chicken or Game *(Geitost saus til vilt)*

⅝ cup (1½ dl) goat cheese or
   Gudbrandsdalost, diced
1⅓ (3¼ dl) cup bouillon

1 cup (2½ dl) sour cream
½ tsp. pepper
6-8 juniper berries

Melt goat cheese in one third of the bouillon. Add remaining bouillon, bring to a boil. Lower heat, add sour cream under constant stirring and let simmer 4-5 minutes until desired consistency. Add pepper and juniper berries to taste. **Makes 2¾ cups.**

Old Fashion Sauce *(Gammaldags duppe)*

½ cup (1¼ dl) 100% goat cheese, grated
2⅔ cups (6½ dl) water
¼ cup (½ dl) flour

¼ cup (½ dl) sugar
⅓ cup (¾ dl) sour cream

Serve with klubb *(large dumplings).*

Grate cheese and bring to boil with 2 cups water. Stir flour into remaining water until smooth. Add to cheese with sugar, and stir until it begins to boil. Let simmer 10 minutes, stirring occasionally. Add sour cream. **Makes 3½ cups.**

Sour Cream Gravy *(Rømmesaus)*

1⅛ cup (2¾ dl) sour cream
3½ tbsp. goat cheese, grated

⅓ cup (¾ dl) chives or dill

Tasty with chicken, veal or game.

Over moderate heat combine sour cream and cheese in saucepan and stir until melted. Stir in finely chopped chives. Heat thoroughly. **Makes 1½ cups.**

Dill Sauce *(Dillsaus)*

1 tbsp. French-type mustard
1 tbsp. vinegar

½ cup (1¼ dl) oil
¼ cup (½ dl) finely chopped dill

Stir all ingredients into a thick smooth sauce. **Makes about ¾ cup.**

Chili Sauce *(Chili saus)*

½ cup (1¼ dl) sour cream
¼ cup (½ dl) mayonnaise
¼ cup (½ dl) chili sauce

1 tbsp. lemon juice
½ tsp. mustard, dry
½ tsp. worcestershire

Mix all ingredients well. Yogurt may be substituted for sour cream. Keep refrigerated. Great with crab. **Makes 1 cup.**

Chive-Parsley Sauce *(Grønn saus)*

½ cup (1¼ dl) mayonnaise
½ cup (1¼ dl) sour cream
1 tsp. mustard, Idun or
   Dijon-type

1 tbsp. parsley, finely chopped
1 tbsp. chives, chopped
1 tsp. lemon juice

Mix all ingredients well. Yogurt may be substituted for sour cream. Keep refrigerated. Serve with crab. **Makes about 1¼ cup.**

Brown gravy (Brun saus)

4 tbsp. butter	**Salt**
5 tbsp. flour	**Pepper**
1 qt. (liter) broth or	**1 tsp. soy sauce**
bouillon	**1 tbsp. black currant juice, if desired**

Melt and carefully brown butter. Stir in flour. And let simmer until nut-brown in color. Whisk fully while adding a little warm broth at a time, and bring to a boil after each addition. Cover and let simmer about 10 minutes. Season and add currant juice if desired. **Makes about 3 ¾ cups.**

Mint Sauce (Myntesaus)

2 cups (5 dl) broth or	**Salt**
pan drippings	**White pepper**
3 tsp. carmel coloring	**2 tbsp. fresh mint or 1 tsp. dried**
3 tsp. cornstarch	

Pour pan dripping or broth into a saucepan. Add enough caramel coloring to make a nice color, and bring to a boil. Dissolve the cornstarch in a little water, and add to the broth in a thin stream, while stirring continually. Let simmer a couple of minutes and season to taste. **Makes 2 cups.**

Currant Sauce (Ripssaus)

Pan drippings	**Salt**
1⅓ cup (3 dl) whipping cream	**Pepper**
1 tbsp. soy sauce	**½ cup (1¼ dl) currants**
3 tbsp. currant jelly	

Strain the pan drippings and add with the whipping cream to a heavy-bottomed sauce pan. Lett simmer until it begins to thicken. Add jelly and soy sauce and stir until the jelly has melted. Add seasoning to taste. Carefully add cleaned currants and serve immediately. **Makes about 1⅓ cups.**

Parsley Butter (Persille smør)

Excellent with steamed or baked fish.

2 bunches parsley	**1¼ cup (385 g) butter**
2 tbsp. fish broth	

Mince parsley and bring to a boil in the fish broth. Add butter and stir until velvety smooth, this takes about 10 minutes. *Do not let it boil.* **1⅜ cup.**

Dessert Sauces

Red Fruit Sauce (Rød fruktsaus)

Red fruit sauce is the crowning glory to mousse, puddings and rice-cream. Make it from currant, cherry, strawberry or raspberry juice, they are all delicious.

2 cups (5 dl) juice of your choice   **2 tbsp. potato flour**
Sugar if needed   **Cold water**

Bring juice to a boil. Meanwhile dissolve potato flour with a little water. Remove juice from heat and slowly add the potato flour thickening, stirring constantly to assure its smoothness. Bring quickly to a boil and remove from heat. If cooking period is prolonged the sauce may become thin or even elastic. The sauce should be smooth and not too thick. Pour sauce into a pitcher or other suitable container and sprinkle a little sugar over the top to prevent film from forming. Chill. **Makes 2 cups.**

Quick Red Fruit Sauce (Hurtig rød fruktsaus)

If you do not keep fresh or canned juice on hand the supermarkets carry reasonable substitutes such as, Junket, Danish Dessert, pudding and pie fillings, etc. Follow directions on package except double the recommended amount of liquid.

Apricot Sauce (Aprikossaus)

¾ cup (1¾ dl) apricots, dried   **¼ cup (½ dl) sugar**
2 cups (5 dl) water   **1 tbsp. potato flour**
                                                           Water

Rinse the apricots and let soak in the water for 3-4 hours. Let simmer in the same water until tender. Force through a sieve and let cool. Add sugar to taste, and potato flour. Pour back into the kettle and bring to a boil while constantly stirring. As soon as it begins to boil, remove from the heat and keep covered until cooled. Chill before serving. **Makes 2 cups.**

It was a real treat for us children when our Sunday dessert, was cream of wheat pudding topped with a red fruit sauce, or once in a great while this delectable apricot sauce.

Goat Cheese Dessert Sauce (Gjetost dessertsaus)

1 cup (2½ dl) Ski-Queen goat cheese   **Touch of anise, cardamom,**
¹/₃ cup (¾ dl) milk   **cinnamon or ginger**
1 tbsp. honey or syrup

Grate the cheese and melt over low heat with the milk and honey. Add your favorite seasoning.

Making this sauce with Ski-Queen Gjetost will give a rich luscious golden sauce with a rich aroma. Remarkably good on ice cream as well as over pears and nectarines.

Blueberry Sauce (Blåbærsaus)

Wash amount of berries needed. Set a side ¼ cup (½ dl) berries, and gently mix with 1 tablespoon sugar. Mash the remainder of the berries with a fork and add with sugar to taste. Serve the sauce in a pitcher, or arrange on individual dessert plates with the dessert. Decorate with the sugared whole berries.

Fruit Sauce from Frozen Berries (Saus av dypfryste bær)

Fresh frozen berries make delicious fruit sauces for puddings or ice creams. Take out as many berries as needed and set to thaw in a sieve placed over a bowl. When defrosted press berries through sieve and add enough of the liquid to make consistency desired. Add vanilla and sugar to taste if needed and desired.

Rich Vanilla Sauce (Fin vaniljesaus)

Most homes used two types of vanilla sauce, *fin* (rich), which was reserved for birthdays, special holidays and guests; and *hverdags,* everyday, vanilla sauce.

½ vanilla bean, sliced lengthwise	3 egg yolks
1 cup (2½ dl) light cream	2-3 tbsp. sugar
1½ tsp. vanilla sugar or extract	½ cup (1¼ dl) whipping cream

Place the split vanilla bean in a heavy saucepan and pour in cream. Bring the cream to a boil over moderate heat. Remove from heat, cover and let stand approximately 10 to 15 minutes so the sauce will absorb the flavor of the vanilla bean. Remove the bean. Using a wire whisk, in a separate bowl, beat the egg yolks and sugar together and add to the cream. Put the sauce over low heat until it thickens, while stirring. Remove from heat and stir from time to time as it cools. Add additional sugar to taste. Whip the cream and add just before serving. Serve with baked apples, chocolate pudding or fruit desserts or pies.

Everyday Vanilla Sauce (Vaniljesaus til hverdags)

1½ cups (3 ½ dl) milk	½ tbsp. potato flour
1½ tbsp. sugar	1½ tsp. vanilla sugar
1 egg, large	

In a heavy saucepan combine milk, sugar, egg, and potato flour. While stirring, bring to the boiling point over medium heat. It *must not* boil. Remove from heat. Stir the sauce from time to time as it cools. Serve chilled. **Makes 1¾ cup.**

Warm Chocolate Sauce (Varm sjokoladesaus)

2 cups (5 dl) water	3 tbsp. vanilla sugar
5 tbsp. cocoa or chocolate syrup	Salt
¼ cup (½ dl) sugar	$^{1}/_{3}$ cup (¾ dl) whipping cream

Combine all ingredients, except vanilla sugar and whipping cream, in heavy saucepan and bring to a boil while stirring. Remove from heat, add vanilla sugar and a pinch of salt. Whip cream and add to warm chocolate sauce. Serve with cold puddings and fruit desserts. **Makes $2^{1}/_{3}$ cups.**

Fish

The beloved Norwegian poet Bjørnstjerne Bjørnson, in his poem *Den norske sjøman er* tells a story of the courage, determination and faith of the men who bravely struggled with the treacherous sea, whether they sailed the seven seas or were fishing the coastal waters of Norway.

Most of us do not quite comprehend the dedication of the fishermen. We know only the enjoyment of the savory delicacies they bring to us - from herring to cod, from mackerel to haddock, from pollack to flounder to salmon, the shining king of the sea. Add to this the myriads of shellfish and you have culinary treats that continue to delight many of us.

Properly prepared fish is not only tasty but sound nutrition. It is comparatively low in calories, and has not been fed hormones, tranquilizers and antibiotics as have domestic animals. The Norwegian Seafood Export council explains:

> There is no longer any doubt about direct links between diet and health. In this respect, food from the sea is extremely important. Fish is a magnificent source of protein. Such proteins are readily digested and have an ideal makeup. Amino acid compositions differ little from species to species. In latter years, fish fat has received much attention for its polyunsaturated, so-called Omega 3 fatty acids. Omega 3 fatty acids protect against cardiovascular diseases. They are vital to development of the brain and nervous system, and the retina of the eye. They are also necessary for fetal and infant development. New research indicates that Omega 3 fatty acids are also efficacious against chronic infections, diabetes and certain types of cancer.
>
> The human body needs vitamins. These are generally divided into two groups, water soluble and oil soluble. A lack of vitamins leads to reduced health and vitality, and even to serious deficiency diseases. Fish and seafood have a high content of a number of B vitamins (water soluble) and particularly vitamin B12. Fat fish are the only natural source of vitamin D in our food. Fish also provide soluble vitamins A and E.
>
> Seafood gives a well balanced intake of a number of minerals. As a benefit to persons with high blood pressure, seafood is low in sodium while rich in potassium. A number of trace elements, including selenium, iodine, and fluorine, are required for proper health, and most of these are found in seafood. Fish supplies us with a natural form of selenium with no dosage risks.

Ever since Viking times, possibly long before, the sea has held a mysterious lure for the Norwegians. It has often brought sorrow to a family waiting for a loved one. But the sea is also generous; it has been the life source for many Norwegians for generations.

With abundant choice of fish available, it is easy to vary our meals. The simplest way to prepare fish is to simmer it in salted water. For variety add a little onion, bay leaf, dill or pepper. Fish baked in the oven, or in foil, retains much of its aroma, juice and flavor, and the resulting broth is simply delicious. Grilled fish is truly tasty and can be prepared with a minimum of fat. Fish casseroles may be varied by the addition of potatoes, vegetables, various spices, sauces and cheese. Fish soup can be made from the water in which fish was cooked or from broth made by boiling fish skin and bones together. Fish broth should never be boiled more than 30 minutes.

My first recollection of truly fresh fish was when our family lived on the island of Kollen at the end of the Oslofjord, where it opens up into the Skagerak. We often caught our first fish in the morning as the sun's first rays illumined the sea's surface. In the fall and spring the wind would often whip the sea up around our row boat, making the fishing more exciting for us youngsters at least. Back on the island, the aroma of

The wrinkled skin, the grayish dark gills and cloudy sunken eyes, are enough to scare the hungriest cat away. If you start out with old fish, deep fry it until the grease is dripping, or broil it until desert dry, or smother it in a thick layer of bread crumbs until any resemblance of the original has vanished; you should not wonder why your family thinks they don't like fish.

slowly simmering, fresh fish was to us, a great payment for our efforts. Fish for breakfast gave lots of energy to young bodies craving nutrients. The memories of those days are a far cry from what some markets today call, "Fresh Fish."

Look for these signs of freshness: Clean fresh smell, clear bulging eyes, bright red gills, shiny smooth and elastic, yet firm flesh. Herring may have red eyes and mackerel may have dark gills, but this does not necessarily mean that either is old and unpalatable. Following your "catch", rush home and let the fish bask for a while in cold running water, or let it rest for about one hour in lightly salted water. This will help bring out maximum flavor.

Preparing fish: All fish after it has been cleaned, and unless freshly caught, should be soaked in water, to which has been added 3 tablespoons salt to 1 quart (liter) water about 20 to 30 minutes. This way any possible taste, intestine, and other matter is drawn into the water.

Boiled, sliced fish: Cod, salmon, mackerel, or pollack slices should be placed in boiling, well-salted water. The fish must *not* boil. Simmer from 5 to 10 minutes depending on thickness of slice and type of fish. Lean fish requires less cooking time than fat. If you are not planning to utilize the fish broth, add 4 to 4 ½ tablespoons salt to each quart (liter) of water and if desired, a teaspoon of vinegar, which results in a firmer and whiter flesh. If you intend to use the broth for sauce or gravy only, use one tablespoon salt to each quart of water.

Boiled whole fish: Lean fish such as ling, cod, pollack, or billet falls apart easily and should not be cooked whole. If you intend to prepare this type of fish whole, bake rather than boil. Fatty fish such as salmon, trout, fresh water herring, or mackerel may be boiled whole in a fish poacher or large kettle, or it may be baked. There should be a rack in the bottom of the utensil for easy removal of fish to platter. In an emergency a piece of foil may be substituted for the rack. If a large fish is placed whole in boiling water the skin will break and the outer parts of the fish will be overcooked and dry by the time the heat reaches the backbone. Therefore, large fish, from 2 to 4½ pounds (900 g - 2 kg) should be placed in cold water; cooking time, from 30 to 50 minutes. Medium fish, from 1 to 2 pounds (450-900 g) are placed in lukewarm water; cooking time, 20 to 30 minutes. Small fish, less than 1 pound (450 g) are placed in boiling, salted water; cooking time, 10 to 20 minutes.

It is difficult to judge when a whole fish is thoroughly cooked. To make this determination carefully prick the fish close to the backbone, and if the meat leaves the bone and has become dull and non-transparent, it is done. Another way is to measure the thickness of the fish. Place fish on flat surface and measure thickness with a ruler next to the thickest part. Then follow cooking time as suggested in the table:

Lean Fish (Cod, pollack, haddock, etc.)

2 inches (5 cm) thick	**13 minutes**
2 ¾ inches (7 cm) thick	**25 minutes**
4 inches (10 cm) thick	**50 minutes**

Fat Fish (Salmon, trout, etc.)

2 inches (5 cm) thick	**18 minutes**
2¾ inches (7 cm) thick	**35 minutes**
4 inches (10 cm) thick	**70 minutes**

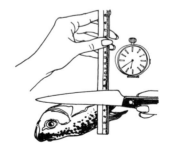

Flat Fish *(Flounder, turbot, etc.) as well as mackerel and herring*

1⅛ inches (2¾ cm) thick	13 minutes
1½ inches (3¾ cm) thick	23 minutes
2 inches (5 cm) thick	35 minutes

Cooking in foil on top of stove: Either whole or sliced fish may be cooked in foil. Cleaned and washed, it is placed on a piece of foil and salted. If whole, salt the fish inside the abdomen as well as the entire outside. Use up to 1 tablespoon salt for each two pounds (900 g) of fish. A squeeze or two of lemon may be sprinkled over the fish. Spices such as dill, chives, parsley, basil, paprika, curry, etc. may be added. Wrap the foil tightly around the fish and place, with the folding side facing up, on top of potatoes which are being boiled in a small amount of water. Cooking time for fish slices or chunks is from 10 to 20 minutes. Fish cooked in this manner will retain its taste and aroma. The resulting broth, contained in the foil, maybe used for gravy.

Cooking in foil in the oven: Butter a piece of foil. Rub salt into a 1 to 2 pound (450-900 g) cleaned and washed fish. Parsley, dill or other spices sprinkled into the abdomen imparts added flavor. Place the whole fish on the foil, wrap tightly and lay in a small roasting pan with the folded side up. Pour a cup of water into the pan and bake at 375°F (190°C) oven. Cooking time varies according to the size of fish, but allow about 45 minutes for a 3½ pound (1½ kg) fish. Remaining broth in the foil can be used for gravy or mixed with some melted butter and served with the fish.

Grilled fish: Fat fish such as salmon, herring, trout is especially suited to grilling. Flounder is also good, but lean fish such as cod falls apart easily. Fish may be grilled whole or sliced. Place in double grill rack which has been greased, and grill for 3 to 5 minutes on each side. Salt the fish after it is cooked. Or add spices to the fish, wrap in lightly buttered foil and grill directly on the coals.

Deep-fat fried fish: Fish fillets or small, whole fish may be deep fat fried in shortening and oil at a temperature of 350°F (175°C). If a thermometer is not available it is easy to determine proper cooking temperature by dropping a bread cube into the hot oil; if it turns golden brown within one minute it is ready to receive the fish. The fish to be fried must be completely dry. It may be fried plain or breaded, but breading results in a delicious crisp crust. Or it may be dipped in salted pancake batter. Do not reuse the oil. It is not good for your health, nor does it lend to the flavor of the fish.

Frozen fish: A great variety of fish is available in frozen form. Although frozen fish is not quite comparable to fresh fish, it is tasty and a great convenience to our busy lives today.

If you are lucky enough to have in your possession more fresh fish than can be eaten in one meal, utilize the freezer. Lean fish has better keeping qualities than fat fish. To prepare fish for freezing, clean and wash well, and slice or cut into fillets. Small fish should be frozen whole. Fat fish should be frozen in blocks of ice, or coated in ice, to maintain its quality.

Block freezing: Clean and wash the fish. Put in large container (square or rectangular fits best in freezer) and cover with water. Freeze. When frozen remove the block from the container and wrap in foil. Put dividers between the fish which has been sliced or fillet for easy removal.

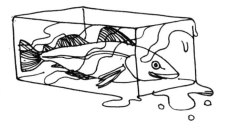

Ice coating: Put cleaned and washed fish in plastic bag and allow to remain in the freezer for 24 hours. Remove and dip in cold water. Return to freezer until the water is frozen. Repeat two or three times until layer of ice is formed around the fish. Wrap for freezing.

Vegetables to serve with fish: Fish has a rather neutral taste, therefore most vegetables are compatible with its flavor. Leek, green beans, broccoli, peas carrots, and cucumber salad is excellent with any fish meal. Boiled rutabaga and cabbage is great with herring. Stewed vegetables are best with fried fish, and salads with either boiled, baked or fried fish.

Which sauce to serve: For years, melted or browned butter was the most widely used accompaniment for fish, but today most people prefer a less fattening sauce, merely fish broth or lemon juice. Use as little butter as possible when frying fish. A thin sauce can be made by using four tablespoons of flour to one quart broth or liquid, varying the taste by adding leek, parsley, dill, celery, mushrooms, asparagus, horseradish, shellfish, tomato purée, curry or basil.

Cod (Torsk)

During one of my visits to Norway a dear friend's face lit up in utter disbelief when, in answer to "What would you like for dinner?", my reply was "boiled cod". She protested, but memories were too vivid, and delectable cod it was.

The Norwegians have always loved cod, ever since Viking times when they were used as both food and in trading. To this day, most Norwegians enjoy at least one cod dinner a week. The mild taste of cod makes it easy to vary the menu, and most vegetables are a fitting accompaniment.

Cod or any fish for that matter has to be fresh - absolutely fresh, to make those taste buds come alive. The advice of Thorstein Diesen from the book *Norsk Mat* is well taken:

When you go to purchase a cod, remember that most people can consume an unbelievable amount. A good cod head is one of the happiest acquaintances one can make. A cod, so fresh there is still a twinkle in his eyes, can spark an indescribable appetite.

As soon as the cod is in the house, prepare it. As with flowers, so with cod - you must talk to it and handle it gently to reap the maximum goodness.

Begin by letting the fish *enjoy* itself under running water. If this is impossible, let the fish rest awhile in lightly salted water. It will produce the same results.

Rule No. 1: A good basic rule when slicing fish into serving portions, is never make the slices thicker than your finger.

Rule No. 2: Use plenty of salt. Double the amount normally called for in most fish recipes. The very best method (not practical in most areas) is to cook the cod in clear sea water, adding an extra portion of salt.

Rule No. 3: Never allow cod to boil. This is a cardinal sin! After the water has reached the boiling point, carefully lower the fish into the boiling water, reduce the heat and simmer gently until done. It is done when the flesh is no longer translucent and separates easily from the bones. Fish which has been overcooked and loses its shape, also looses its serving attractiveness. If you are preparing a large quantity of fish it is advisable to use more than one utensil, or just cook a portion at a time, even if it is necessary to keep your guests waiting. The cod must be served steaming hot.

Remove fish with a slotted spoon, if you are not lucky enough to own a steamer with perforated tray. Place carefully on a heated platter, and insert a small bunch of parsley in the cod's mouth. Garnish with lemon slices and sprinkle with chopped parsley. Nothing but melted *butter* (no substitutes) will do for such a dish, but please melt carefully so as not to scorch it.

Rule No. 4: Serve the cod on heated dinner plates. In fact heat two plates per person in case of second servings. Since the cod in itself is quite colorless, it is of great importance to set an attractively, colorful table. A bright red tablecloth with contrasting blue dishes, and a centerpiece of fresh flowers will impress your guests as a dinner well remembered. The usual accompaniment to a cod dinner is tiny, boiled, steam-dried and buttered potatoes. A melon ball cutter is useful in shaping the potato balls. Serve in a heated bowl with butter and chopped parsley. Cheese and crackers, together with some fruit, make a grand finale to a delicious meal.

Party Cod (Festtorsk)

Slice cod fillets into uniform, square serving pieces. Dip in slightly beaten egg white and salted zwieback crumbs. Lightly brown fish in margarine. Lay half of fish pieces in an oven-proof casserole. Mix a few chopped, pickled onions with a little butter and top each section of fish with a spoonful. Make a second layer of remaining fish. Sprinkle one tablespoon grated Jarlsberg, or other mild cheese, on each section and top with cooked spinach mixed with a little mayonnaise. Bake in 450°F (230°C) oven for 5 to 8 minutes. Serve at once. Decorate with tomatoes and parsley.

Lutefish (Lutefisk)

Lutefisk (dried cod treated with lye) must surely be the strangest culinary effort credited to the Norwegians, but what a treat when prepared properly. Everyone of course is not a devotee of lutefish, but those who are defend it vehemently. Others go to the opposite extreme and claim it's a national disgrace. In years past the homemaker had to go through the complicated task of treating the dry fish with lye, but now, even in America, frozen lutefish is readily available at selected fish markets and at Scandinavian Delicatessens.

Every country has its culinary specialties. Nostalgic memories tug at your heart-strings if, when separated by distance, these favorites are set before you. Norway's lutefish is such a specialty to many.

Cooking lutefish the old fashioned way: Do not cook in aluminum vessels as it will darken the kettle. Use 3 level tablespoons salt to each quart water. Bring water to boil, add salt and return to boil. Add fish which has been sliced into serving pieces and again return to boil, then remove from the heat. Skim, and let fish steep for 5 to 10 minutes depending on thickness. Serve at once.

Without added water: Put the serving pieces of lutefish in a kettle, season each pound (450 g) of fish with ½ tablespoon of salt and place over low heat. This allows the water to be "drawn" out. Bring to a boil and remove from heat. Let steep 5 to 10 minutes. Serve at once.

Baking in foil: Heat oven to 400°F (205°C). Skin side down, arrange lutefish on a sheet of double aluminum foil and season with salt. Wrap foil tightly about fish and place on rack in a large pan and bake 20 minutes. Cut corner from foil and drain out excess water. Serve at once.

Lutefish with a firm texture can be obtained by first sprinkling with coarse salt and allowing to stand several hours. Rinse well in cold running water, and soak in unsalted water. Then cook or bake as desired.

Lutefish must be served hot on piping hot plates. Accompaniments vary from bacon or pork drippings, white sauce, mustard sauce, or melted butter which seems to remain a favorite. Boiled and steamed potatoes, stewed whole, dry green peas are a must as a vegetable accompaniment. The only other necessary additions are freshly ground pepper, lefse or flatbread. In some parts of Northern Norway lutefish is served with melted goat cheese.

Marinated Salmon (Gravlaks)

At one time salmon was so abundant along the coast of Norway and served so frequently, that servants required a special guarantee clause in their contract which limited the serving of salmon to two or three times a week. Today salmon is expensive, and considered *festmat*, gourmet food. *Gravlaks* may be served as an appetizer or as a main course, usually served with dill sauce and creamed potatoes

3 lbs. (1,350 g) filleted salmon,	**¼ cup (½ dl) sugar**
center cut	**20 white peppercorns, or**
1 large bunch of dill	**substitute with black**
¼ cup (½ dl) salt	

Ask your fishmonger to cut the salmon in half lengthwise and remove the backbone and all small bones. At home, rinse fish well and dry in towel. Wash the fresh dill and dry on paper towels. Place a thick layer of dill into a deep casserole or baking dish. (If the dill was grown in a greenhouse, it will not be as pungent, in this case, chop the herb to release its flavor and sprinkle it over the fish instead.)

In a separate bowl, combine salt, sugar, and crushed white pepper. Sprinkle some of the spices over dill. Rub the fillets with some of the spices, and place one fillet skin side down in the dill. Again sprinkle the salmon generously with the spices and dill. Add the second piece of fish, skin side up. Make sure the thicker part of one fillet is pressed against the thinner part of the other. Finally, add the remaining dill and spices. Cover with aluminum foil or clear wrap. Place a wooden board slightly larger than the salmon on top and add a light weight to press it down, three to four food cans, distribute the weight evenly. Let the fish stand from 24 to 36 hours in the refrigerator. Turn the fish every 12 hours, but make sure the two fillets remain pressed closely together. Baste the salmon with the liquid marinade that accumulates, separating the halves a little to baste the salmon on the inside. Replace the wooden board and weights each time.

When the *gravlaks* is ready to be served, remove the salmon from its marinade, scrape away the dill and spices and gently pat dry with paper towels. To slice, place the separated halves skin side down, and use a sharp knife to cut across the fish at a sharp angle, slicing thinly and detaching each slice from the skin. It should be served cold and maybe kept in the refrigerator for several days if necessary. Serve decorated with dill and twisted lemon slices. If used as a main course serve with boiled/steamed potatoes, fresh peas and dill sauce.

Baked Salmon (Ovnstekt laks)

	Garnish:
1 whole salmon (whatever size needed)	**Lemons, juice and slices**
Butter	**Dill or parsley**
Water, fish bouillon, milk or cream	**Tomatoes**
	English cucumbers

Have your fishmonger clean the fish. As soon as you bring it home wash it under running, cold water. The blood and the dark membrane must be rinsed or brushed away. By rubbing a little salt in first it will come off easier. Quickly dry the fish after rinsing. Rub in the salt and place on buttered heavy aluminum foil. Place a pat or two of butter in the cavity, and add a few tufts of dill or parsley. Cover tightly and follow baking direction for fat fish. The salmon is ready when the back fin comes off and when a toothpick inserted in the thickest part is easily penetrated.

Carefully remove salmon to a hot platter. Remove the skin off the top layer. Tuck some dill or parsley, tomato wedges and cucumber slices around the salmon. Slit thin lemon slices, twist and garnish the delicate fish, add some greens if needed and sprinkle with paprika. Strain the broth, and serve as is, or use to make sauce of your choice, such as rémoulade. Or serve the traditional way, with hot melted butter to which chopped fresh chives have been added. Serve with boiled/steamed potatoes, vegetables and traditional cucumber salad.

Baked whole salmon is marvelous with a smorgasbord, or julebord.

Salmon Platter (Laksekabarét)

4 lbs. (1,800 g) salmon, cooked
6 eggs, hard boiled
6-8 tomatoes, small
2 lbs. (900 g) shrimp
1 bunch radishes

1 head Boston lettuce
1 English cucumber
Mayonnaise to taste
Light cream
Lemon Juice
Parsley

A wonderful dish for a party, and a good way to make the salmon go further is to make this salmon platter. An added bonus is that most can be prepared a day in advance. Serve with hard rolls or fresh bread.

The day before, clean, and carefully steep the salmon. (See Fish chapter). Remove skin and bones while still warm, and place them back in the fish broth. Cool salmon and place in covered container. Boil the eggs, cool, shell and put in a covered container. Clean the shrimp and place in plastic bag. Wash and dry lettuce and place in plastic bag.

Just before the guests arrive arrange the lettuce with the salmon on top on a large platter. Add chopped eggs, quartered tomatoes, sliced cucumbers and shrimp (save a few out). Stir mayonnaise with a little light cream, and a few drops of fresh lemon juice. Pour mayonnaise over all and decorate in diamond shapes with finely chopped parsley and shrimp. **Serves 12.**

Trout In Sour Cream (Ørret med rømme)

2 trouts
1 tbsp. salt
Parsley, chopped
2-3 tbsp. butter or margarine
3 tbsp. flour

Salt and pepper to taste
½ cup (1¼ dl) sour cream
Lemon slices
Paprika

Clean fish under running water. Make a couple shallow diagonal cuts in the thickest part of the fish. Sprinkle inside lightly with salt and stuff with parsley. Carefully brown butter in skillet. Roll fish in mixture of flour, salt and pepper. Brown trout over medium heat, turning once. Add sour cream and continue to simmer over low heat until done. Baste the fish from time to time. When done, remove fish to platter, adding all the gravy from the pan. Add a little water to the pan, bring to a boil and stir well, add this to fish platter just before serving. Decorate with parsley and twisted lemon slices. Sprinkle with paprika. **Serves 2.**

Mackerel Fillets (Dillstekt makrellfilet)

In the spring the mackerel is low in fat (approx. 3%). However in the autumn it can contain as much as 30% fat, which means an abundance of Omega 3 fatty acids. And don't forget mackerel is a rich source of vitamin D and B12.

2 lbs. (900 g) mackerel, approx.	**1 bunch dill**
2 tbsp. oil	**2 tsp. salt**
¼ cup (½ dl) water, scant	**Pepper to taste**
Juice of 1 lemon	**Butter or margarine**

Clean and fillet fish, or have your fishmonger do it. Make a marinade of oil, water, lemon juice and finely chopped dill. Leave the fillets in marinade for 1 hour. Remove fillets and drain but allow the dill to remain on the fish. Fry in butter or margarine over moderate heat for approximately 3 minutes on each side. Serve with steam/boiled potatoes, steamed carrots and cauliflower and cucumber salad. **Serves 4.**

Pickled Mackerel (Syltet makrell)

2 mackerel, small	**1½ tbsp. salt**
1½ quarts (liters) water	**10 pepper corns, whole**
¼ cup (½ dl) white wine	**3 bay leaves**

Clean and wash the fish. Combine remaining ingredients in a kettle and allow to boil 15 minutes. Add the cleaned mackerel to the brine and steep approximately 20 minutes. Remove mackerel to a bowl and pour boiling brine over. Cool, cover and refrigerate until the next day. Delicious served with sour cream and a pinch of sugar. Serve with hot potatoes, salad and flatbread. **Serves 2-3.**

Dishes of Salted Herring (Retter av spekesild)

Salted herring must be cleaned and fillet before it is soaked. By placing the herring to soak in a mixture of water and milk, one is assured of a firm, white and delicate fish. Heavily salted herring should be soaked a minimum of 12 hours. Herring dishes improves in flavor as they stand.

Pickled Herring (Sursild)

For this dish you will need salted herring, available at Scandinavian delicatessens. Friday was salted herring day in our home, a very inexpensive food at the time. No freshly ironed tablecloth this day. Mamma would spread out a double sheet of wax paper for each, then she'd place the cooked potatoes and herring on each place setting. That was it! Pappa loved this meal, he would take 1 herring fillet at a time and meticulously cut them in even pieces and eat them with the potatoes.

2 to 4 salted herring fillets	**1 cup (2½ dl) water**
2 onions, yellow or red	**½ cup (1¼ dl) sugar**
3 bay leaves	**1 tbsp. black peppercorns, whole**
²/₃ cup (1½ dl) wine vinegar	

Clean herring, cut off tail and head and rinse well in running cold water. Make shall cut in skin backbone and peel off skin, pulling towards tail end. Fillet. Put in mixture of milk and water, enough to cover, and allow to stand about 12 hours. Remove and drain. Cut fillets in 1 inch (2½ cm) pieces. Thinly slice onions. Layer the herring and the onion slices alternately in a glass jar. Add bay leaves. Bring vinegar, water, sugar and pepper to a boil, let cool. Pour over herring and refrigerate. Let stand at least overnight before serving. Standing improves flavor. **Makes about ¾ quart.**

Spiced Herring *(Kryddersild)*

2 lbs. (900 g) salted herring	4 whole cloves
Milk and water, to cover	4 whole allspice
1 tbsp. vinegar	1 bay leaf, large
8 black peppercorns	4 slices onion

Soaking: Clean herring, cut off tail and head and rinse in running water. Make shallow cut in skin along backbone and peel off skin, pulling toward tail end. Fillet. Put in a mixture of milk and water enough to cover. Allow to stand 12 hours. Remove and drain. Bring all other ingredients to a boil. Cool, and pour over fillets. Let stand at least 24 hours before using.

Spiced Herring in Dill *(Kryddersild i dill)*

Spiced Herring	Potatoes
Coffee cream	Dill
Mayonnaise, light	Fresh dill tufts

Use as many spiced herrings as needed. Mix a little cream with light mayonnaise and add plenty of chopped fresh dill. Pour the sauce on a deep platter. Roll up spiced herring fillets and place on their side in the sauce. Add a tuft of fresh dill to the center. Chill thoroughly and serve with piping hot potatoes and hardtack.

Herring in Tomato Sauce *(Tomatsild)*

3 spiced herring	⅔ cup (1½ dl) sugar
⅓ cup (¾ dl) tomato purée (not paste)	¾ tsp. whole pepper
¼ cup (½ dl) white vinegar	1 onion, large
2 tbsp. water	3 bay leaves, large
2 tbsp. oil	Dill

Follow soaking directions for Spiced Herring. Cut into bite size pieces. Mix all ingredients except onion, bay leaves and dill. Slice onion very thin. In a glass bowl layer onion, herring and bay leaves. Sprinkle with chopped dill. May be made up to 2 weeks in advance, but chill 24 hours before serving.

Herring in Mustard *(Sennepssild)*

4-6 spiced herring fillets	3 tbsp. pickle juice
⅔ cup (1½ dl) sour cream	½ cup, scant (1 dl) fresh dill or,
2 tbsp. mustard, prepared	2 tbsp. fresh chives, chopped, or 1 tbsp. dry

Follow soaking directions for Spiced Herring. Cut herring crosswise in bite-size pieces. Place in serving dish. Add mustard and pickle juice to the sour cream to taste. Add dill. (Lots of fresh dill is delicious). Pour over herring, reserving a few herring pieces for decoration. Sprinkle with chives.

Scrumptious Herring Salad (Herlig sildesalat)

Rinse equal amounts of bite-size pieces of soaked herring, (dried on paper towel), and boiled, cold potatoes. Add finely chopped onion, as much as desired. Whip sour cream, add 1 tablespoon sugar to 1 cup (2½ dl) sour cream, and plenty of capers. Add a couple of drops of green food coloring or until the sauce is light green. Mix with the salad. Serve with pumpernickel bread.

Haddock (Hyse)

The ingeniousness of the Norwegian homemaker to utilize every particle of food with which the earth and sea blesses her, is manifested in the following five recipes made from one large haddock.

Freshness is all important, both for taste and success in making these dishes. Get acquainted with your fishmonger and his expected arrival of fish. Have him give you a ring when your particular delicacy arrives - then waste no time getting there. Hurry home just as quickly, and prepare your fish immediately. From experience I know you will have a most rewarding few hours.

For the following recipes:

FISHBALLS (Fiskeboller)
FISHPUDDING (Fiskepudding)
FISHCAKES (Fiskekaker)
FISH GRATIN (Fiskegrateng)
FISH CHOWDER (Fiskesuppe)

You will need:

One 8 to 9 lbs. (3¼-4 kg) haddock,	**4 stalks celery, large**
7 large eggs	**½ cup (1¼ dl) salt pork**
½ cup (1¼ dl) potato starch flour (not corn starch)	**4 onions, medium**
1 qt. (liter) cold milk, very fresh	**1 cup (2½ dl) coffee cream**
1 tbsp. nutmeg, grated	**½ lb. (225 g) shrimp**
	Salt to taste

Have the fish cleaned and fillet. Be sure to ask for the head, fin parts, and backbone. If your fishmonger is as nice as mine (he probably is) he no doubt will throw in an extra head or two for broth. Rinse fish well in cold, running water and dry on paper towels. Place the heads, fins, and backbones in a large kettle, cover completely with cold water and add two generous tablespoons of salt. Cover and bring to boil. Boil gently for 30 minutes.

Now, back to the fillets. If using a meat grinder, grind the fish three times, (or use food processor, or place small amounts of fish and onion at a time in a blender, and blend for 1 minute at high speed) blend together with 2 peeled onions. Discard the slivers of fish that adhere to the grinder blades. In order to salvage all bits of fish in the grinder it is helpful to put through a cut-up, peeled raw potato. Put entire amount of pureéd fish in a large bowl, add 1 tablespoon salt and 1 tablespoon grated nutmeg, and mix thoroughly. Add 3 eggs, one at a time, beating at least 5 minutes after each addition. Add ½ cup (1½ dl) of potato starch flour and beat again. Add 1 quart (liter) fresh, whole milk, 1 ounce (2 tbsp.) at a time, mixing well with each ounce. When all the milk has been added continue to beat for another 15 minutes.

Drain kettle containing fish parts and transfer fish broth to another large kettle. After fish parts have cooled, remove all fish meat and place in a covered container and refrigerate. This will be used for gratin and chowder, which may be made at a later date-but within one week.

Divide the ground fillet mixture into thirds, refrigerating two thirds and reserving one third for immediate use.

Fish Balls (Fiskeboller)

Dip a tablespoon in cold water and pick up an amount of dough the size of a large egg. Shape in the palm of your hand. Drop the egg into boiling fish broth and simmer gently for 25 to 30 minutes, never allowing the boiling to stop. The fish balls will float to the surface. When cooking period is completed they will slowly sink. You may remove the fish balls and store them in a container for later use, or make a white sauce with shrimp, or season with curry, and pour over the hot fish balls. May be frozen. **Serves 4.**

Fish Pudding (Fiskepudding)

Preheat oven to 350°F (175°C). Take one third of the fish dough and pack down firmly in a well-greased loaf pan, using a spoon which has been dipped in water. Place this loaf pan in another pan filled with 1½ inches (3¾ cm) of hot water, and bake 45 minutes, or until done. If an inserted toothpick comes out clean, the pudding is done. May be served with white sauce and shrimp or curried white sauce. Or slice to thickness of your finger and brown in a little butter. May be frozen. **Serves 4.**

From the sea leaps
like a troll in a box
the long fresco:
Reddish gray granite
a gray-green dawn.
A sunburst amidst
a cloud - of lead.
Reiis-Andersen

Fish Cakes (Fiskekaker)

Using the remainder third of the dough, shape as for fish balls. Melt butter or margarine in a heavy fry pan. Flatten the balls to ¾ (2 cm) inch depth and fry slowly to a medium brown. Transfer to another skillet until all are browned. Leave at least 3 tablespoons of the butter in the pan; brown well, but do not burn. Remove from heat add 3 tablespoons flour and blend. Add 1½ cups (3½ dl) fish broth all at once, and whisk until smooth. Return to heat and add more liquid if needed to make a smooth gravy. Pour gravy over the fish cakes and cook gently 25 to 30 minutes. A sliced onion may be browned and added to the gravy. May be frozen. **Serves 4.**

Fish Gratin (Fiskegrateng)

Make a white sauce and add ¼ teaspoon grated nutmeg. Add 2 cups (5 dl) of fish (gleaned from fish parts) to sauce and mix well. Beat 4 egg whites until stiff; fold into white sauce mixture until thoroughly blended. Place in buttered casserole. Sprinkle with topping of bread or zwieback crumbs. Dot with butter. Chopped chives added to the butter makes a delicious flavor. Bake at 350°F (175°C) for 50 minutes. Test for doneness with toothpick. Must be eaten at once. Serve with baked or boiled potatoes and melted butter. **Serves 4 to 6.**

Fish Chowder (Fiskesuppe)

Clean and dice 4 large stalks of celery. Cook in small amount of water until tender. Dice ½ cup (1¼ dl) of salt pork and fry gently, but well. Dice one medium onion. Make cream sauce with coffee cream. Dilute with fish broth, resulting in a rather thick sauce. Then add celery and water in which it was cooked, the fried salt pork and diced onion. The final addition is 1-1½ cups (2½-3¾ dl) fish meat. Cook gently for 30 minutes. When serving, sprinkle individual bowls with fresh, chopped chives. **Serves 4 to 6.**

Creamsauce: Melt ¼ cup (½ dl) of butter, add 2 heaping tablespoons of white flour and blend. Dilute gradually with 2 cups (5 dl) milk until desired thickness. Simmer 7-8 minutes. Season to taste.

Shellfish (Skalldyr)

Shellfish such as lobster, shrimp, crab and crayfish, although expensive, is by many considered a much-appreciated luxury food. Shellfish does not keep well and must be kept refrigerated, and eaten as soon as possible after being cooked. Shrimp, lobster, and crayfish change color during the cooking process because the dye in the shell is destroyed when exposed to heat.

Boiled Lobster (Kokt hummer)

Place the live lobster in cold water and bring to a boil. Boil 5 minutes, reduce heat and simmer 15 minutes more. (By this method the lobster becomes drugged at the lower temperatures).

Or, to drug the lobster before boiling, place in heavy salted water 1½ cups (3½ dl) salt to each quart (liter) of water for a couple of minutes. Then plunge into boiling water. Use high heat so the water does not stop boiling when the lobsters are added. Add ¼ cup (½ dl) salt for each quart of water and dill, if desired. Boil 5 minutes, reduce heat and simmer 15 minutes. After the cooking period, plunge the lobster into cold water to stop the cooking action. When cooled, place lobster on its back, and with a sharp knife, cut in half lengthwise from head to tail. Discard all organs. Remove the black vein which runs along the back and underside of the tail meat. Crack the claws with a nutcracker.

Broiled Lobster (Ristet hummer)

Plunge live lobster head first into rapidly boiling, salted water, enough to cover. Cook for two minutes. Remove. Follow preceding recipe regarding cleaning. Head may be removed at this time. Place lobster under broiler with shell side up, about 5 inches (12½ cm) from the flame, and broil 7 minutes. Turn, flatten lobster open to expose the meat. Brush with melted butter and broil another 7 to 8 minutes. Serve with melted butter and lemon.

Oysters (Østers)

A few hundred years ago oysters were harvested in abundance on the west and south coast of Norway, but today this delicacy has become very scarce. Norway's high-quality live oysters are now harvested in isolated bays. The shell of young oysters is white, whereas the older oysters have a yellow, brownish color. The shells of live oysters are tightly closed. If it is partly open and does not close when handled, the oyster is dead and must not be eaten. Oysters must be kept refrigerated.

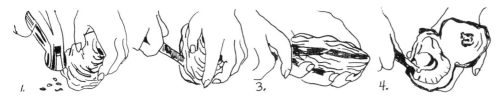

Wash and rinse oysters well in cold water. Place oyster flat on counter or table to open. Secure with the left hand and with the right hand force an oyster knife between the shell and at the narrowest part. (see illus. 2). Many prefer to hammer the edge of the shell first which allows the knife to be inserted more easily (see illus. 1). Cut across the large constrictor muscle by sliding the knife close to the flat shell where the muscle is fastened (see illus.3). Cut across the underside of the same muscle by cutting deep into the round part of the shell (see illus. 4) and leave the oyster lying loose in the shell. If oysters are to be served out of the shell, collect them in a bowl or pan until all the cleaning is completed. Then carefully check the oysters for any pieces of shell which may have been overlooked.

Fried Oysters (Stekte østers)

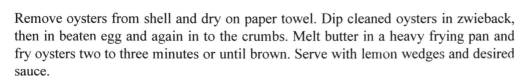

Oysters   Crushed zwieback
1 egg, beaten   Lemon

Remove oysters from shell and dry on paper towel. Dip cleaned oysters in zwieback, then in beaten egg and again in to the crumbs. Melt butter in a heavy frying pan and fry oysters two to three minutes or until brown. Serve with lemon wedges and desired sauce.

Cauliflower With Shrimp Sauce (Blomkål med rekesaus)

1 head of cauliflower, medium   **¼ cup (½ dl) cream**
2 tbsp. butter   **Salt**
2 tbsp. flour   **Pepper**
2 ½ cups (6¼ dl) whole milk or use   **2 lbs. (900 g) shrimp, cooked and shelled**
    part cauliflower broth

In late summer when cauliflower is rather inexpensive, this dish is much enjoyed in Norway. Served with French bread and a green salad it makes a tasty supper anytime of the year.

Remove leaves and trim base from cauliflower. Boil or steam cauliflower in, or over, salted water until just tender. Do not overcook. Keep hot. Melt butter in saucepan, add flour, and stir in milk or broth, bring to a boil. Stir in cream. Simmer over low heat 5 to 8 minutes. Add seasoning and shrimp, and simmer long enough for shrimp to heat through. *Do not boil.* Lift head of cauliflower carefully to a large heated platter or shallow bowl, and pour sauce over. Sprinkle with paprika, and add a tuft of parsley.
Serves 4-6.

Crabs (Krabber)

Use a large utensil and fill with water. Salt as you would for potatoes and add a sprig of dill for exciting flavor. Sea water can be used for cooking crabs, but even then additional salt should be added. Bring water to a rapid boil and add crabs, only a couple at a time, so the water does not stop boiling. Depending on their size, they should be done in 15 to 20 minutes. Allow to cool in the same water. When cool, remove both large and small claws carefully. A nutcracker is a helpful tool.

  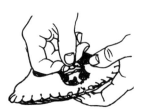

If the shell is hard use a hammer and tap carefully on the large claws to extricate the delicious meat in one piece. Pull off top shell, remove the spongy parts such as gills, stomach and intestines; remove the semi-transparent membrane covering the body. Remove small apron-shaped piece on bottom of crab and the projecting parts opposite. Break body in two. Serve crab with melted butter, a little mayonnaise or vinegar. Toasted French bread is excellent served with crab.

Crab Feast (Krabbelag)

Plan 1 whole crab per person. Prepare and clean crab as in previous recipe. Give each person a nut cracker and a seafood fork. Set the table with lemon wedges, pepper, and mayonnaise. French bread and butter, or choose a delicious sauce, like Chili Sauce or Chive-Parsley Sauce.

Sardines (Sardiner)

To my mind there are sardines and then there are Norway sardines. And there is no comparison. It is said that, "In Norway they catch the fish to fit the can. Elsewhere they *cut* the fish to fit the can". You can tell a Norwegian sardine by its smoky, savory flavor. A sardine from Norway tastes different because of the smoking. Slow-burning oak fires - used to preserve the delicate flesh even before canning methods were perfected by Stavanger Hermetiske Fabrik in 1879 - render a rich, mellow savoriness found in no other canned sardine. Laurels should be heaped on the two enterprising Norwegians, Martin Gabrielsen and John Mejlænder whose inquiring minds, discovered how to preserve the sea's bounty of small ocean fishes in the summer for enjoyment the year round.

"Caught and canned in a day." First, a quick brine bath descales the sardines and makes them more receptive to the smoking. Then the fish are sorted to size automatically, threaded by machine onto thin steel rods where they are suspended individually by heads and conveyed into the ovens to be lightly smoked for one hour over slow-burning selected oak wood which heightens natural flavor and adds special tang. After the smoking, mechanized knives cut off the heads.

Trained packers carefully hand-layer the smoked fish into cans. Each can is checked by inspectors to insure uniform filling.

Pure oil or sauce is added automatically by machine. (The olive oil, natural sardine oil, tomato and mustard sauce must pass strict Norwegian and U.S. inspection). Then the lids are put on and the can is hermetically sealed, washed and placed in steamer for one hour to cook and to thoroughly sterilize the contents.

How to tell a Norway winter caught brisling (or sprat) from a Norway summer caught brisling: Each can of sardines from Norway is required by Norwegian law to be labeled with a thorough description of contents, kind of oil, weight, packer, etc.

Summer-caught brisling: very tender flesh, often so juicy and plump it's hard to remove the fish whole from the can. Ranges in size from 3½ to 4¾ inches (8⅝ to 12 cm) long. Packed only in pure virgin olive oil.

Winter-caught brisling: firmer in flesh and texture, can be larger in size, ranging from 3¾ to 6¾ inches (7½ to 15 cm) long. Usually packed in light natural oil from the fish itself, highly refined and specially developed by the test laboratories of the Norwegian Canning Industry.

Today, medical researchers are discovering what seafaring Norwegians have known for centuries: Seafood is good for you! Salt water fish are also an excellent source of iodine. Tiny Norwegian sardines are excellent as a source of bone-building calcium and vitamin D.

Each three-ounce (85 g) serving contains 372 milligrams of calcium - more than an eight-ounce (2½ dl) glass of whole milk. Sardines also provide 10 percent of the U.S. RDA for energy important iron and riboflavin (vitamin B12).

Fish are rich in omega-3. But not all fish are created equal. Fattier fish living in icy, northern waters - such as Norway sardines - seem to yield especially high levels of omega-3 oil. A 3½ oz. serving of drained Norway sardines contain 5.1 g of Omega-3. As one of the cold-water fish with the highest omega-3 counts, sardines offer a convenient way to incorporate the nutritional benefits of fish oils in a diet. (For recipes see Index.)

Adieu, farewell, for the last time

Farewell, farewell my ancient land
I am now onboard
I am too impoverished to live
and build my future here.

Happiness is beckoning from afar
with a rose-colored hand
Here at home I have to toil
in poverty's domain.

Farewell, farewell my proud Norway,
my native land farewell!
I love you dearly - your fjords,
your mountains and your woods.

You are so beautiful my native land,
when shrouded in the colors of spring.
When birch trees burst and sway in green
and *blåveis* peek from beneath the snow.

Marius Elvinus

Many emigrants can relate to the words above. As their ships set out for distant lands they were grasped with a melancholy and sadness only emigrants can understand. Often this longing for their native land stays with them throughout life.

Meat, Poultry and Game

Lamb (Lam)

Has a mild, and yet singular flavor. The meat has fine fibrous structure, and is tender and juicy.

Frozen lamb: Like all meat, it should be defrosted in the refrigerator or in a very cold room. Quick defrosting in a warm room causes the meat juices to seep out leaving the meat less flavorful and juicy.

Cooking: Never boil meat hard, but let simmer. Use this procedure; Bring water to a boil, add meat, and return to a boil. Skim well, and add ingredients recipe calls for. Let the meat simmer until tender. The length of time depends on the thickness of the meat.

Frying: Dry the meat pieces well with a paper towel. Add butter to frying pan, let it melt, foam-up, and turn a nut brown. Be careful not to burn. When foam subsides add the meat. Add one serving portion at a time into the pan. Add salt and spices after the meat is browned. Let pan cook a minute or two after meat is removed and before adding additional pieces. This will assure an even hot surface in the pan. Pour the strained meat juice over the meat in a kettle and simmer until done.

Roasted: You will get the best result when it bakes at 265°F (130°C). Always use a meat thermometer. Insert into the thickest part of the lean meat, and do not let it touch fat or bone. The cooking period depends on weight and thickness of meat, and how you like it baked. Lamb ribs are baked at a higher temperature, 350°F (175°C), to secure golden brown and crisp ribs.

Ribs of Lamb with a Touch of Birch (Pinnekjøtt)

Most Scandinavian delicatessens will be able to supply you with *pinnekjøtt*. Cooking directions are the same as for your home-cured ribs. Figure on 10-12 ounces (285-340 g) of *pinnekjøtt* per person. It is not by chance that Christmas and *pinnekjøtt* are so closely associated. They belong together! The sheep that have been getting fat from their summer-time grazing on the mountain farms, are slaughtered in September and October, and it is from these animals the ribs are taken.

4½ lbs. (2 kg) cured lamb ribs-pinnekjøtt
Boiling water

Cooking: Soak ribs overnight in lots of water. Cooking the lamb rib to perfection is part of the preparation. Use a large kettle with very little water in the bottom. Position an interlaced "bridge" of small birch branches (with bark removed) just over the water in the kettle (or use a rack). A dexterous person will have no problem building a firm "bridge" so the meat will not receive an involuntary dunking!

Distribute the meat evenly on this structure, cover tightly and put a weight on top. Place over moderate heat and cook for approximately 2 hours. More water may be added as necessary. Do not remove the meat until tender or until it is ready to be served.

Boiled/steamed potatoes are usually served with *pinnekjøtt*, and mashed rutabagas with the addition of a generous amount of butter and some cream makes this a royal feast. Let each guest season with pepper to taste. A large serving platter is ideal for

The western area of Norway, has given Norwegian food culture a delicious dish that is reserved, in most cases, for Christmas. Some vestlendinger *insist that the anticipation is even better than the taste, if that is possible.*

both the rutabagas and *pinnekjøtt*. Mound the mashed rutabagas in the center of the platter. Arrange the ribs so that the cutlet end borders the platter and the ribs point upwards, encircling the heaped rutabagas. What a magnificent sight! A choice lamb rib is fat enough that no additional sauce is needed, but if so desired, the cooking broth may be served on the side. And yes, using both hands to eat *pinnekjøtt* is quite acceptable.

Dry-salting: Rub the lamb ribs well with salt to which has been added a large pinch of saltpeter, which will give meat a red, more delicate appearance. (Saltpeter is optional.) Put a generous layer of salt, mixed with a little saltpeter, in the bottom of the salt tub. Lay the ribs on top with the bone side up and cover with another blanket of salt. The salt will draw the blood out from the meat and create a brine which is used for basting the meat from time to time. Some Norwegian cookbooks recommend the mutton remain in this salt for 2 days, but 36 hours is sufficient. Dry the mutton rib well and it is ready for hanging. Many maintain 3 to 4 days' drying time is enough, but *pinnekjøtt* experts insist on a much longer time - from butchering season until Christmas, or not less than 2½ months. It is important that the drying process gets off to a good start, so the use of an electric fan for the first 3 or 4 days is recommended. Hang in the airiest, driest and darkest place possible. When finished drying, remove the rib with cutlet attached. It is necessary to soak the cutlet in water for a couple of hours after such a long hanging period.

A stabbur - storage house. One could tell the wealth of its owner by the amount of decorative carvings displayed on doorposts and gables.

Norway's national dish! Dr. Thor Heyerdahl, world renowned Norwegian ethnologist, author and explorer of Kon-Tiki and RA II fame, shared his favorite version of this recipe with us.

Lamb and Cabbage (Fårikål)

A welcome sign of fall in my youth was a pot of *fårikål* simmering on our black wood stove. The cherished sunlit summer evenings, replaced by the pitch black September nights was a perfect setting for this dish. The whole pepper corns hidden in between cabbage leaves and under chunks of meat is part of the "tradition", but if you want to avoid the "nuisance" inclose them. I usually double the peppercorns recipes call for.

6 lbs. (2¾ kg), breast or shoulder   **1 tbsp. black pepper corns**
2 large heads cabbage   **1 tbsp. salt**
                                           4 tbsp. flour

Wash the lamb in lukewarm water and cut into small pieces. Blot dry, dip in flour and layer in pot with a little more than half the cabbage which has been washed and coarsely cut. Add boiling water until it reaches half the level of the meat. Add salt and pepper. Simmer for 1 hour; then add reminder of the cabbage. Simmer well covered for about 1 hour longer, or until meat and cabbage are tender. Serve with steam/boiled potatoes, carrots and flatbread. **Serves 10-12.**

Fricassee of Lamb (Lammefrikassé)

2 lbs (900 g) of lamb w/bone   **2-3 carrots**
   neck, shoulder, ribs   **1 parsnip**
   or shanks   **1 head cauliflower**
2½ cups (6¼ dl) water   **1 leek**
                                     1½ tsp. salt

Bring water to a boil and add the meat. Return to a boil and reduce heat and simmer about 45 minutes. Clean, peel and slice vegetables. Add to the meat the last 10 minutes. Season. Serve with rice or steam/boiled potatoes. **Serves 4.**

Lungemos from Telemark (Lungemos fra Telemark)

After several years absensce from Norway, I rather embarrassed my aunt Esther on my first return trip there. She had waited to do the final grocery shopping until I arrived, thinking I would enjoy choosing our meal. I was delighted, and knew exactly what I wanted.   The last few days before leaving America, for Norway, *lungemos* had come to mind, and that is what I desired. When I spotted it in the store, I excitedly exclaimed, *"Lomos!"* In my broken slang, that was like using "ain't" for "am not". "Ssh! It is called *lungemos*! Besides it is not fit to serve guests from America", my aunt explained obviously embarrassed.

Well - when we topped off our *lungemos* dinner, with an elegant marzipan cake, she felt somewhat better. As for me I was very happy. And my aunt - she never let me forget that bizarre meal.

This recipe, using veal and lamb, is somewhat different from the original recipe, yet very tasty. Lungemos means finely chopped lungs, or intestines, cooked in stock.

1 lb. (450 g) veal or lamb	½ tsp. pepper
1 cup (2½ dl) stock	½ tsp. ginger
1 onion, small	Salt
1 tbsp. butter	

Grind or mince the meat. Add meat, stock, onion and butter into a saucepan. Simmer about 30 minutes. Add spices and salt. If needed add a little barley flour to thicken to the consistency of porridge. Delicious served with flatbread, potatoes and lingonberries. **Serves 4.**

Potato Dumplings with Meat (Kumler med kjøtt)

Some cooks put meat or salt pork in the dumplings, others serve the meat on the side. Some serve potato dumplings with a sauce made from Norwegian goat cheese, *geitost*, while others pour melted butter over their dumplings.

Kumle recipes and traditions vary from place to place and home to home. This is Ingrid Espelid Hovig's, Norwegian culinary expert and television chef's recipe as used in her home in Bergen.

1½ lbs. (675 g) salted and smoked mutton	1 lb. (450 g) salt pork, approx.
	3 quarts (liter) water

Soak the meat and salt pork overnight. Bring to a boil, uncovered, in fresh cold water. Skim. Simmer meat and salt pork, covered, until tender, about 1-2 hours. Remove from pan and keep warm in a little of the stock.

Potato Dumplings:

1 lb. (450 g) raw potatoes, peeled	2-3 tbsp. flour
¼ lb. (115 g) boiled potatoes	1 rutabaga, small
1 tsp. salt	Melted butter
¾-1 cup (1¾-2½ dl) barley flour	Thyme

Grate the raw potatoes on the finest part of the grater or grind them in a food mill with the finest attachment. Mash or grind the boiled potatoes and mix the two. Add salt and flour at once to prevent potatoes from darkening. If the potatoes have a high water content you should pour off some of the water before the flour is added or you will have to add more flour and then the dumplings will be too firm. The amount of flour needed depends on the quality of the potatoes. Make a small dumpling to test this. The mixture should not be so thin that the dumplings spread out into the stock, nor should they be so firm that they are heavy and tough.

Shape the dumplings with a tablespoon dipped in warm stock and drop them into the simmering stock. The meat stock should simmer at all times while the dumplings are cooking. The kettle should be so large that there is plenty of room for the dumplings or they may stick together. Simmer for about 30 minutes or until they are cooked through. To test cut a dumpling in two.

Peel the rutabaga and cut into bite-sized pieces. Boil tender in a little of the meat stock or in lightly salted water. If there is room in the kettle, the rutabagas may be cooked with the dumplings.

Cut the salt pork in slices and the meat in cubes. Place meat, pork and rutabagas on a platter with the dumplings. Serve, using the melted fat skimmed from the stock, or a little margarine as a sauce. The next day season the stock with salt and thyme to taste, and serve as a soup with the dumplings or alone. **4-6 servings.**

Cured Meat (Spekemat)

Salt-cured meat has been a traditional part of Norwegian gastronomy since Viking days. In olden times it was necessary to build stocks of dried food as insurance against the uncertainties of the future.

Before salt was used, meat was probably heat-smoked at home in the open-hearth living room and then hung in the larder for further drying and maturing.

The arrival of salt on the household scene meant a change in the method of curing, from salting to drying (maturing) and often smoking. And many were the handsome storehouses (stabbur) in rural districts, all well filled with years-old hams, legs of lamb and sausages.

Today, the production of salt-cured food in Norway is a skilled process carried out in modern slaughterhouses under constant government supervision. And salt-cured food is more popular than ever: it provides renewed contact with the simple, romantic ways of the past and, of course-it tastes so good!

The roots of this tradition rich food grows deep in Norwegian food culture. The taste is novel and exciting with innumerable possibilities for variation. Exciting entrees may be prepared in moments, and it tastes delicious all year round. It is also suitable around the clock, on a piece of bread in the morning, in a salad for lunch, in a picnic basket, together with dill-stewed potatoes for dinner. For parties or evening snack, or on a buffet, cured meat is welcome. Always keep some type of cured meat on hand, you can always count on somebody dropping in, right?

Cured Meat Buffet (Spekematbuffet)

The serving of Norwegian salt-cured meat abounds with attractive possibilities. The salt-cured buffet, with its numerous variations and combinations is easy to prepare because most of the dishes can be placed ready on the table before the guests arrive. Suitable all year around - genuine Viking food which invariably attracts a great deal of well-deserved attention.

Scrambled eggs and salt cured meats go together naturally in the Norwegian diet. The scrambled eggs may, if desired, be served cold. Beat together 4 eggs, 3 tbsp. cream, ¼ teaspoon salt and 1 tablespoon chopped chives. Pour into medium-hot frying pan containing 1½ tablespoon melted butter. Gently heat the mixture until it begins to coagulate, stirring with a fork.

Sour cream and Norwegian flatbread make an excellent accompaniment to this type of food; as do fresh-fried chipped potatoes and mushrooms fried in butter.

Omelettes, either plain or vegetable filled - asparagus, cauliflower, celery or leek are particular favorites.

Baked tomatoes with butter and Norwegian flatbread add a novel touch.

Potato salad with sour cream is very easy to make. First prepare some boiled potatoes. Mix ¾ tablespoon of French-type mustard sauce and 1 cup (2½ dl) sour cream. Pour this over the sliced potatoes and sprinkle liberally with chopped chives.

Slicing cured meat: Slice the meat on a chopping board using a sharp knife. Start slicing from the thickest muscle near the shank and then cut slices across the muscle fibers so that the meat will be tender. White bread or Norwegian flatbread and butter should accompany the dish. In Norway sour cream is a favorite accompaniment.

Preserving cured meat: Meat being hung to dry should be placed in a bag of porous material such as cheesecloth (not plastic), which should not come in contact with the meat. A stiff wire frame around the meat can prevent this. The top opening of casing should be tightly closed at all times. The cured meat may be cut into smaller portions and frozen.

Salt-Cured Ham (Spekeskinke)

The ideal weight for a good salt-cured ham is 8½-11 pounds (4-5 kg). In the preparation of salt-cured ham the same method is used as for salt-cured leg of lamb, but because the ham is larger more salt and a longer curing period is required. The ham may be either brine-cured or dry-salted. Prepare brine, thoroughly clean a suitable container and chill both. Rub the ham well with salt using approximately ¼ cup (½ dl) to each 2¼ pounds (1 kg) of meat (the addition of ½ tablespoon sugar is optional). Place a generous layer of salt mixture beneath the meat as well as between the layers and carefully pour the brine into the container to completely cover.

Pour *carefully* to avoid washing away the rubbed-in salt. If a large quantity of meat is being cured and is therefore tightly packed, it leaves less room for the brine, so be sure to salt extra well. Place a weight on the meat so that it will be completely submerged at all times. Salted meat must be carefully observed. If a grey scum appears on the surface, remove and add more salt, bring to a boil and skim well. It is not advisable to make a fresh brine as this will remove additional meat juices and affect the flavor of the meat. Whether the dry-salt or brine-cured method is employed, the meat should cure for 6 to 10 weeks before being hung to dry. Remove ham from the brine, rinse well in cold water and hang to dry in a well ventilated, comparatively dry and not too warm area. The ham may also be smoked. If so, first soak in cold water for 24 hours to remove excess salt. It should be thoroughly dried before being smoked. It takes from 4 to 5 months for the ham to be cured and ready to eat.

Winter Brine (Vinterlake)   Summer Brine (Sommerlake)

10 quarts (liters) water   **10 quarts (liters) water**
3 lbs. (1 kg 350 g) salt (not iodized)   **4½ lbs. (2 kg) salt (not iodized)**
1½ lbs. (675 g) sugar   **1½-2½ cups (3¾-5¾ dl) sugar**

A stronger brine is required if meat takes place during summer weather or in a warm, humid room. The brine can be made from either coarse or regular salt. Combine all ingredients and bring to a boil. Do not use aluminum pans. Stir occasionally as the brine scorches easily. Skim well and boil from 5 to 10 minutes. Cool *completely* before pouring over the meat. Discard sediment but include any salt which may have settled on the bottom. Sugar has a tenderizing effect and gives added flavor.

Cured Leg of Lamb (Fenalår)

Fenalår another Norwegian delicacy which emanates from a period when our people struggled to preserve enough food to last through the long winters. Surely our forefathers would be amazed that what to them was a necessity, would in future generations become a favorite in Norwegian culinary culture.

In ages past most slaughtering took place in November. In the old Norwegian language the month of November was known as gormanadr (the month for butchering). It was an especially busy and taxing month as they needed to butcher a sufficient number of animals to meet their meat and bacon needs for the year. The meat was either dried, salted or smoked, or a combination of all three. It was quite a status symbol to have your *stabbur* (storehouse built on pillars) filled with food, and not at all unusual to find a cured ham or leg of lamb which had hung there for 5 or 6 years and often much longer. Experts agree, however, that for meat to be at its tastiest best it should not hang longer than from 1 to 2 years.

The preparation of salted and cured meat, *spekemat,* requires dry air, the drier air the better the meat. The size of the leg of lamb is also important. Small ones have a tendency to dry out while the larger ones remain juicy and flavorful. The fresher the meat the better the end result. Dry-salting is the best method for curing a leg of lamb, however, if more than one is being cured, use the brine method.

Dry-salting: Dry-salting extracts the juice from the meat and produces a strong brine with which meat should be basted often and evenly. Vigorously rub the salt into the meat. In a wooden tub, crock, glass or enamel container put a generous layer of salt to cover bottom. Place the meat on top of the salt with the bone side up. Sprinkle the top with a blanket of salt. If sugar is used add ½ cup sugar (1¼ dl) to 2 pounds (900 g) of salt.

New Year's Eve Game (Viltgryte)

The first time I tasted this dish was in "Sami country" in Northern Norway. I thought maybe it tasted so good because I was in "Sami surroundings", but I have never been disappointed with later servings.

This dish tastes good all year long, not only on New Year's Eve. It is the best known Sami dish in Norway. Accompaniments are boiled potatoes and stirred lingonberries. It calls for reindeer meat but any game will do.

1 lb. (450 g) half frozen reindeer shoulder thinly sliced	**½ cup (1¼ dl) milk, scant**
Butter for browning	**¼ cup (½ dl) sour cream**
½ cup (1¼ dl) mushrooms	**3 thin slices Norwegian goat cheese**
1 cup (2½ dl) water, scant	**5 juniper berries, crushed**
1½ tbsp. flour	**Salt and pepper**

Shave thin pieces off the half defrosted meat. Brown quickly in butter in hot pan. Clean and slice the mushrooms and fry in separate pan, add to meat. Stir in flour mixed with a little water. Bring to a boil, then reduce and let simmer 10 minutes. Stir milk into the sour cream and add to the kettle with goat cheese and juniper berries. Season with salt and pepper. **Serves 4.**

Marinated Meat (Gravet kjøtt)

An old tradition almost lost, and now revived. How lucky for us! You can use any tender meat of pork, beef, lamb, or game.

1¼ lb. (675 g) meat (fillet)	**½ to 1 tsp. black pepper, ground**
2 tbsp. salt	**½ tsp. fresh basil, crushed**
2 tbsp. sugar	

Carefully cut away any membranes and fat from meat. Mix salt, sugar and spices, and turn meat in it. Place on a platter, cover with foil and plastic wrap. Place in refrigerator from 4 to 5 days. Turn a couple of times a day. Scrape off the spices and slice paper thin before serving. Serve with mustard sauce, pickles, pickled or sliced onion and dark bread. **Serves 4.**

Meatballs (Kjøttkaker)

A favorite! The flavor is rather mild, however, and you might want to add a little more seasoning. Serve with boiled potatoes, peas, and lingonberry jam.

1 lb. (450 g) ground chuck or round	**1 tsp. salt**
1 can evaporated milk, small	**2 eggs**
¼ tsp. pepper	**3½ tbsp. flour**
¼ tsp. allspice	**2 tbsp. butter**

In a bowl, thoroughly blend ground chuck or round with evaporated milk. Add spices and eggs, mixing well. Fully stir in the flour. Add butter to frying pan. When melted, and pan is hot, form balls and add to the pan., flatten slightly with back of tablespoon. Remove to platter and make the gravy.

Gravy:	
Butter	**2 tbsp. flour**
2 onions, diced	**Water**
1 cube Knorr-Swiss bouillon	

Dice onion and sauté in butter. Add meatballs, bouillon and water; let simmer for a few minutes. Mix the flour with a little water and stir into mixture in saucepan. Let simmer for a few minutes. If a darker gravy is desired use a little Gravymaster.

Stuffed Cabbage Leaves (Kålruletter)

1 cup (2½ dl) milk	**¾ lb. (340 g) ground round**
2 slices bread, French or	**2 tsp. salt**
Vienna, crust removed	**12 cabbage leaves, white**
½ tsp. pepper	**1½ qts. (liters) water**
¼ tsp. ginger	**3 tsp. salt**
¼ tsp. nutmeg, freshly grated	

Pour milk over bread and spices and mix until smooth. Grind the meat with the salt, three or four times. Fully mix meat and bread paste. Carefully loosen cabbage leaves and parboil in salted water until limp enough to handle, or parboil whole head, making it easier to separate leaves. Remove heaviest veins from cabbage leaves. Save cooking water. Place spoonful of forcemeat on each cabbage leaf, wrap, and tie with cotton string. Boil for 15-20 minutes in water used for boiling cabbage. Remove from water, drain and remove string. Serve with a basic white sauce, spiced with a little grated nutmeg. Some prefer these cabbage rolls browned in butter and served with the brown butter. **Serves 4.**

Meat and Vegetable Loaf (Kjøtt og grønnsakpudding)

This tasty loaf is quickly made with your food processor or mixer. Make a large portion, and freeze part of it for busy days. The addition of cabbage is not only flavorful and nourishing but enables you to cut down on the meat.

½ lb (¼ kg) cabbage   1½ tsp. pepper
Water   1 tsp. nutmeg, freshly ground
Salt   2 tbsp. potato flour
1½ lb (675 g) ground meat, lean   2 cups (5 dl) milk
2 tsp. salt

Wash and core cabbage and parboil in lightly salted water 10-12 minutes. Remove from water, drain and cool. Thoroughly mix the salt into the ground meat. Stir in potato flour and nutmeg, and add milk a little at a time. Blend well after each addition until it reaches a thick, viscous consistency. Butter an oblong pan or loaf pan. Place the meat and cabbage in layers, beginning and ending with meat, and having meat all around the sides of the pan. Preheat oven to 300°F (150°C) and bake approximately 1 hour. Make the following sauce:

½ cup, scant (1¼ dl) broth   ¼ cup (½ dl) water, cold
    from meat loaf   1 tbsp. tomato purée
1¼ cups (3 dl) potato water   Touch of cayenne pepper
1 bouillon cube   1 tsp. sugar
1½ tbsp. flour   1-1½ tsp. salt

Bring meat broth and potato water to a boil. Add bouillon cube to dissolve. Make a thickening from flour and water and whisk into the broth until smooth. Let simmer 6-8 minutes. Add tomato purée, spice, sugar and salt. Serve the meat loaf with rice or boiled potatoes, and sauce. **Serves 4.**

Sausages, Simple and Delicious (Pølser - så enkelt, så godt)

A few simple rules and your sausages will be delicious every time. And why not make your own? It is neither difficult nor time consuming.

Many meat grinders and kitchen machines have optional sausage attachments. It is satisfying to know one can enjoy sausage without so many preservatives, that one feels embalmed before the meal is through.

To Cook: Never boil sausages, they should only simmer. Bring the water to a boil and turn the heat down before you add sausages. With a cooking thermometer it is easy to control the temperature of the water. Around 180°F (82°C) is the right temperature for all sausages. Simmer thin Wieners, hot dogs and other small sausages about 10 minutes. Knockwurst, bratwurst etc. about 15 minutes, and large dinner sausages, pork sausages, etc. about 20 minutes. Use this time for raw, cooked or smoked. If you need to use the sausages direct from the freezer add another half time to it. If desired, for added flavor, simmer the sausages in bouillon, add a few slices of onion or your favorite spices.

To fry: Fry over medium high heat in very little fat, and remove sausages as soon as they are browned.

To grill: When grilling outside or in the oven, make two to three slits on each of the sausages or hot dogs, or punch small holes in them. It will keep them from splitting open. Remember to turn often, sausages soon scorch on a hot grill.

Pork Sausage or Patties (Medisterpølser/kaker)

2 lbs. (900 g) lean pork   ½ tsp. sugar
¼ lb. (115 g) bacon   ½ tsp. cloves
½ lb. (225 g) veal   ½ tsp. ginger
3 tbsp. potato flour   ½ tsp. nutmeg, freshly grated

1½ tbsp. salt
1½ tsp. pepper

2 cups (5 dl) cold milk
Sausage casings

Grind meat 6 times, and add spices. Add milk a little at a time, and mix well. Add the potato flour, and work well. Stuff casings loosely. Tie. Cook a small ball to taste for correct seasoning. Simmer sausages 15 to 20 minutes. Keep in the refrigerator in the stock, on which a "lid" of fat will form. If this lid is not broken the sausage will keep quite some time. Before serving cut into 3-4 inch (7½-10 cm) lengths and brown lightly over low heat in butter or margarine.

Note: In place of sausages, patties can be made from this mixture. Fry slowly over medium heat.

Voss Sausages (Voss pølser)

Do find a butcher who will smoke these sausages for you, their delectable flavor lingers on your taste buds.

5½ lbs. (2½ kg) mutton, from
    shoulder, neck and flank
1¹/₈ lb. (450 g) fresh pork fat
¼ cup (½ dl) salt
⁷/₈ cup (2 dl) potato starch
3½-4 cups (8-9 dl) stock or water

2 tbsp. sugar
½ tbsp. pepper
¼ tsp. nutmeg
¼ tsp. ginger
Sausage casings, 4 yds. (meters)

Beautiful Voss! (Birthplace of Knut Rockne, Notre Dame's famous football coach.) I first tasted this type of sausage while overlooking the serene Voss lake, basking in the beauty surrounding it - mountains dotted with little farms. The memory will always remain.

Debone the meat and cut into strips. Cut pork fat into strips. Crack the bones, cover with water and bring to boil. Skim, let simmer to make stock, approximately 1 hour. Strain and chill. Grind meat and fat once. Add the salt and refrigerate 12 hours. Whisk the potato starch, sugar and seasonings into the cold stock. Gradually add to the meat mixture. Do not overwork the meat. Rinse the sausage casings well. (Read directions, they might have to be soaked in water for several hours). Then stuff with mixture, but not too tightly which might cause sausages to burst open. Tie securely at 16-inch (40 cm) intervals. Smoke 3-4 hours. Simmer in lightly salted water about 20 minutes. Serve with boiled potatoes and mashed rutabagas, preferably along with *pinnekjøtt*. Cold Voss sausages are good as sandwich meats and add a delicious flavor to soups and stews. **Serves 20.**

Veal Patties (Kalvekarbonader)

1 lb. (450 g) veal
¼ lb. (115 g) pork (do not remove fat)
4 zwieback, finely crushed
½ tsp. ginger
½ tsp. nutmeg
1½ tsp.salt

¼ tsp. white pepper
1 egg
½ cup (1¼ dl) light cream
½ cup (1¼ dl) soda water
1 egg
4 zwieback, finely crushed

Grind veal and pork together 3 to 4 times, or have your butcher do it. Add 4 crushed zwiebacks, seasoning and egg. Mix cream and soda water together and add. Mix well until smooth. Form into oval patties. Dip in beaten egg; roll in zwieback crumbs. Fry in butter to a light brown and serve with browned butter. **Serves 4-5.**

Reindeer Roast with Game Sauce (Dyrestek med viltsaus)

5 lbs. (2¼ kg) leg of reindeer	Sauce:
Strips of suet, ¼ inch (5 mm) thick	1½ tbsp. butter
½ cup (1¼ dl) butter	2 tbsp. flour
Salt and pepper	2 cups sour cream
1 cup (2½ dl) whole milk, warm	2 tsp. red currant jelly
1 cup (2½ dl) water	1 slice brown goat cheese

Wash meat in cold water and dry well. Trim off fat and excess skin (not the membrane that keeps muscles together). Game meat tends to be rather dry and should be larded. With thin, sharp knife, make deep holes or pockets in meat and stuff in strips of suet. Tie the roast, and rub with salt and pepper. Brown butter in large, heavy pot on top of stove. An iron pot is preferred. Grease thoroughly with butter or margarine before using. Place meat in pot, meaty side down. Brown well on all sides, adding more butter as needed. Turn with two wooden spoons to avoid pricking meat. When brown, pour on the warm milk and water, and reduce heat. Cover, leaving lid slightly ajar allowing steam to escape. Cook slowly 2 to 2½ hours, basting meat occasionally. Add more milk and water as needed to keep meat covered about two thirds. When cooking is completed, remove meat and keep warm.

Sauce: Brown butter, stir in flour, add drippings from roast a little at a time, stirring constantly to make a smooth, medium thin sauce (the sour cream will thicken it). Cook 5 to 8 minutes. Stir in sour cream, currant jelly and goat cheese. Add salt, if necessary. Let simmer a while, but do not boil. Slice and arrange meat on warm serving platter. Decorate with parsley and tomatoes. Serve sauce in separate dish. Accompanied with parsleyed, steam-dried potatoes, or small browned potatoes, and any kind of green vegetable (brussels sprouts or peas are very good). If available, rowanberry jelly with its sharp flavor is an excellent accompaniment to any game.

The Sami people are usually thought of as different groups according to the activities they carry out. The "Mountain Sami", the nomad people of Northern Scandinavia and Russia, are the typical Sami. The precious reindeer means life to the Sami people, they use every part. Bones and horns are used for objects and ornaments, skin for clothes and boots, and the priceless meat sustains life.

Veal Roast (Kalvestek)

May be treated in the same manner as reindeer roast, without the larding, and tastes delicious served with the above sauce.

Beef (Oksekjøtt)

When defrosting take from freezer and leave in refrigerator until defrosted. This prevents too much of the juice to seep out and keeps the meat tender. Be sure frying pan is well heated before adding butter or margarine. Use just a little butter/margarine, let melt thoroughly and let the foam subside before adding the meat. Fry beef of about the same thickness at the same time. And do not put too much meat in the pan at the time, this cools the pan too much. Wait to add salt until meat is done. Salt draws the juices out and leaves the meat dry. Do not puncture the meat when turning, this too will cause juice to seep out.

Hash (Pytt i panne)

1-1½ lbs. (450 - 675 g) beef, lamb, or pork leftovers or stew meat	1 large onion
	Butter
4 to 6 potatoes, cooked and cooled	Salt and pepper

Dice meat and potatoes in ½ inch (1¼ cm) cubes. Coarsely chop onion and fry lightly in a large skillet. Add meat, potatoes and seasoning (should be well seasoned). Fry slowly until nicely browned, adding butter as necessary, and turning frequently. Serve with a fried egg on top of each portion if desired. **Serves 6-8.**

Swiss Steak (Bankekjøtt)

1½ lb. (675 g) beef roast or	10 whole peppercorn
1 inch (2½ cm) thick round steak	1½ tsp. salt
Margarine for frying	3 tbsp. flour
2½ cups (6¼ dl) water	2 onions, med., sliced
1 bay leaf	

Cut meat in thin slices and dry well with paper towels before browning in margarine. (If round steak is used, pound with meat mallet; it breaks up tough fibers.) Proceed as with roast.

Remove meat from pan to kettle. After each browning, add a little of the 2½ cups (6¼ dl) water and bring to a boil, pour over meat. Eventually add remaining water. Add bay leaf, salt, pepper and simmer until meat is tender. Make a paste of flour and a little water and stir into meat juice to make gravy. Simmer 6-8 minutes. Add onion which has been browned in a little margarine. Taste for seasoning. **Serves 4-5.**

Boneless "Birds" (Benløse fugler)

½ lb. (225 g) marrow (buy marrow	1 tsp.salt
bones) or 3-4 oz. (85-115 g) fat	½ tsp. white pepper
2 lbs. (900 g) round steak	½ tsp. cloves
1 lb. (450 g) finely ground top round	½ tsp. ginger
Milk or water	

Cook marrow bones in salted water (skim water as necessary) long enough to remove marrow in one piece. Continue cooking bones to make bouillon for sauce. Have meat cut into thin slices as for steak rolls. Pound meat lightly. Work ground meat and spices together with a small amount of milk or water. On each slice of meat (individual serving size) put one tablespoon ground meat and flatten. Top with a portion of marrow. Roll up and tie with string. Brown well in butter. Add strained bouillon from bones, to cover. Allow to simmer about an hour, or until meat is tender.

Brown sauce: Brown 2 tablespoons butter and stir in 1½ tablespoon flour until smooth. Gradually add stock from the "birds," stirring constantly. Boil 6 to 8 minutes, salt to taste. Add a dash of Worcestershire sauce if desired. A small can of drained, sliced mushrooms may be added. **Serves 8.**

Roasted Pork Loin with Fruits (Svinestek med frukt)

8 medium-sized prunes, pitted	5 lbs. (2 ¼ kg) pork loin,
8 medium-sized apricots, dried	cut and deboned
1 Granny Smith apple, large	Salt and freshly ground pepper
Lemon juice	Butter and oil

Cover prunes and apricots with cold water and bring to a boil. Remove from heat and let fruit rest in water for half an hour. Peel, core and cut apple in 1-inch (2½ cm) pieces. Sprinkle with lemon juice to prevent discoloring. Push the handle of a wooden spoon in through the center of the meat; repeat on other side. Remove fruit from water and pat dry with paper towels. Mix with apples and push fruit into the meat with the wooden spoon handle until all fruit is used, and fruit is within ½-inch (1¼ cm) of either side. Season roast well with salt and pepper. Tie string firmly around the roast and secure at ends. Preheat oven to 350°F (175°C).

In a casserole large enough to hold pork loin, melt a little butter and oil over moderate heat. Let foam subside, then add pork loin, turning it from time to time with two wooden spoons. It will take about 20 minutes to brown the loin evenly on all sides. With a bulb baster remove all the fat from casserole. Pour in 2 cups water and bring to a simmer. Cover the pan tightly and place in preheated oven for approximately 1½ hours, or until the meat shows no resistance when pierced with a sharp knife. Serve with boiled-steamed potatoes, green beans, cauliflower, and stirred lingonberries or jam. **Serves 6-8.**

Pork Loin with Rib Section (Ribbe)

Ribbe is a must sometime during the Christmas holidays in Norway, always accompanied with sweet sour cabbage and stirred lingonberries, or lingonberry jam. Read the whole recipe before purchasing meat.

4 lbs. (1 kg 800 g) pork loin	1 tsp. pepper
rib cage with rind	1 tsp. ginger
1 tsp. salt	

If you purchase the center ribs have your butcher saw across the bones between the chops so that they will be easy to separate when serving. The ribs also needs to be sawn slightly apart with 2¼ inch (5½ cm) intervals. If you do it yourself use a hacksaw to be sure the bones are nearly cut through, otherwise it will be difficult to get nice serving pieces. Generously rub salt and pepper into the rind, place with the rind side down, cover and refrigerate for 48 hours before baking.

Rub salt, pepper and ginger liberally into the rind. To get a crisp crackling make diamond slits in the rind, being careful not to make the slits too deep into the rind. In a large roasting pan place the rib cage on a rack with the rind side facing down. Pour 1 cup (2½ dl) boiling water into the pan. Cover the whole pan completely with aluminum foil, place on the lowest rack in oven preheated to 450°F (230°C), and steam 15 minutes; this helps to retain the juices. Remove from the oven. Reset oven to 350°F (175°).

Remove rib cage and foil and build an even bed of foil on the rack to allow the ribs to be evenly baked, place the ribs with rind up on top of the foil and return to the baking pan. Place uncovered pan in center of the oven. Baste with drippings from time to time and bake until done. 2-2½ hours should do nicely. During the last half hour no basting is required. If the rib cage browns too quickly, place a piece of foil on top. If you desire an even crisper crackling, place the rib cage, rind-side up, under the broiler for a few minutes. Watch carefully to prevent burning. Pour off and strain the fat from the ribs and serve as sauce with the ribs. **Serves 6-8.**

Roasted Suckling Pig (Helstekt gris)

1 suckling pig	2 cups (5 dl) boiling water
3 tsp. salt	4 tbsp. butter
Vinegar and water	
1 tsp pepper	

Preheat oven to 450°F (230°C). Clean and scrub the suckling well. Soak overnight in a solution of 2 cups (5 dl) salt and 2½ tablespoons vinegar to 5 quarts water. Remove

Fishing in Lofoten

Pollock Party Soup

Lutefish ↑

Top back row left: Spiced Herring, Herring in Mustard. Front row left: Herring in Tomato Sauce, Pickled Herring. ↓

Marintated Cheese ⬆

Lamb and Cabbage ⬇

Potato Dumplings with Meat.

Tray with cured meat. Serve with your favorite potato salad and orange sauce. ↑

Lamb Roll ↓

Cheese makes any occasion festive.

Dessert Cheese ↑

Nøkkelost Quiche ↓

and dry well. Rub inside and out with seasoning. Remove eyeballs and close lids. Insert an ovenproof object approximately 2-inch (5 cm) in depth into the suckling's mouth. Pull the forelegs forward and bend the hind legs into a crouching position. Secure legs. Rub suckling with butter, transfer to a roasting pan, and pour in boiling water. Cover ears and tail with aluminum foil. Do not baste the pig with drippings but rather rub with butter or baste with oil every 15 minutes. Bake uncovered in preheated 450°F (230°C) oven for 15 minutes. Reduce heat to 325°F (165°C) and roast until tender (30 minutes to the pound). Remove suckling from the pan and keep warm.

Gravy: Pour off all but 3 tablespoons grease from the roaster. Add 2 to 3 tablespoons flour and stir until smooth. Add pan juice which has been degreased and supplemented with enough milk to make 1½ cups (3½ dl). Pour into flour mixture all at once and stir constantly until smooth. Bring to a boil and simmer 10 minutes. Add seasoning to taste and a few drops caramel coloring if desired. Remove object from the suckling's mouth and replace with a shiny, red apple. Place on a large platter or board. Garnish with greens and pickled crab apples.

Roasted Fresh Ham with Crackling (Skinkestek)

12-14 lbs. (5½-6¼ kg) fresh ham	2 tbsp. flour
3 tsp. salt	½ tsp. mustard
1 tsp. pepper	1½ tsp. red wine or
2 tbsp. margarine	1 tsp. vinegar

Have your butcher remove the ham hock. Wash ham well. One of the bonuses of fresh ham is the crisp crackling. To achieve this crisp crackling the rind must be quite moist. Soak the ham in cold water overnight with the rind side completely submerged in the water. Or steam, rind side down, 10 to 15 minutes on rack over boiling water in the roaster (reserve this water to be used later for basting). Steaming the ham makes it much easier to carve. Remove from the roaster and, with a very sharp knife, make diamond slits in the rind, being careful not to cut into the fat or meat. Rub salt and pepper thoroughly into the rind.

Return to roaster and bake in preheated 450°F (230°C) oven for 20 minutes. Reduce heat to 275°F (135°C) and bake until done, at 25 minutes per pound. Baste ham with the drippings every 20 minutes up to the last half hour. Allow the ham to remain in oven for balance of roasting period with the oven door slightly ajar. Remove all grease from drippings and add boiling water. Make a brown gravy from margarine, flour and drippings. Simmer 10 minutes. Add seasonings and red wine or vinegar to taste. Remove rind carefully and serve with the ham as an added delicacy. Serve with boiled potatoes, sweet-sour cabbage, and lingonberries. **Serves 10-12.**

In our home it would not be Christmas Eve without skinkestek. For others it is a must sometime during the Christmas season. There is not a great demand for fresh ham with the rind on in America, but keep looking you will find a butcher who knows what you are talking about.

Roast Duck (Stekt and)

Ducks are easy to prepare and are a true taste treat. Brussels sprouts, green peas or onion are vegetables that combine well with either duck or goose. If frozen, allow it to defrost in refrigerator.

1 4-5 lb. (1¾-2¼ kg) duck	½ lemon
Salt	¼ cup (½ dl) consommé, boiling
White pepper	1 cup (2½ dl) beef bouillon
2 oranges	Cornstarch

Preheat oven to 450°F (235°C). Wash duck under cold running water and dry with paper towels. Rub cavity with salt and pepper. Prick the surface of the *lower* part of the breast, around the thighs and back with a small sharp knife to produce a crisper crust. Truss the bird securely. Place on rack in shallow roaster and bake until light brown. Remove fat from roasting pan with a bulb baster. Reduce heat to 350°F (175°C) and continue roasting. Baste with boiling bouillon from time to time. After 1½ hours' roasting time pour off juice into separate pan. Add to this consomme, juice of 2 oranges and ½ a lemon, and thicken with a little cornstarch. Salt to taste. Bring to boiling point but do not boil. Pour gravy evenly over duck and return to 450°F (235°C) oven until a golden film is formed on the bird. Remove to heated platter. Decorate with greens and orange slices. Let bird rest 10 minutes for easier carving. Duck may be baked with or without stuffing using same dressing as for goose. To test for doneness, pierce the thigh with a small sharp knife. If the juice that runs out is clear yellow, the duck is done. **Serves 4-5.**

Roast Goose (Stekt gås)

1 goose, 9 lbs. (4 kg)	**1½ lbs. (675 g) apples**
Lemon	**½ lb. (225 g) prunes**
Salt	

Preheat oven to 450° (235°C). Wash the goose under cold, running water, dry with paper towels. Rub salt and lemon in cavity and outside of bird. Pour 2 cups of boiling water over prunes and soak until limp. Drain and chop. Peel and dice apples. Combine with prunes and pack loosely into cavity of bird. Fasten neck skin to back of goose and truss bird. For crisper skin, prick the lower part of breast. Place bird on rack in large, shallow pan, and reduce heat to 350°F (175°) allowing 25 minutes per pound. Remove fat with a bulb baster. The goose is rather fatty which makes basting unnecessary. Pierce the thigh with a small sharp knife to determine doneness. If the juice that runs out is clear yellow, the goose is done. For easier carving turn oven off and with oven door ajar let goose rest in the oven for 15 minutes. **Serves 6.**

Roasted Ptarmigan Breasts (Stekt rypebryst)

4 ptarmigans	**Pepper**
1 tsp. salt	**Butter**

Broth:

Water to cover meat	**Juniper berries**
1 carrot, sliced	**White pepper, to taste**
1 stalk celery, chopped	**Thyme to taste**
2 tbsp. onion, chopped	

Gravy:

1¾ cup (4¼ dl) ptarmigan broth	**3 tbsp. cornstarch**
1/2 cup (1¼ dl) whipping cream	**Salt and pepper to taste**
3-4 tbsp. sour cream	

Defrost the ptarmigans in refrigerator, and rinse in cold running water, dry with paper towels. Cut away breasts. Chop the remainder of meat and brown in butter. Add cold water to cover, and remaining ingredients for broth. Bring to a boil, skim, and let simmer uncovered for about 1-1½ hours. Strain and let it simmer until it is condensed to 1²/₃ (3¾ dl) cups. Add cream, sour cream, and thicken with cornstarch. Season to taste with salt and pepper. In a warm pan brown the breasts in butter. Salt and pepper, and bake in warm oven, 435°F (225°C) for 7-8 minutes. The meat should be juicy and pinkish. Remove from oven and let rest covered under aluminum foil 10-15 minutes. You can serve the breasts whole or sliced. Serve with gravy and cooked small red potatoes. Carrots, baby peas, cauliflower or broccoli are good vegetable accompaniment. So is lingonberries or a tart jelly. (Troll Cream or Veiled Wilderness Girls make a perfect dessert). **Serves 4.**

Hare or Rabbit (Stekt hare eller kanin)

Norway was occupied by the Germans who rounded up many construction workers, including Pappa, and sent them on work projects far away. Mamma was left with four children to care for, and began to raise rabbits. They multiplied fast, and when some time later word came that the Germans were coming to check every farm, mamma killed, skinned and canned everyone of the 93 rabbits, and shared this great food with family and neighbors.

It is impossible for me to think "rabbit" without remembering the year 1943 when we lived at Nesodden.

1 rabbit or hare	***Gravy:***
Vinegar and water	**2½ tbsp. margarine**
5 tbsp. margarine	**4 tbsp. flour**
1 tsp. salt, scant	**1²/₃-2 cups (2¾-5 dl) broth**
1½ cups (3¾ dl) milk	**1 cup (2½ dl) sour cream**
1½ cups (3¾ dl) water	**Salt**

Wash rabbit thoroughly. Place in vinegar solution (1 tablespoon vinegar to 1 quart (liter) water overnight. Remove heavy membranes and sinews, (they are not present in domestic rabbits). Be careful not to cut or tear the meat. Chop off thighs and forelegs. Divide back in two and then cut into appropriate-size serving pieces. Melt margarine in a cast iron pan. When foam subsides, add the meat and brown well on both sides. Season. Remove from pan while making gravy of margarine, flour and broth. Return meat to the gravy and let simmer over low heat for about 1½ hours. Domestic rabbit usually takes less cooking time than hare. Just before serving transfer to heated platter; keep warm. While stirring, add sour cream to gravy and bring to a quick boil. Pour over meat. Serve with whole lingonberry or cranberry sauce. **Serves 4-6.**

Sandwich Meats

Lamb Roll (Lammerull)

2 lbs. (900 g) lamb flank	**1½ tbsp. salt**
½ tsp. pepper	**1 tsp. sugar**
½ tsp. ginger	**2½ tbsp. unflavored gelatine**

At Christmas time and other festive days, many Norwegians make their own sandwich meats. Why? Tradition! Once you taste them, you will want to make it a tradition as well.

Carefully remove the thin membrane without cutting into the meat. Trim the meat into a rectangular shape, about 8 inches (20 cm) long piece. Distribute the excess trimmings evenly in the roll. Mix spices and gelatine and sprinkle over the meat. Roll tightly, beginning with the thickest end of the roll to get an even shape. Fasten with

toothpicks and tie securely with cotton thread. Place in a plastic bag in the refrigerator for 24 hours, to help the salt and spices to be absorbed into the meat before cooking. Wrap in a cloth, cheesecloth or cotton towel and tie again with cotton thread. Place in boiling unsalted water and let simmer approx. 1½ hours. (Timing depends on thickness of roll).

When cooked, remove from water and let rest 10-15 minutes before being placed in press. Place between 2 small trays with a weight on top, approx. 12 pounds (5½ kg). The roll will keep in the refrigerator in a light brine for about 10 days. It may be frozen before being cooked.

Pork Sandwich Sausage (Fleskepølse)

A sausage with the consistency similar to liver paté. Served with dark bread, butter pickles or pickled beets.

1 lb. (450 g) veal	1¼ tbsp. salt
¾ lb. (340 g) pork, lean	½ tsp. nutmeg, freshly grated
¼ lb. (115 g) pork fat	¾ tsp. ginger
1/2 cup (1 ¼ dl) onion	1¾ tsp. pepper

Grind meat, fat, and onion well together. Place in a mixing bowl, and beat 5 minutes. Add spices and salt, and beat another 2-3 minutes. Stuff sausage casings and tie off securely. Place in a kettle with near boiling water. Leave them in this water until they expand and look tight and the fat melts. Remove to another pan with boiling water. Keep the water close to the boiling point for 20 minutes. Remove from heat and place in cold water. Keep turning the sausage in the water so that the melted fat is distributed evenly and solidify in an even layer underneath the sausage casings. Refrigerate. Spread on sandwiches.

Pressed Headcheese (Persesylte)

As I reminisce, I can see Mamma working on a pig's head, preparing our Christmas *sylte*. As a child it was always a puzzle to me, why the placing of a heavy object on the headcheese could make it so delicious.

Sylte may be served as a main course with boiled potatoes and pickled beets, most often, however, it is used as pålegg - *sandwich meat.*

½ pig's head	**Filling:**
Boiling water	1 tbsp. salt
1 to 2 tbsp. salt	½ tsp. peppercorns
8 to 10 peppercorns	¼ tsp. cloves
2 bay leaves, optional	¼ tsp. allspice
2 lbs. (900 g) veal shoulder	2 tbsp. gelatin, optional

Clean pig's head thoroughly and soak in cold water overnight. It can soak as long as two to three days, but in that case the water should be changed often. Place head in boiling water to cover, together with salt, peppercorns and bay leaves. When it has boiled about 1 hour, lift from water and remove all the rind. Keep it warm. Continue cooking head until meat is tender, preferably with a little added rind. Simmer veal shoulder separately. Soften gelatine in a little water. Gelatin may be omitted if as much veal is used as called for in the recipe. Mix salt and spices. When head is cooked remove meat and fat and keep separate. Remove all meat-colored spongy spots, *eitel*, small lumps in the meat. Dip a piece of strong cheesecloth in warm water, wring out and place in pan or bowl. Arrange a layer of rind in bottom and sides. On top of this put strips of pork fat, making sure edges meet, but do not overlap. Sprinkle with spices. Layer fat, pork and veal, beginning and ending with fat, and sprinkle spices between each layer. (If gelatin is used soften and spoon between layers). Cover all with layer of rind. Wrap cloth tightly around the head cheese, and sew together with needle and thread. Return to broth in which head was cooked and heat thoroughly, about ½ hour. Remove from boiling water, drain and return to pan in which it was formed. Place a fairly heavy object on top, but not so heavy that too much juice and fat is forced out. After an hour or so add enough extra weight that the head cheese will be squeezed into desired shape, will be firm and hold together when sliced. Cool as quickly as possible and leave weight on overnight. Soak in brine about 2 to 4 days.

Brine: To 1 quart water add ½ cup salt. Add black pepper corns and a bay leaf if desired.

Pickled Pork Loaf (Sylte)

3-4 lbs. (approx. 1,800 g) pork shoulder when deboned	½ tsp. pepper
1 tsp. salt	1 tsp. allspice
	1 tsp. cloves, or more

Do not remove rind or fat from pork. Fill a large heavy-bottomed pan with water, bring to a boil and add salt, 1 tsp. per quart (liter) of water. Stir until dissolved. Add pork and let simmer 1½ to 2 hours or until tender. Rind may become cooked before meat. If the tip of a spoon penetrates the rind is done. Then carefully remove rind from meat, and if necessary continue cooking meat until done. In the meantime combine spices and salt. Line a pan (square, round or loaf) with a cloth which has been wrung out in warm water. Work with the pork as soon as it has been removed from the boiling water.

Place a layer of rind on bottom and sides of pan, making sure the edges meet but do not overlap. Slice lean meat and fat separately and place in alternate layers beginning and ending with fat. Arrange any small pieces in center of sylte. Sprinkle mixed spices between each layer. Cover *sylten* with rind, and fasten with toothpicks, or sew together with needle and heavy cotton thread. It should be about 5 inches (12½ cm) thick when sewn together. Wrap cloth tightly around and secure with string. Return to water in which the meat was boiled and let simmer about 30 minutes, or until heated through. Remove from boiling water, remove cloth, and drain. Stud with whole cloves 1 inch (2½ cm) apart. Return to pan in which it was formed and place a fairly heavy weight on top, but not so heavy that too much of the fat and juice is forced out. After an hour or so add enough extra weight that the *sylte* will be squeezed into desired shape, be firm and hold together when thinly sliced. Cool as quickly as possible and leave weight on overnight. Loosen cloth and scrape off any fat or juice. Soak in brine for 2 to 4 days. If only part of *sylte* is used at this point, again secure in cheesecloth and return to brine, but for no longer than 7 days. Keep refrigerated after removal from brine.

Brine: To 1 quart (liter) water add ½ cup (1¼ dl) salt.

Liver Paté *(Lever paté)*

1 lb. (450 g) pork liver
8 oz. (225 g) pork fat
1 onion, small
4 anchovies (Scandinavian)
  and some liquid
2 eggs
2 tbsp. flour
1 cup (2½ dl) coffee cream

¾ lb. (340 g) fresh pork fat
  cut into ⅛ inch (5 mm) thick strips
1½ tsp. salt
⅛ tsp. pepper
½ tsp. allspice, optional
¼ tsp. ground cloves, optional
¼ tsp. sugar, optional

Wash and dry liver and cut into chunks. Coarsely chop the pork fat, onion and anchovies and combine with the liver and 2 tablespoons anchovy liquid. Grind 4 or 5 times. Or divide the mixture into fourths and purée each batch in an electric blender set on high speed, or run through a kitchen machine. Transfer each completed batch to a large bowl. Beat the eggs with flour, coffee cream and spices and add to meat mixture a little at a time. Preheat oven to 350°F (175°C). Line a 1-quart mold or loaf pan with the strips of pork fat, making sure they overlap slightly and fully cover the bottom and sides of pan. Spoon the liver mixture into the mold and top with additional pork fat strips. Cover with heavy aluminum foil, sealing edges tightly. Place in a large baking pan and add enough boiling water to the pan that it reaches at least halfway up the sides of the mold. Bake in the center of the oven from 1¼ to 1½ hours. Remove from oven and lift off foil. When it has cooled to room temperature remove from pan and wrap in aluminum foil. Refrigerate. **Makes 1 quart.**

Vegetables

Cucumber (Agurk)

European cucumbers, sometimes called English cucumber, are about twice as long in length as the American variety. They are smaller in circumference, have less seeds and is crisper. The Norwegians call them *slangeagurk,* or snake cucumber. They should have a fairly smooth surface and be as straight as possible. Use a Norwegian cheese slicer to get paper thin slices.

Onion (Løk)

It is difficult to imagine a delicious meal without onions in one form or another. In Norway the most widely used onions are, *kepaløk* (yellow or red onions), *purre* (leek), and *gressløk* (chives). Onions keep well the year around and is a culinary additive with some rank, but too many use it only as such. Onions are versatile, add flavor to soups, sauces, casseroles, salads, meat and fish, and are delicious served separately as a vegetable. Boiled, onions acquire a rather sweet taste and are easier digested than when fried. Onions should be kept in an airy and dry place.

Hasselback Onions (Hasselback-løk)

Plan about 1 medium onion per person. Peel and slice onion thinly, being careful not to slice all the way through. Place in a baking dish, cut side up. Brush with a little melted butter. Sprinkle with salt and paprika, and some shredded cheese. Bake at 390°F (200°C) about 30 minutes. Serve with meat or chicken, and a green salad.

Baked Onions for Roast (Bakt løk)

No more tears if you add whole un-peeled onions to boiling water and simmer for 15 minutes. Drain, cool and peel, and add to roast in the oven. They are delicious!

Tips on frying Onions (Steketips for løk)

The warmer the fat is, the crisper the onions will be. If you mix a little oil with the butter, or use straight oil you can use a higher temperature, and your onions will be crisper. If you desire soft onions, add 1-2 tablespoons of water when the onions have reached the light golden state. Simmer covered a few more minutes, and soft onions are guaranteed.

French Fries Onion Rings (Frityrkokte løkringer)

Peel and slice onions thinly. Divide into rings and place in a bowl. Pour milk over to cover and let stand for 30 minutes. Beat an egg and dip the onion rings in the egg, then in flour, and fry until golden brown in hot shortening. Drain on paper towels. Serve immediately.

Onions with Cheese Sauce (Løk med ostesaus)

6 onions, medium	1 tsp. salt
3 tbsp. butter	1 tsp. paprika
3 tbsp. flour	1 tsp. curry
1⅛ cups (2¾ dl) coffee cream	3 tbsp. bread crumbs
½ cup (1¼ dl) cheese, Jarlsberg or Gouda	

Boil onions until tender. Place in baking dish. Make white sauce using butter, flour and cream. Add grated cheese, salt, paprika, and curry and pour over the onions. Sprinkle with bread crumbs and bake at 350°F (175°C) for 15 minutes. **Serves 4.**

The Glorious Leek (Den herlige purren)

The leek has been cultivated along the Mediterranean for 5000 years. In Norway it was cultivated as early as 1694. Norwegians use them in every conceivable way. It is a vegetable rich in iron and C vitamins. It adds a savory taste to numerous cooked dishes and soups, and great zest to salads. It keeps best in humid and dark places and freezes well. Cut in chunks and parboil or slice thin and freeze.

Boiled Leeks (Kokt purre)

Select large leeks. Cut off tops. Leave about 2 inches (5 cm) of the green part. (The green part may be frozen, cut up or whole, and used later as an excellent addition to vegetable or meat soups). Slice the leek lengthwise and wash well. Tie together with cotton string. Place in a small amount of boiling, lightly salted water and cook until tender, about 15-20 minutes. Serve with butter, margarine or your favorite sauce.

Rutabagas (Kålrot)

This unpretentious, tasty vegetable supplies vitamin A (carotene), minerals, and 45 milligrams of vitamin C in 3.5 ounces (100 g), about our minimum daily requirement. It tastes good raw, in salads, or with other vegetable snacks, cooked, or fried in slices, and keeps well. It has earned the name, "orange of the North".

The summer of my ninth year, my sister Eva and I weeded our neighbor farmer's rutabagas fields. We joined nine other young people, all older than I, at Mellom-Granerud farm on Nesodden. We rode in a rickety hay wagon pulled by a large stocky horse. The vegetable fields seemed to stretch endlessly. We started to work at 9 a.m. and worked with great enthusiasm until the lunch bell rang. It was wartime in Norway and food was scarce. However, this lunch was a feast, with meat, boiled potatoes, gravy, and mashed rutabagas with nutmeg. I have loved rutabagas from that day. When I worked in the rutabagas fields I knew nothing of their value. Most of the rutabagas were cattle and horse feed. Lucky animals!

Many people shun this lowly vegetable, not knowing how to prepare it, however it can be prepared any number of ways to compliment numerous recipes. Remember to wash the rutabagas thoroughly, slice in thickness desired, and peel.

Mashed Rutabagas (Kålrotstappe)

Mashed rutabagas is the traditional accompaniment to pinnekjott, (cured ribs, of lamb). Use milk, cream, broth or a combination in your rutabagas. Using milk or cream or adding potatoes or a carrot gives it a milder flavor.

2-3 lbs. (900-1,350 g) rutabagas	*Pinnekjøtt* broth (optional)
Water to cover	Salt
2 potatoes, medium, cook	White pepper
Table cream	Nutmeg, freshly ground (optional)

Wash rutabagas thoroughly, slice in ½-inch (1¼ cm) thickness and peel. Place in lightly salted boiling water to cover and cook until tender, about 30 minutes. Drain and mash together with the warm potatoes. Add salt, pepper, and nutmeg if desired. Add a little cream and broth. Serve decorated with parsley.

For a delicious flavor, when you are cooking *pinnekjøtt*, place peeled and sliced rutabagas on top of meat. When the meat is cooked the rutabagas are tender. Steaming rutabagas on top of the ribs give them an indescribable flavor. When cooked, proceed as above.

Cotter's Kettle (Husmannsgryte)

If you are concerned about preparing a nutritious meal and there is no time to cook, try this recipe. It is bursting with nutritious, colorful vegetables.

1 bouillon cube	1½ cups (3½ dl) rutabagas, cubed
¾ cup (1¾ dl) boiling water	¾ lb (340 g) medisterpølse
2 large carrots, sliced	or bratwurst
2 medium parsnips, diced	Dash of dry mustard
1 large leek, sliced,	Salt and pepper to taste
including the green	

Dissolve bouillon in boiling water. Add all the vegetables and let simmer 15-20 minutes or until vegetables are barely done. Remove skin from sausage, cut in thick slices and add to vegetables. Add mustard, salt and pepper, and let it simmer covered for a few more minutes. Do not overcook. Serve with mustard, potatoes, and dark bread. **Serves 4.**

Cauliflower (Blomkål)

Buy firm heads which are white and spotless. Sometimes they will be a pale yellow, but the leaves should always have a fresh green color.

Use the whole head, even the leaves if desired. For salad grate the center stem, or dice it. It is best to steam the cauliflower. If it is cooked in water, do not overcook, 10-15 minutes will do for an average size head, and 5-10 minutes for florettes. When cooking a whole head it cooks quicker if you cut a crisscross deeply into the bottom of the stem. When cooked cauliflower is to be used in salads it will keep its delicate color if it is dipped in cold water immediately after cooking. Place left over florets in the pickle jar, and use as pickles.

Cauliflower may be added to soups, purées, salads and souffles. It will keep for several days in the refrigerator if kept in a plastic bag.

Celeriac (Sellerirot)

Celeriac, a white round tuber with firm flesh, adds a wonderful flavor to soups and stews. It is hard to find in America, but the produce manager of your market can order them when in season.

Parsley Root (Persillerot)

Smooth leaved wild parsley originated in a small area around the Mediterranean. The first recordings of curley parsley comes from the late 16th century. In Scandinavia the smooth-leaf, turnip-rooted parsley is popular for soups and casseroles. it has a large, white fleshy root. The produce department of your market can help you get it.

Creamed Green Peas (Grønn ertestuing)

It is amazing how inexpensive, traditional, good food can be. I remember these creamed peas served with mammma's delectable meatballs (they taste good with any meat), or when we ate *lutefisk*. The dried peas cost only pennies a pound. If unavailable at your food market, check out your Scandinavian delicatessen or natural food stores.

2 cups (5 dl) dried peas	**3 tbsp. flour**
1 qt. (liter) water	**2 tsp. salt or more**
3 tbsp. butter	**1 tsp. sugar**

Rinse the peas well and pick out any foreign objects. Place in water to soak overnight in a cool place. Let them simmer in the water they were soaked in, approxemately 1½-2 hours. Mix the flour with the butter and add to the peas and let simmer about 10 minutes longer. Add salt and sugar to taste. If you wish you may add a peeled or diced carrot to the peas during the last ½ hour of cooking. No sugar is needed if you add a carrot.

Sweet/Sour Cabbage (Surkål)

A traditional vegetable which tastes delicious with meatballs and all pork dishes. It can be made with green or red cabbage. Red cabbage makes it a more colorful dish.

1 head red cabbage, about 1½ lb. (¾ kg.)	**1-2 tbsp. caraway seeds**
¹/₃ cup (75 g) pork fat or butter	**1 cup (2½ dl) currant juice**
1 apple, chopped	**or vinegar**
2 tsp. salt	**2 tbsp. sugar if vinegar is used**

Remove the outer leaves of the cabbage and rinse the cabbage in cold water. Divide in fourths and remove core. Lay flat side down on cutting board and slice thinly. Add the fat to a heavy saucepan. Peel and chop apple. Layer cabbage and apple in saucepan. Pour currant juice over the cabbage, or add sugar to vinegar, if used, and pour it over the cabbage. Place saucepan on burner. Cook over low heat until very tender. It is best to let is simmer, for about 1-1½ hours or until done. If you keep the heat on low there is no need to stir, but watch from time to time so it does not burn. If necessary add a small amount of water. Serves 4-5.

Lets Talk Potatoes (Potetsnakk)

Norway in years past was thought of as a fish, meat, potato, and porridge country. When planning dinner, the first thing a homemaker thought of was potatoes. Mostly cooked until wonderfully mealy. (There is a special trick to that, see recipe that follows).

However, Norwegians did not just cook potatoes enough for one meal, but would cook enough to be used with breakfast, or for *Pytt i Panne, lomper* or lefser.

We know potatoes are one of our most nourishing foods, and are not fattening. The culprits are what we put on them, gravy, butter, sour cream, melted cheese, and bacon bits, or the hot fat we fry them in.

Potatoes are one of the most inexpensive nutritional foods, nearly fat free, (0.1 % fat). They have starch which help fill you up, gives energy, fiber to help with digestion, and minerals, particularly iron so important for blood, and vitamins B and C to help strengthen the body.

In ages past, grain was the staple food in Norway, and the Norwegians, like many other Europeans, were reluctant to accept potatoes when introduced. South America had cultivated the potato for thousands of years before it came to Europe. In the 1700's food was scarce in Norway, but following hundreds of years of raising grain it was difficult to convince people of the benefit of the potato, until a minister, P. H. Hertzberg, took up the cause of the potato in his sermons. In fact, he wrote a book about the cultivation of the potatoes, a best seller and sold out of three printings. Before long the knowledge of the benefit of potatoes, as they understood them in those days, spread across Norway, and today, it remains Norway's most important vegetable.

Boiled/Steamed Potatoes (Kokte melne poteter)

Bring water to a boil and add even sized potatoes. Just enough water to cover. If the potatoes are un-peeled you do not need salt in the water. (Obviously cooking the potatoes with the peel on saves nutrition). Quickly bring thinly peeled potatoes to a boil and cook until easily penetrated by the tip of a sharp knife, about 20 to 30 minutes. Let simmer, do not overcook or they will become soggy and fall apart easily. Drain immediately. Return to low burner, shake pan gently to prevent sticking, and continue steaming until the pan is completely dry. This produces a dry, mealy potato. Cover with cloth, not a lid, until ready to serve. *Note*: the potatoes will not stay mealy if cooled and reheated.

Hasselback (Roasted) Potatoes (Hasselbackpoteter)

This easy way to prepare potatoes is becoming increasingly popular in Norway. And it is simply delicious. Once I watched a Norwegian chef place a peeled potato in the hollow of a large wooden spoon, and began to slice it in $^1/_8$ inch (¼ cm) slices till about ½-inch (1¼ cm) from the end. (The spoon prevented the knife from slicing all the way through the potato). So easy! Preheat oven to 425°F (215°C).

4 oval baking potatoes, medium	**Jarlsberg cheese, grated**
1 tbsp. butter	**Paprika**
2 tbsp. butter melted	

As you peel the potatoes drop them into cold water to prevent discoloring. Slice as explained above. Butter an oven-proof dish. Drain the potatoes and pat them dry with a paper towel. Place the potatoes side by side, cut side up, in the dish brushed with butter. Brush the potatoes with melted butter, and sprinkle with salt. If needed brush again with melted butter after 30 minutes. About 5 minutes before they are baked sprinkle with grated cheese and paprika. Total baking time 50 minutes. **Serves 4.**

Raw Potato Dumplings (Klubb, kumle, kumpe)

This dish is well known all over Norway, and its names and recipes vary from district to district. The foundation of these dumplings is potatoes with variations achieved by adding different ingredients. In eastern Norway *klubben* is made from barley and pea flour and eaten with *myssmørdupp* (a sauce of soft cheese made from whey) On the southern coast these dumplings are called *kumpe*, and further north they are known as *ball*. *Ball* is often served with fish. Generally this type of dumpling is large - about the size of a medium size apple. These old, traditional dumplings have numerous stalwart fans.

Potato Dumplings from Agder (Kumpe fra Agder)

Grate potatoes, drain most of the liquid and add enough barley flour or other flour until the dough is firm. Add a little salt. Form into round or oblong shapes with your hands, enclosing a piece of bacon or suet in the center of each dumpling. Simmer dumplings in lightly salted water ½ to ¾ hours, depending on size. Cold dumplings may be sliced and fried in bacon drippings.

Potato Dumplings with Bacon, North Norway (Klubb og fett, Nord Norge)

Grate raw potatoes and blend with barley flour until a proper consistency. Some ground, boiled potatoes and a little salt may be added. Form round or oblong dumplings with your hand. Bring salted water to a boil, add dumplings and simmer until done. Serve with boiled rutabagas and fried bacon. Some people enjoy these dumplings served with syrup.

Potato Dumplings From Ryfylke (Klimpor fra Ryfylke)

These dumplings are smaller and were used in meat soups at banquets and weddings. Follow directions for previously described dumplings but use white flour, boiled potatoes, a little salt, sugar and cinnamon. The addition of an egg is optional. *Klimpor* may also be cooked in milk.

Tradition Rich Cheeses

Our way of purchasing cheese at the supermarket, differs greatly from the days when the Norwegian dairy maids labored on the mountain farms from before sun up until late evening. In Anders Sandvig's book *Seterliv og Seterstell*, he says that the dairy maid's workday could last from 12 to 16 hours.

Norway is a cheese loving nation. In Norway, cows thrive on sparsely populated areas. By crystal clear rivers and unspoiled mountain sides they produce first grade milk for raw material all important in cheese making.

The cattle would often get to lick a few grains of salt from the dairy maids hand before she began the milking which took place in a shed or *utsel*, a building on the mountain farm.

She used wooden pails, which were made from pine, or juniper. The height of the bucket could be about 8 inches (20 cm) and the breadth between 12-13 inches (30-30½ cm). Usually bands made from hazel held the wooden staves together, seldom did they use iron for this. The pails had no handles, but a protruded pole to hold onto. Following the milking, the milk was strained

through a wood strainer. In the center it had a round, cross shaped hole. A knitted hair strainer was placed in the center of this utensil and the milk then poured through the outlet hole. In later years the strainer was made from tin metal netting. If the milk was to be poured into a separate container they used a funnel also made from wood. After the containers were filled they placed these *melkekoller,* low milk bowls, on top of each other in 4 to 6 rows where they were left standing until they skimmed the cream off.. Many would place the *koller* on top of each other on a stone bench, in pyramid fashion.

It seems, in the olden days the milk was left standing a week before it was skimmed. By this time it would be quite sour, and thick, it would have consolidated and was viscous, and it could be skimmed off like a piece of skin. Then the cream stood another week before they began to churn the cream. In later years they began to churn the cream after 4-5 days. The left over sour milk was used in cooking or made into *gamalost* or other sour milk cheeses.

Gradually the cream was poured into the sour cream tubs. The sour milk was poured into *skjørkolken*, the sour milk container, where it would stand until they made cheese of it, or it was brought back into the valley on the pack horses.

Subsequently the dairy maid now had to clean the vessels used. First they all needed to be rinsed in lots of cold water from the streams. Then they were scrubbed inside out in warm water. Following which juniper branches were placed in the vessels and boiling water poured over, this was left standing until it cooled. The water was then poured out and the vessels were overturned onto cloth, ready for use the following morning.

The dairy maid's work continued through the day making rennet and the many different cheeses, and painstakingly preparing the food for other dwellers on the mountain farm.

When I contemplate on the work of the dairymaids, I cannot help but think how fortunate we are to be able to pick up almost any cheese we desire in a grocery store or a Scandinavian Delicatessen.

You may not live in an area where Norwegian cheeses are readily available, but many are now obtainable by mail in the USA. Knowing a little about them and their content will help you choose the proper cheese for the right occasion.

Aged Cheese (Gamalost)

Gamalost is more than food, it is a part of the Norwegian culture.

It has been said that the name *gamalost*, (aged cheese) was the name given to the cheese because the old technique and method of making it had been handed down for generations. Other explanations are that since an abundance of newly made cheese was eaten in earlier times, and *gamalost* was the only cheese that was stored, it got its name because it was the oldest cheese on the farm.

Today *gamalost* is ready for sale within 5 weeks. It was, and is an art to make good *gamalost*. In the past hand skimmed milk was used, and special utensils and tools were needed. During the ripening process the cheese was kept in a chest or box which was only used for *gamalost*. Blessed the homemaker who had good *gamalost* mold in her coffer. This mold would be on the tools and in the chests for years. The storage temperature was important, and who knows, maybe the stories of some having kept the cheese in their straw mattresses were true.

Gamalost is not produced outside of Norway, yet the Norwegians have made *gamalost* for hundreds of years. It truly is a distinctive cheese and authentic Norwegian.

In days past nearly every farm and *seter* produced their own *gamalost*, but with the advancement of time, the imported cheeses made with rennet became more popular. The dairies took over the production of *gamalost* in the 1890's, the making of which is quite a sight.

The cultivated *gamalost* mold grows fast, and within a few days the cheese looks like huge, long haired balls of yarn. The mold is then brushed back into the cheese, and it ripens from the outside in, which is the reason the cheese is lighter in color toward the center and darker on the outer edges. The cheese should have a light golden color, be firm and moist and have a piquant appetizing flavor. If the cheese has an unpleasant odor it has become too ripe. The cheese should be kept cool, and well wrapped or in a covered cheese dish.

Serving gamalost: It is best sliced thin, preferably served on rye or any dark bread, maybe with an extra dab of butter. Some use dark syrup with it, others spread a thin layer of honey on top, or a little lingonberry jam.

Lefser or flatbread makes a good accompaniment. Thin slices of gamalost with a little sour cream and good butter rolled up in a scroll is a delicacy.

Sharp, Creamy Cheese (Pultost)

Pultost is also a very old cheese, and extremely easy to make. Made from soured skimmed milk or kefir, with the addition of caraway being the most popular. It is said that Norway has ten varieties of *pultost* with a thousand delicate distinctions. The cheese is known for being rich in protein and has a low fat content. Many feel it has not attained the acclaim it deserves. It is reasonable and goes along way. Served with butter on coarse bread it truly wakes up your appetite.

Norwegian Swiss Cheese (Norsk Sveitserost)

In 1856, more than 150 years ago, when the first Norwegian Dairy, Rausjødalen Dairy, was established in Tolga, they hired a Swiss to head it. Being aware of the Swiss people's knowledge of cheese making, the Norwegians wanted to learn the very best method. The dairy's first year production consisted of 140 cheeses. Hundreds of Swiss came to Norway in the 1800's, they had a great influence on Norwegian cheese production in the beginning stages. It was only natural then that Swiss cheese would be among the first produced in Norway.

From that period until the 1950's the Norwegians made Swiss cheeses weighing 155 pounds (70 kilos). It was as big as a mill-wheel and extremely difficult to produce, as well as unwieldy. Finally the size was changed to the smaller Norwegian *sveitser* of today.

The Norwegian Swiss cheese is matured for at least 5 months. By then the sweet nut-like flavor characteristic to Swiss cheese is developed.

Of utmost importance in the production of Swiss cheese, is the quality of the milk. The cheese should have a firm consistency with large holes. Many believe if there is a drop of salt water in the holes, the cheese is fully ripe.

The Norwegian Swiss cheese is above all intended for sandwiches and cheese trays, but may also be used in cheese dishes. In fondue for example, this Swiss cheese is tops.

Jarlsberg *(Jarlsberg)*

This cheese was first produced in the early 1800's on the old Jarlsberg estate, its namesake, on the western shore of the Oslofjord. Difficult times and reasonable cheese imported from Holland abated the cheese production at Jarlsberg. Nonetheless, its reputation and unusual qualities was not forgotten over these years, and more than 100

years later the cheese specialists at Norway's Agricultural School, under the direction of Professor Ola Martin Ystgaard set out to reconstruct the Jarlsberg cheese. It took several years and hundreds of experiments before Professor Ystgaard would allow the cheese on the market in the early 1960's. Anyone who has tasted the exquisite Jarlsberg cheese knows Professor Ystgaard succeeded with his goal. The cheese is exported around the world as well as thoroughly enjoyed at home in Norway. Cheese experts worldwide have searched for the secret, but so far in vain.

Jarlsberg is made into 22.5 pounds (10 kilos) round wheels with rind, and rind free cheeses. Foremost it is a marvelous party and sandwich cheese, but lends itself remarkably well to warm cheese dishes.

Gouda-Type Norvegia Cheese *(Gouda-type Norvegia ost)*

Norwegian cheese of the gouda-type have in the last few years been named Norvegia, speaking of both the one without rind and the little round mini Norvegia with rind. The Norvegia is loved in most Norwegian homes and used daily. Norvegia's ancestors hailed from Holland. It obtained its name from the town of Gouda in southern Holland. Since those early days it has gone through innumerable changes, and one can safely say that the Norvegia of today is a typical Norwegian cheese. It has a mild, but rich flavor with a pliant consistency, and has small even eyes.

In Norwegian homes it is above all others, known as the sandwich cheese, and is included both on the breakfast table, in the lunch pack and for evening snacks. And today, the youth enjoy it on a pizza, yes indeed times have changed.

Edam Cheese *(Edamerost)*

Originally this cheese came from the town of Edam, Holland. It is round, it is said, because in days of old they used to roll the cheese in small wooden chutes onto the ships which transported them around the world.

It takes 4 months to prepare Edam cheese. The homemakers in olden days began the preparations for their Christmas cheese in August, 4 months ahead. Today it still takes 4 months to produce Edam cheese, but homemakers buy them in the stores except for rare exceptions. Cut the Edam cheese in layers, in little triangles from the top down. It tastes best thickly sliced, and is delicious with grapes.

Normanna *(Normanna)*

Norway's Normanna, is somewhat similar to the French Roquefort cheese, both in flavor and looks. Originally one would allow mildew to grow on slices of *loff*, a white bread similar to french bread. The bread would then be dried, crushed and added to the cheese containers. Today, the fungus needed is cultivated and added. The cheese is made from cow's milk. It has a sharp aromatic taste. A versatile cheese, it is appetizing both as a sandwich spread and as an addition to soups, sauces, lamb chops, and in salads. As a snack with red grapes, radishes, and celery it is tops. On a buffet or in cheese trays it is a must.

Nøkkelost (Nøkkelost)

In times past when *nøkkelost* was imported from Holland, the cheese factory in Leyden stamped the city emblem, two crossed keys on it, hence the name nøkkelost, or Key cheese. Today the *nøkkelost* made in Norway is typical Norwegian. The dairies began producing them as early as the middle of last century. Since then there have been many renditions and variations.

The Norwegian's think of the nøkkelost as an every day cheese, but with what flair!

Nøkkelost is delicious on an open-face sandwich, served on dark bread and accompanied with fruit. The cheese is elegant used in cooking. Its aromatic spices of cumin and cloves, opens the door wide for any creative cook. Try it in salads, sauces, souffles or cakes. It's unique flavor is loved by everyone. The Americans, in time, insisted on a softer and more pliant cheese. The Norwegians solved the problem by making a gouda-type cheese with the *nøkkelost* spices. This delicious cheese now has gained popularity in Norway as well. The *nøkkelost* matures for three months before it appears in the grocery stores.

Ridder Cheese (Ridder)

This is a true aristocrat. Ridder literally means knight. It is a cheese for our times created for those who relish a generous slice of cheese. It is produced from rich, high quality milk in a small dairy by one of the most beautiful *fjord* arms in Norway. It came on the market in the late 60's, is round and approximately 8 inches (20 cm) in diameter. Weighs about 3 lbs. (1 kg 350 g). It is surface ripened for 5-6 weeks and has a soft texture.

This is a true aristocrat. Ridder literally means knight, it is a cheese for our times. Created for those who relish a generous slice of cheese. It is produced from rich, high quality milk in a small dairy by one of the most beautiful fjord arms in Norway.

Ridder is a distinctive dessert cheese. When served, *Ridder* should be accompanied with the season's berries and fruits, such as strawberries, kiwi, and ripe grapes.

The cheese gets it's full aroma at room-temperature, and has an aromatic, piquant flavor, and should be cut with a sharp knife.

Tilsiter (Tilsiter)

The Belgian Limberger cheese is thought to be the forerunner to the *Tilsiter* cheese now produced in many countries. The orginal went to Holland, Germany and Austria. Some Dutch emigrants brought the cheese with them to East Prussia, among the emigrants there was a lady who made a cheese she named after Tilsit, the town in which they settled.

The production of Norwegian *Tilsiter* began in the 1950's, when the opportunity presented itself to export cheese to Germany and the continent, including Holland. The production of *Tilsiter* was started because it was a cheese much loved in many countries. Before the European import restrictions started Norway produced some 2000 tons of *Tilsiter* yearly, half of which was exported.

The Norwegian *Tilsiter* differs from the Norvegia in that it is more pliant, and of a very different texture. It is by covering the cheese with a special culture during the ripening process which gives it it's unique flavor. It is a marvelous cheese for sandwiches, lends itself well to be served with milder cheeses on cheese trays. It has a strong aroma and is therefore not suitable in warm dishes.

Goat Cheese (Gjetost)

The Norwegian Dairy Association (Tine) says gjetost is as native to Norway as trolls and fjords. It all started, they say, more than 100 years ago on a small summer farm high up from the Gudbrandsdal valley, famous for it's rich farming traditions.

The milk maid had just made the curd cheese from cow's and goat's milk. The left over whey was boiling in a great iron kettle in the fire place. Usually she would allow almost all the liquid to evaporate. The golden paste that was left at the bottom of the kettle, was used for sandwich spread. A particular night she expected visitors and wanted to serve them something special. She added cream and some goat milk and poured the hot mixture into a

mold. Unbeknown to her, that night she probably served the very first golden gjetost ever made. This is how the sweet golden *gjetost* became the staple breakfast treat in every Norwegian home.

Today *gjetost* still is made the same way, but modern techniques and equipment have taken over. The Norwegians' appetite for goat cheese, however, is insatiable.

As children in Norway we were all fed school breakfasts. In memory, they never varied. A glass of milk, *skonrok*, a hard roll or hardtack, or a course dark rye bread with *gjetost*, and an apple or orange. Every morning it tasted just as delicious, especially when in the freezing winter mornings we entered heated schoolrooms, with our breakfasts ready for us on the *pult*, school desk.

The goat cheese is a 100% natural product, no sugar or color is added. The sweetness comes from the milk sugar caramelizing when cooked.

Remember to serve the cheese in wafer thin slices. Here, nothing but a Norwegian cheese slicer will do, (you need one anyway) available in any Scandinavian shop, or fine department stores.

Take Care of the Cheese (*Ta vare på osten*)

Cheese keeps well, but certain guidelines should be followed. A cheese which is vacuum packed keeps for about 2 months. Never keep several kinds of cheese together in one package as they will take on the different flavors. Wrap tightly and with care. Air, moisture and acid causes mold to appear.

Mold should be cut off, and the cheese wrapped in new foil. White cheese should not be frozen, the texture is easily destroyed. Shredded cheese, however, lends itself to freezing. Wrap in small portions. Cream cheeses, *Gamalost* and Normanna freezes well. All cheese tastes best when close to room temperature. Keep in mind that cheese is a superb food product to have in reserve.

Mountain Dairy Maid's Favorite (*Seterjentas favoritt*)

⅞ cup (200 g) butter
⅞ cup (200 g) 100% goat cheese

¼ cup (½ dl) confectioners' sugar, scant
1 tsp. cardamom

Use this spread on your favorite lefser, waffles, or hard rolls. Delicious!

Cream butter until soft, grate cheese, and add to butter. Add confectioners' sugar and cardamom.

Cooked Cheese (*Kokaost*)

2½ qt. (liters) whole milk
1 qt. (liter) kefir or cultured milk
1 small egg, or a half one

⅔ cup (1½ dl) raisins
Cinnamon and sugar

A tasty side dish with homemade waffles and lefser. So simple to make, and so nourishing.

In a heavy-bottomed pan bring the milk to the boiling point. Beat kefir and egg together and add in a thin stream to the milk, stirring continually. Let stand until whey separates from the cheese mass. Strain through a cheesecloth placed in a strainer. Press the cheese into a mold or spring-form pan, with layers of raisins in between. Sprinkle sugar and cinnamon on top.

Egg Cheese From West Agder (*Egg ost fra West Agder*)

1 qt. (liter) milk
6 eggs

1 cup (2½ dl) sugar
1 cup (2½ dl) kefir or cultured milk

A cheese served with sugar and cinnamon. It is simple to make and tasty.

In a heavy pan bring the milk to a boil. Let cool slightly. Beat eggs, sugar and cultured milk together. While stirring vigorously pour the egg mixture, a little at a time, into the warm milk, and bring to a boil. (Strain off the whey, and use in your bread baking). Serve with sugar and cinnamon.

Creamy Sharp Cheese (*Pultost*)

1 qt. (liter) kefir, or
   unflavored non-fat yogurt
¼ cup (½ dl) sour cream

½ tsp. salt
Caraway seed, dill or chives

You choose the flavor. Caraway is what I remember best, but dill, chives or leek is also delicious.

In a heavy saucepan over low heat, heat the milk or yogurt until it separates, it is very important to let it do so slowly. Do not stir. Strain the cheese mass through double cheese cloth placed in a sieve over a bowl. When most of the whey has drained off, pick up the four corners of the cheese cloth and squeeze out the remainder. Do not discard the whey, but use in bread-baking or as a healthy drink. Place the cheese in a bowl and add sour cream and seasoning of your choice. I use ¼ cup (½ dl) of caraway to a quart, you might want to use less. Let the cheese stand for 24 hours to develop flavor. Keeps in covered container in refrigerator for up to two weeks.

Nøkkelost Quiche (Nøkkel quiche)

It is easier to make a pie dough with a mixture of shortening and butter, but an all-butter dough is superior. A quiche should always be served hot or luke warm.

⅝ cup (150 g) butter	**Filling:**
⅞ cup (200 g) flour	6 slices bacon
2 tbsp. water	9 oz. (250 g) nøkkelost, grated
	4 eggs, slightly beaten
	1 cup (2½ dl) half and half
	2 tbsp. chives
	½ tsp. salt
	½ tsp. white pepper

Cut butter into flour with pastry blender until the size of small peas. Add water and mix to a soft dough. Work the dough as little as possible to prevent unnecessary shrinkage. Press into a 9½-inch (24 cm) quiche pan. Fry bacon until crisp. Drain on paper towel and break into pieces. Grate cheese and sprinkle on the bottom of the pie crust. Whisk eggs, half and half, chives and pepper together. Carefully pour the egg mixture over the cheese. Sprinkle with bacon on top. Bake until firm, on the lowest rack in the oven at 350°F (175°C). **Serves 6-8.**

Nøkkelost Omelette (Nøkkelost omelett)

3 tbsp. butter	2½ cups (565 g) cups nøkkelost, grated
6 eggs	2 yellow peppers, chopped
⅜ cup (½ dl) water	1¼ cup (285 g) ham, cooked and sliced
½ tsp. salt	Parsley, chopped

Melt butter in skillet. In a bowl beat together eggs, water and salt. Pour into skillet. Sprinkle cheese evenly onto the omelette mixture. Sprinkle peppers on top. Cook covered over moderate heat until eggs are set and cheese is melted, 8-10 minutes. Do not stir. Serve immediately, sprinkled with parsley, and accompanied with ham. **Serves 4-6.**

Jarlsberg Cod (Jarlsberg torsk)

2 lbs. (900 g) cod fillet	1 small leek, thinly sliced
1 tbsp. butter	3 tomatoes, small
1 tsp. salt	1¾ cup (4 dl) Jarlsberg, grated
½ tsp. white pepper	⅔ cup (1½ dl) half and half cream
1 clove garlic, minced	

Clean and dry fish. Cut into serving size portions and place in a greased shallow baking dish. Season with salt, pepper and garlic. Arrange sliced leek and tomato slices over fish. Top with cheese and pour half and half over all. Bake in 350°F (175°C) oven until done. **Serves 4-6.**

Jarlsberg Filled Peppers (Jarlsbergfylt paprika)

4 large peppers, red or green	**1 lemon, juice of**
2 tsp. coarse salt	**²/₃ cup (1½ dl) French bread crumbs**
1 lb. (450 g) ground meat,	**1¼ cup (3 dl) Jarlsberg, diced**
low fat	**3½ tbsp. butter**
½ tsp. Tabasco	**Garlic salt**
½ tsp. garlic salt	
½ tsp. pepper, coarsely ground	

Divide peppers in two, remove stem and seeds. Sprinkle the coarse salt on baking pan. Mix meat, Tabasco, garlic salt, pepper, lemon juice, crumbs, and half of Jarlsberg cheese. Divide evenly between the peppers. Top the peppers with remainder of the cheese. Melt butter, add garlic salt and brush over the peppers. Place on top of coarse salt on baking sheet, and bake in 350°F (175°C) oven about 35 minutes. **Serves 4-6.**

Norvegia Filled Potatoes (Norvegiafylte poteter)

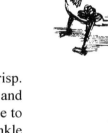

4 baking potatoes	**2 tbsp. green pepper, diced**
6-8 slices bacon	**2 tbsp. red pepper, diced**
1 cup (225 g) Norvegia, grated	**Salt and pepper**
or other swiss cheese	**Sour cream**
2 small onions, diced	**Chives**
1 egg	

Bake the potatoes till almost done. While potatoes are baking fry bacon until crisp. Drain on paper towel, and break in pieces. Prepare vegetables. Cut potatoes in two and remove most of the inside. Mash potatoes and mix with bacon, cheese, (save a little to sprinkle on top), onions, egg, peppers, salt and pepper. Fill the shells and sprinkle cheese on top. Put potatoes back in the oven and let bake until warm throughout (about 15 minutes), and cheese is melted. Serve with sour cream and chives, and a nice green salad. **Serves 4.**

Norvegia Spinach Pie (Norvegia spinatpie)

Filling:	**Pie dough:**
2 cups (5 dl) chopped spinach,	**7 tbsp. butter**
frozen and thawed	**²/₃ cup (1 ½ dl) flour**
7 slices bacon	**1 tbsp. water**
1¹/₃ cup milk	
3 eggs	
1 tsp. salt	
½ tsp. nutmeg, grated	
²/₃ cup (1½ dl) Norvegia, grated	
or other swiss cheese	

Thaw and drain spinach of all water. Cut butter into flour with pastry blender until pieces are the size of small peas. Add water. Mix and form into ball. Chill. Fry bacon until crisp, drain on paper towel and crumble. In a bowl, slightly beat the milk, eggs, salt and nutmeg together. Set aside. Line a 9-inch (23 cm) pie plate with pastry. Trim ½-inch (1¼ cm) beyond rim and tuck under. Flute edges. Spoon spinach into pie shell, add bacon and shredded cheese. Pour egg mixture over. Bake in moderate oven, 350°F (175°C) 30-40 minutes or till knife inserted halfway between center and edge comes out clean. **Serves 6-8.**

Ascent to the Mountain Farm (Til seters)

The seter, mountain farm, has always held some sort of magic for me. Here the mountain peaks seem to touch the sky, crisp mountain air fill my lungs, while the wide expanse of the miniature world unfolds below.

However, dairy maids, whose day often lasted 16 hours, may not have enjoyed the mountain top views as much as I, a mountain hiker. And yet, I still hope for the time when I will have the experience of a few weeks on a mountain farm. For a glimpse of what travel up to the *seter*, used to be, I have translated an excerpt from Hans Aanruds book, *Sidsel Sidserk;*

Across the valley a procession is working its way up the mountain path. Kjersti Hoel watches through the chamber window, following the procession with her eyes until they disappear over the grassy mountain side far into the interior of the mountain plateau.

It is the livestock leaving for the seter today. *Budeia,* the dairy maid, leads, riding the *jegerhest*, Chasseur horse, dressed in her Sunday best, with a white kerchief, she rides high on the horse in a ladies saddle with a high frame resembling an arm chair. She is rosy, round, and self-asserting. Today she is in charge, and is the one who feels important.

Following her are two fellows, each leading a horse positively straining under it's heavy burden. The livestock follows as in a grand parade. First, the lead cow, then Brandros with her crooked horn, then Krokhorn and Morkhei followed by others (except Farskall and Litage who remained at the farm in the valley to train the calves to follow). The large bull, as if to watch over all, comes last.

The goats following the cattle closely, would love to pass them. Then the sheep in a close clump, followed by four large hogs. At the end are the assistant (second) dairy maid and Sidsel Sidserk with her filled rucksack. This is the first time Sidsel Sidserk was allowed to come to the *seter* with the cattle. From our childhood we had remembered we anxiously wondered if she could manage her job this summer...

(At the *seter*) "Sidsel Sidserk stood atop the turf covered roof ridge of the cow stable and scanned the view. With her birch bark hat, shepherd rucksack, goat horn bugle tied to a string around her neck, and her stick in hand she was ready for work...

When summer ended, the animals penned inside the enclosure rambled impatiently about and understood that *bufarsdag*, the day for leaving the *seter*, had arrived. Laced panniers with butter and cheese tubs stood in a row. Horses loaded with panniers and packed saddles stood by the *seter* walls. In front stands the Chasseur horse with the lady saddle.

Men who herded the animals stood by with pipe in mouth waiting for the dairy maid busy making *bufars* cheese with the last milk, milked this morning which could not be left behind.

Visiting a Mountain Farm *(En setertur)*

It is impossible for me to think of Norway in the summer time without thinking *rømmegrøt*, sour cream porridge. Like the summer my cherished friend, Else Aas, had heard of a mountain farm not too far from her family cottage at Gullverket; where we could buy fresh sour cream for our porridge. Else, Bjarne Nordli, another treasured

friend, my sister Gro, and myself, drove a short distance, parked the car, and then started our hike into the mountains to find the little *seter*.

Our hike was slowed by picking the wild raspberries, blueberries, and lingonberries which grew in profusion, as if beckoning us to partake. The climb to the *seter* was beautiful and invigorating. As we made our ascent, the view below increased in magnificence, filling us with joy and anticipation to reach the *seter*.

We took a few wrong paths, after which the little mountain farm came into view. Mr. Soløst, it's friendly owner, a trump of a "homemaker," welcomed us.

His simple cottage had a living room, kitchen and bedroom. The sun shone brightly through spotless windows framed by checkered curtains. And on the floor we admired the polished wood stove by a stack of logs, the ends cut evenly and appearing to be part of the wall. There also were a few unpretentious pieces of furniture in the room.

His small kitchen was filled with gleaming pans neatly arranged on wall racks, equipment to make butter, cheese and sour cream, a wood stove and small sink left just enough room for one or two people to turn around.

Mr. Soløst showed us around the *seter*, the chicken coop, and the barn for his sheep and 26 cows which was as clean as his cottage. After our tour he showed us how he made cheese, butter and his delicious sour cream. We bought two quarts of sour cream and began our decent.

Later, in the evening of the same day, we visited Bjarne's quaint cottage at Hol Lake.

Bjarne is an expert rømmegrøt maker, and a lover of Norwegian food traditions. We watched by the lake the bright rays of the setting sun, while relishing every mouthful of Bjarne's steaming hot sour cream porridge, served with sugar, cinnamon, and black currant juice. And as we did, we sent grateful thoughts up to Mr. Soløst on his little summer mountain farm...

Sour Cream Porridge (Rømmegrøt)

Rømmegrøt, sour cream porridge, has always held a hedersplass,, in high esteem, in Norwegian food culture. It was and in many places still, is used at celebrations to commemorate certain days, such as Misummer, Olsok, weddings, births, etc.

In the past, though the recipes were similar, the porridge was given different names like *slåttegraut*, usually served to celebrate the end of haying. It was customarily cooked with thick sour cream, and served with flatbread and milk. Or if the porridge was served the day the cattle were moved to or from the summer mountain farm, it was called *bufarsgraut*. Some used *dravle*, simmered curds and whey. The dairy maid either cooked the porridge at the seter or on her return to the farm. The curds and whey served as an accompaniment, were always prepared at the summer farm. Even at weddings and at births the sour cream porridge was a welcome *sending*, contribution.

These offerings would arrive in intricately carved, or rosepainted wooden vessels made especially for the porridge, and delighted and nourished the happy recipients. The porridge itself, in some areas, was decorated with diamond shapes of sugar and cinnamon.

Rømmegrøt was a must for Midsummer festivities, June 24th, and for Olsok, July 29th, this holds true as well to day. Today it is usually served with *spekemat*, salt-cured smoked meat, and flatbread as accompaniments.

Rømmegrøt is a heavy meal, but our forefathers, whose day began before sun up and continued long past sun down, were more concerned with nourishment than calories. The porridge is not recommended for everyday use, but rather to be saved for celebrating special days.

Rømmegrøt cannot be made in a hurry - patience is the key to success. Ingredients used must be the very best quality.

Today much of the butter fat, a necessary ingredient for this porridge, has been removed from the cream. If sufficient butter does not ooze out while cooking, supplement with 2 to 3 tablespoons of unsalted butter.

Sour Cream Porridge I (Rømmegrøt I)

This *rømmegrøt* cannot be made with our commercial sour cream which is processed to prevent butter separation, which is so essential to the dish. If non-commercial sour cream is not available, make your own as described below.

2 cups (5 dl) heavy cream, or non-commercial sour cream	1 cup (2½ dl) flour
2 tbsp. lemon juice	½ tsp. salt
	2 cups (5 dl) milk, hot

The milk is minimum amount. You could need as much as 1 cup more to achieve proper consistency. Pour cream into saucepan and stir in lemon juice. Let stand for 15 minutes. Bring cream to a boil and simmer gently for 5 minutes. Sprinkle with ½ cup (1¼ dl) of the flour and blend thoroughly. Continue cooking for 10 minutes or more, or until butter comes to the surface. Beat constantly. According to your taste the butter may stay in the porridge, or you may skim it off and keep hot in a separate pan. When no more butter oozes from the mixture, under constant stirring, sprinkle in the remaining flour. Add hot milk a tablespoon at a time, stirring constantly until porridge is thickened and smooth. Salt mildly to taste. Serve hot, with butter, sugar and cinnamon. Serve delicious fresh currant or raspberry juice as an accompanying beverage. Some people prefer milk with *rømmegrøt*, but I feel that a refreshing fruit drink is a must with such a rich, though delectable porridge.

In certain places in Northern Norway they serve their *rømmegrøt* with a little grated mild goat cheese.

Sour Cream Porridge from Tinn (Rømmegrøt fra Tinn)

2 cups (5 dl) water
⁵/₈ cups (1½ dl) butter
1 qt. (liter) whipping cream
2 cups (5 dl) kefir
1 egg

1²/₃ cup (4 dl) flour or more,
  ¼ cup (½ dl) or more should be
  barley flour mixed with white
  flour
2 tsp. salt

In a heavy-bottomed kettle bring water and butter to a boil. Whisk together cream, kefir and egg. Pour into water in a thin stream while stirring continuously. Simmer for 15 minutes stirring frequently. Sift in flour while beating constantly. Let simmer for another 10 minutes. Beat constantly. After a few minutes butter will separate from porridge. Skim off butter and save in a small bowl, keeping it hot. Add salt to porridge. Serve the porridge with sugar and cinnamon. Pass melted butter for those who would not think of eating the porridge without it. Enjoy with red berry juice or milk.

Rice Porridge (Risgrynsgrøt)

1²/₃ cups (3¾ dl) water
1 cup (2½ dl) rice, long grain
1 qt. (liter) milk, boiling

1½ tbsp. butter
Salt and sugar to taste
Cinnamon

In a heavy-bottom pan sprinkle rice into the boiling water, and stir until it returns to boil. Reduce heat and cover, cook slowly until most of the water has been absorbed. Add boiling milk, stir, and continue to simmer until rice is tender and porridge has thickened. Total cooking time about 1½ hour. Add butter and salt. Serve hot, with milk, or currant juice, sugar and cinnamon. **Serves 4.**

Party Rice Porridge (Festrisgrøt)

Use the previous recipe, omitting butter, and substituting 2 cups (5 dl) of sour cream for two cups of the milk. Add the sour cream when the porridge has thickened. Bring to a boil stirring continually. Add the salt. Serve hot, with milk or currant juice, sugar and cinnamon. **Serves 4.**

> *The giant trolls of Norway roam through the mountains and valleys, and have even been seen on Karl Johan, Oslo's main street. Many are huge, and some have several heads with but one eye between them. They are incredibly stupid, and are easily outwitted by the smart Norwegian children. Their troll hags are also giant, lazy and not very creative in preparing meals. Porridge is a favorite among trolls.*

Ja, vi elsker dette landet
(Norway's national anthem)

Ja, vi elsker dette landet,
som det stiger frem
furet værbitt over vannet
med de tusen hjem,
elsker, elsker det og tenker
på vår far og mor
:og den saganatt som senker
drømme på vår jord.:

Norske mann i hus og hytte,
takk din store Gud!
Landet vilde han beskytte,
skjønt det mørkt så ut
Alt, hvad fedrene har kjempet,
mødrene har grett,
:har den Herre stille lempet,
så vi vant vår rett.:

Richard Nordraak

Desserts

Pity those who have never had the opportunity to go berry picking in the wild. To gather baskets and pails and head for the large mysterious forest where we as children, even in the middle of the day, imagined that behind the trees and hillocks, *hulder* and trolls were surely lurking. The lush woods and meadows at Nessodden where I grew up, totally satisfied our families needs for berries and our childhood imagination for play. Among my fondest memories of summer in Norway are our family's berry-picking excursions. They included parents, grandparents, uncles, aunts and children. We brought open-face sandwiches and drank water from the pristine, rushing brooks. Our dessert was fresh berries. We younger ones did not wait for dessert time for as soon as we saw the plants, heavy laden with berries, we rushed to taste them (like the children in the *Blueberry Outing*). At the end of the day our telltale blue-black teeth and lips were proof that possibly as many berries were eaten as had found their way into the pails we were supposed to have filled.

Another highlight was when we returned home and mamma made *pannekaker* (crepés) and blueberry soup from the berries we had gathered. During the week it was more blueberry soup, blueberry compotes, and fresh blueberries with milk (cream was a luxury) and sugar. And not many things tasted as good as mamma's homemade bread with her homemade blueberry jam. Oops, guess we are talking about dessert.

Norwegians often enjoy fruit soups or compotes. Many revel in picking their own berries, (more so in days past than today), wild strawberries, raspberries, blueberries, blackberries, lingonberries, and cloudberries. Norwegian children, like their elders, were excited when wild blueberries were ready to be picked. Alf Prøysen, Norway's beloved folk song writer, wrote this delightful song about berry picking in Norway, you can enjoy it in Norwegian or English.

Blueberry Outing

It was a pretty summer day when Pelle said to Kari;
"Let's go to the woods, they are brimming with berries!"
Let's bring Lillebror, and Kjelleman and Mari
there are plenty berries, mounds are everywhere.
But we must have a gathering cup, and it must be large!"
They all stormed into mother's kitchen:
And Pelle grabbed a milk pail, and Kari got a mug
and Mari got a coffee cup and Kjell he got a cone.
They ran towards the woods a glad and boisterous flock
and Lillebror came last to gather berries in a lid.

When they reached the woods they came to a plateau
with blue on blue as far as their eyes could see.
They sat down topsy turvy and ate until they were filled,
then each found a mound, and shouted, "This one is mine!"
"Let's see whose cup will first be filled; all gave it a try!"
The plateau resounded with "Kling" and "Pling" and "Plang".
First the milk pail sang, and then the mug clanged,
something danced in the cup, and jangled in the cone,
But from the smallest mound came a rush of "Plingelings"
because Lillebror sat and picked berries in a lid.

Blåbærturen

Det var en deilig sommerdag at Pelle sa til Kari:
"Nå går vi ut i skauen for det er så mye bær!
Så får vi med oss Lillebror og Kjelleman og Mari
for det er nok å ta av, det er mange tuer der.
Men vi må ha en plukkekopp og den må være stor!"
Så stormet alle sammen inn i kjøkkenet til mor:
Og Pelle fikk et melkespann og Kari fikk et krus
og Mari fikk en kaffekopp og Kjell et kremmerhus.
Så fløy de opp i skauen i en gla og vilter flokk
- og lillebror fløy sist og skulle plukke i et lokk.

Så kom de opp i skauen, og så kom de til ei slette,
der var det bare blått i blått så langt du kunne se.
Så satte de seg ende ned, så spiste de seg mette,
så fant de seg en tue hver og ropte: "Fritt for det!"
"Nå ser vi hvem som først får fullt, nå setter vi igang!"
Og over hele sletta sa det: "Kling" og "Pling" og "Plang."
Først sang det i et melkespann, så klang det i et krus,
det danset i en kopp og raslet i et kremmerhus,
men fra den minste tua sa det "Plingeling" i flokk,
for oppi den satt Lillebror og plukket i et lokk.

Fruit Soups and Compotes

Blueberry Soup (Blåbærsuppe)

3 cups (7½ dl) blueberries
¾ cup (2 dl) sugar
4 cups (10 dl) water, boiling

1½ tbsp. potato starch flour
Water

Rinse berries and remove any foreign objects. Layer with sugar in cooking utensil. Pour the boiling water over. Cook until tender. Remove from heat. Make a thin paste of potato flour and a little water, and gently stir into the soup in a thin stream. Return to a boil while continuing to stir. Immediately remove from heat and keep covered while cooling. For best consistency cool quickly. Also enjoyable used as a hot drink on chilly days. **Serves 4-6.**

Apple Soup (Eplesuppe)

²⁄₃ cup (1½ dl) sugar
1 qt. (liter) water
4-5 tart apples, sliced

1 stick cinnamon
1½ tbsp. potato starch flour
Lemon juice, fresh

Bring sugar and water to a boil. Wash, peel, and core apples. Slice apples and add to the sugar water with the cinnamon stick. Cook until tender. Do not overcook. Remove from heat and set aside ¼ of the apple slices, and remove the cinnamon stick. Place the remainder of the apples in the food processor and run a few seconds to reduce to sauce. Pour back into saucepan. Make a thin paste of potato flour and a little water and stir into the soup in a thin stream. Return to the heat and bring to a boil while stirring continually. Immediately remove from heat, and add the sliced apples and lemon juice. Cool with lid on. Chill before serving. Serve with crisp cookies or rusk, and a dab of whipped cream if desired. **Serves 6.**

Rose Hip Soup (Nypesuppe)

My siblings and I spent many happy years at Nessodden where these roses grew abundantly along the roads and on the hillsides. We picked and ate the rose hips by the handfuls. Eating the flesh and discarding their woody little seeds, not knowing at the time that we were eating large quantities of Vitamin C.

The rose hips are one of our best sources of vitamin C, containing as much as 1200 to 1800 milligrams of vitamin C per half cup. They make a delicious soup or compote, and a rose hip herb tea. The dried rose hips can be bought in certain import stores, Natural Food Stores and in most Scandinavian Delicatessens.

2 cups (5 dl) rose hips
1¼ qts. (liters) water
¾ cup (2 dl) sugar

2 tbsp. potato starch flour
½ cup (1¼ dl) whipping cream
½ cup (1¼ dl) almonds, slivered

Wash rose hips, removing stems and blossom ends, and discarding the seeds. In a saucepan combine rose hips, water and sugar and cook until tender. Purée in blender or food mill. Return to pan. Make thin paste of potato flour and water; add to soup while stirring constantly. Return to heat and continue to stir until it comes to a boil. Remove from heat. Cool. Whip cream and add to soup a little at a time. Sprinkle almonds on top. **Serves 6.**

Rhubarb Soup *(Rabarbrasuppe)*

1 lb. (450 g) rhubarb	**Water**
1¼ qts. (liters) cold water	**1 tsp. vanilla extract, pure**
¾ cup (2 dl) sugar	**Red food coloring, optional**
3 tbsp. potato starch flour	

Wash and trim rhubarb and slice into ¾-inch (1¾ cm) lengths. Combine rhubarb, water and sugar and cook until tender. Remove from heat. Add enough water to the potato starch flour to form a thin paste and add slowly to soup, stirring constantly. Return to heat and continue stirring until it boils and thicken. Remove instantly. Add red food coloring if desired. This soup can be served hot or ice cold; plain or with a dab of whipped cream, sprinkled with slivered almonds. **Serves 6-8.**

Savory Plum Compote *(Herlig plommekompott)*

1½ lbs. (675 g) plums	**2 tbsp. potato starch flour**
2½ cups (6 dl) water	**Water**
¾ cups (2 dl) raisins	**Lemon juice**
¾ cup (2 dl) sugar	

Serve fruit compotes with a dab of whipped cream, vanilla sauce or milk. Many feel, however, that the only way to eat a compote is with a little sugar, and a pitcher with ice-cold half and half.

Wash plums. Remove stems and leaves. Cut in half and pit. Place in saucepan with water, raisins and sugar. When they come to a boil, turn heat down and let simmer until plums are tender. Remove from heat. Mix potato flour with a bit of cold water. Add to plums in a thin stream while stirring gently but constantly. Place saucepan back on stove and return to a boil while continuing to stir. As soon as it comes to a boil remove immediately. Add a little lemon juice. Pour into an appropriate dessert bowl or individual ones. Sprinkle with a little sugar to prevent film from forming on surface. **Serves 6-8.**

Apricot Compote *(Aprikoskompott)*

4 oz. (115 g) apricots, dried	**¼ cup (½ dl) sugar, or more**
2 cups (5 dl) water	**1½ tbsp. potato starch flour**

A luscious dessert which is always welcome. It takes but minutes to prepare.

Place apricots, water and sugar in a saucepan, bring to a boil and simmer approximately 10 minutes, or until apricots are tender. Remove from heat. Dissolve potato starch flour in a little cold water and add to the soup in a thin stream while stirring constantly. Place back on the burner, and continue to stir while it simmers until thickened. Cool slightly, pour into dessert bowl and sprinkle with a little sugar to prevent a skin from forming. Serve with a dab of whipped cream or a pitcher of half and half. **Serves 3-4.**

Strawberry Compote (Jordbærkompott)

1 quart (liter) fresh strawberries
²/₃ cup sugar (1½ dl)
3 cups water, boiling

2 tbsp. potato starch flour
Water

Layer washed and hulled strawberries and sugar. Add water. Return to boil and let simmer until berries are cooked, but not falling apart. Remove from heat. Blend potato flour in a little water to dissolve. Carefully stir into the compote, return to heat and bring to a boil while continuing to stir. Remove from heat. Let cool slightly; then pour into an appropriate serving dish or individual dessert bowls. Sprinkle with sugar to prevent skin from forming. Serve chilled with a pitcher of coffee cream. **Serves 5-6.**

Prune Compote (Sviskekompott)

A truly traditional dessert, tasty and satisfying. In Norway this dessert was once a much sought after wedding dessert.

1 lb. (450 g) prunes, pitted
3¾ cups (9½ dl) water (part currant
  or apple juice)
½ cup (1¼ dl) sugar

3 tbsp. potato starch
Water
½ tsp. each pure vanilla and
  almond extract

Soak prunes overnight. Bring water (juice), prunes, and most of the sugar to a boil and simmer until tender, about 15 minutes. Add additional sugar if needed. Follow recipe for Strawberry compote. Add flavorings. **Serves 6.**

Troll Cream I (Trollkrem I)

Troll cream was a magical part of our New Year's Eve Celebration. To us youngsters it was truly wizardry because the volume expanded as we stirred. And we did not mind sitting and stirring as long as we had a good book in our hands.

Today, of course, we use electric mixers to make the magical troll cream. You may substitute cranberries for the lingonberries, but be sure they are *very* ripe, and adjust sugar accordingly.

2 cups (5 dl) lingonberries,
  or ½ cup (1¼ dl) lingonberry jam

²/₃ cup (1½ dl) sugar
2 egg whites, from large eggs

Wash berries and remove all unripe berries and foreign objects. Combine all ingredients in a mixing bowl and beat until the volumes quadruples, about 15 minutes. If you are using lingonberry jam omit sugar. Serve in a crystal dessert bowl sprinkled with a few lingonberries. If available add a few mint leaves. Cookies are a great accompaniment, or serve in Crisp Wafer Cups (Krumkakeskåler). **Serves 8.**

Troll Cream II (Trollkrem II)

A different kind of troll cream combining the lingonberries with currants and strawberries, and topping it off with vanilla sauce.

1½ cups (3-4 dl) lingonberries or
  1 cup (2½ dl) red currants plus
  ½ cup (1¼ dl) strawberries or
  raspberries

1 cup (2½ dl) sugar
2 egg whites

Follow directions in preceding recipe. Serve with vanilla sauce. For Vanilla Sauce see Index. **Serves 6-8.**

Cloudberry Cream (Moltekrem)

Plump, orange-yellow cloudberries resemble raspberries in appearance, they do belong to the same family; but their flavor is unique, resembling that of the magnificent mountain marshlands where they flourish. Abundant in vitamin C, cloudberries are mainly used for jam and desserts. Cloudberry cream can be prepared with fresh, or frozen berries which have been pressed through a sieve to remove the seeds, then combined with whipped cream and sugar to taste, or you may use cloudberry fruit spreads, or jam. This is no everyday dessert, and the berries are rather expensive. But if you want to please a Norwegian, you will make a hit with this dessert.

One fall while hiking in the famed Rondane mountains we unexpectedly came across a large patch of cloudberries, and we spent some time enjoying our unanticipated afternoon delicacy.

1²/₃ cups (4 dl) whipping cream	1 tsp. vanilla extract, pure
4 tbsp. sugar	1¼ cup (3 dl) cloudberries

Whip the cream and sugar, add vanilla extract. Carefully fold in the cloudberries, save a few for decorations. Pour into a pretty bowl and decorate with saved cloudberries. *Krumkaker* are an excellent accompaniment, or serve in *krumkakeskåler*. Almond flavored cookies also tastes good with cloudberry cream. **Serves 4.**

If you are unable to obtain cloudberries, use the following recipe;

1½ cups (3¾ dl) whipping cream
½ cup (1¼ dl) cloudberry jam

Lightly whip the cream. Gently fold in the jam. Serve in pretty dessert bowls with crisp cookies. **Serves 4-6.**

Rice Cream (Riskrem)

Today the Norwegian homemaker can buy ready-made frozen rice cream in the grocery store! Though it is good, nothing tops the home-made one. It is mainly a Christmas dessert in most Norwegian homes, and I say, so very delicious it is worth waiting a year for! Do not mistake rice-cream for rice pudding. A whole almond is added to one of the bowls just before serving on Christmas Eve. The lucky finder receives a marzipan pig with a bright red bow, and in some homes the finder passes out the Christmas gifts which spills from underneath the tree.

¾ cup (1¾ dl) white rice, not Minute Rice	2 cups (5 dl) heavy cream, whipped and sweetened to taste
1 tsp. salt	1 tsp. almond extract
1 qt. (liter) milk	½ cup (1¼ dl) almonds, chopped
½ cup (1¼ dl) sugar	1 almond, whole
1 tsp. almond extract	

Cook rice, salt, and milk in double boiler until rice is soft and mixture is thick, about 1½ hours. Add sugar and almond extract. Chill. Add chopped almonds and 1 whole one. Stir in whipped cream. Serve with red fruit sauce. It is difficult to tell you how many this recipe serves, some people cannot get enough of it. However, you should be able to easily **serve 8.**

Rum Pudding (Rompudding)

2 eggs, separated
1/3 cup (¾ dl) sugar
1 cup (2½ dl) whipping cream
1 tsp. rum extract

1 tbsp. gelatine, unflavored
½ cup water, boiling
Whipped cream
Red fruit sauce

Beat egg yolks with sugar. Beat egg whites separately. Whip cream. Mix all together carefully and add rum extract. Soften gelatin in a little water for 1 minute. Add enough boiling water to make ½ cup, and stir until gelatin is completely dissolved, about 5 minutes. Cool, but do not allow to set. Add to rum mixture and stir. Turn into 4 dessert dishes or a dessert bowl; chill until firm. Garnish with whipped cream. Serve with red fruit sauce. **Serves 4.**

Caramel Pudding (Karamelpudding)

A delicate and much loved traditional dessert in Norway. Somehow, we Norwegians never tire of it. It is best when prepared a day in advance, as thorough chilling is a must.

There are many variations of caramel pudding. It is made from eggs, cream, or milk, either of which the end result should be a smooth, delectable pudding. It can be made in an oven-proof mold or in an oblong or round cake pan of a size in proportion to the pudding recipe. The container can be filled completely as caramel pudding, properly prepared and baked, will not rise. Use caution when working with caramel as it is extremely hot and if it comes in contact with any part of the body, a deep burn will result.

   If vanilla sugar or extract is used, add to the egg/milk mixture last. If only cream is used, carefully bring it to a boil before adding the vanilla bean. If the eggs are small, use more. If all, or mostly cream is used, more eggs are required than with milk only.

2½ cups (6¼ dl) milk, or coffee cream
¼ cup (½ dl) sugar
½ vanilla bean, cut lengthwise
3 to 4 eggs

Caramel:
¾ cup (1¾ dl) sugar

In a heavy-bottomed pan, simmer milk or coffee cream together with sugar and vanilla bean for 10 minutes. Cool to lukewarm and remove the vanilla bean. Thoroughly blend eggs, but do not beat excessively as this causes the pudding to become porous. Combine milk and eggs and strain through a sieve to remove stringy parts of the egg yolks. Cool. Both the caramel and the egg mixture should be at room temperature. If the mixture is too hot it will melt some of the caramel which will mix with the pudding and cause it to turn brown.

   Sprinkle the sugar over the bottom of a small, heavy skillet, and let it melt over low heat. Do not stir before sugar has completely melted or lumps may form which are difficult to reduce. Watch carefully so the sugar on the bottom does not brown before that on top has melted. When completely melted, increase the heat and stir constantly to achieve an even color. The heat should be high enough to maintain the caramel in a fluid state and yet allow for a gradual browning; but not so hot that the caramel boils and foams. Test by dropping some on a plate - it should be a golden chestnut color and easy flowing. This may take up to 10 minutes. As soon as the syrup reaches the proper color and consistency pour into a pre-heated mold, grip a pot holder in each hand, and tip and swirl the mold until the bottom and sides are evenly coated. The caramel stiffens quickly, so work fast. Set the mold aside until the caramel has hardened.

Set mold in pan with boiling water to reach halfway up the sides of the mold, and place in preheated 300°F (150°C) oven. The water should not boil or the pudding will rise and have air pockets. A small amount of pudding requires about 1 hour to bake, and larger amounts from 2 to 3 hours. To test for doneness, use a toothpick - if it comes out clean the pudding is done. Remove from the oven and chill.

To remove the pudding, run a sharp knife around the edge and dip mold briefly in hot water. Place a platter on top and invert. The caramel has now melted to a sauce. A successful caramel pudding should be light, golden, and velvet like. Use a decorator tube to glamorize it with "flowers" of whipped cream. **Serves 4-6.**

Victoria Pudding (Victoriapudding)

5 ½ oz. scant (150 g) rusks, sweet
  or zwiebacks, crushed
⁵/₈ cup (150 g) almonds, scalded
⁵/₈ cup (150 g) butter
¾ qt. (liter) half and
  half, good measure

8 eggs, separated
2 tsp. vanilla sugar
½ cup plus 1 tbsp. (115 g)
  potato starch flour
1 tsp. baking powder

This is an elegant and practical dessert which can be made in advance for a large dinner party. Use fresh berries or canned fruits in addition to, or in place of the red fruit sauce.

Crush the rusks or zwieback. Chop almonds. Add the rusks, butter, cream, and finely chopped almonds into a heavy-bottomed pan. Bring to a boil over low heat, while stirring. Set to cool. Separate eggs. Add egg yolks, vanilla sugar, potato starch flour and baking powder to the cream mixture. Whisk gently until mixed. Beat the egg whites until a stiff foam forms, and carefully fold into the cream mixture. Pour into 1½ qt. loaf pan, buttered and sprinkled lightly with crushed zwiebacks. Bake in pan of hot water on the lowest rack in 250°F (125°C) preheated oven for about 2 hours. From time to time check and see if the hot water around the loaf pan has evaporated. Add more water as needed. Remove from the oven and the water bath when done and place on a rack to cool. Let cool awhile before turning out on platter. Serve with warm or chilled red fruit sauce. **Serves 8.**

Chocolate Pudding (Sjokoladepudding)

¼ cup (½ dl) cocoa, unsweetened
6 tbsp. sugar
5 tbsp. cornstarch, leveled

3 cups (7½ dl) milk, whole
1½ tsp. vanilla extract, pure

No, no, not from a package! It has to be velvety smooth, achieved only by preparing it yourself. Yesteryear Sundays were peaceful, filled with family enjoyment and church going. All ages looked forward to the special Sunday dessert, and chocolate pudding was a favorite.

Mix cocoa, sugar, and cornstarch in a saucepan. If the cocoa is lumpy, sift it before use. Add the milk, a little at a time to begin with, and stir after each addition. Place the saucepan over medium heat and bring to a boil, stirring. Stir constantly while the pudding simmers a couple of minutes. Add vanilla to taste. If the pudding is to be unmolded, pour it into a mold that is first rinsed in cold water. Cover the pudding while it cools, so a skin doesn't form on top. You need only use 4 tablespoons of cornstarch if pudding is not to be unmolded. Serve with Vanilla Sauce. **Serves 4.**

Crêpes (Pannekaker)

4 eggs, well beaten
1 cup (2½ dl) whole milk or
  thin cream

¾ cup (1¾ dl) flour
1 tsp. sugar

Norwegians love crêpes. In the summer they are served warm, sprinkled with sugar, and accompanied with fruit soups.

Beat eggs and add to milk. Sift together dry ingredients and add to liquid gradually, stirring well. This makes a thin batter. If the batter should become lumpy strain it through a coarse sieve. Add eggs and mix thoroughly. Heat frying pan and add a small amount of butter. When foam subsides pour in about ¼ cup (½ dl) of batter, enough to make a thin layer when pan is tilted from side to side. Bake quickly over high heat on both sides. **Makes 8 crêpes.**

Prince Harald's Crêpes (Prins Harald's pannekaker)

Make the batter early in the morning for the night it is to be served, this will cause the flour to swell.

3 eggs, well beaten	**Filling:**
2 cups (5 dl) coffee cream	**Vanilla Egg Custard (see index)**
2 tbsp. flour	
1 tsp. sugar	**Decoration:**
2 tbsp. butter, melted	**Strawberry jam**
¹/₈ tsp. salt	**Confectioners' sugar**

Beat eggs. Add cream, flour and sugar to the egg mixture and blend thoroughly. Add cooled, melted butter and salt. Pour into a pitcher, and leave several hours. Proceed as for crêpes. Make vanilla custard and fill crepés. Decorate with jam, sprinkle with confectioners' sugar.

Yogurt Mousse (Surmelkfromasj)

20 almonds, scalded	**¼ cup (½ dl) sugar**
1½ tbsp. gelatin	**1 tsp. vanilla extract, pure**
¼ cup (½ dl) water	**3 tbsp. raisins**
2½ cups (5¾ dl) yogurt	**1 cup (2½ dl) whipping cream**

This delightful, mild flavored mousse recipe has stood the test of time. It should be accompanied by red fruit or apricot sauce.

Finely chop the almonds and set aside. Sprinkle gelatin over the cold water, let stand for 3 minutes. Beat the yogurt, sugar and vanilla together well. Add almonds and raisins. Whip the cream until stiff and fold into the yogurt mixture. Dissolve the gelatin over boiling water. Cool slightly and pour the gelatine in a thin stream into the yogurt as you beat the mixture. Stir now and then as it thickens to prevent the raisins and almonds from settling on the bottom. Rinse a proper size mold in cold water and pour mixture into it. Tap the mold against a towel on the counter top to break any air bubbles in the mixture. Refrigerate the mousse for 4-5 hours to set. Before serving, dip the mold in hot water for a moment. Place a platter over mold and invert. If difficult to unmold you may lay a towel wrung out in hot water over the mold or dip quickly once more in hot water. See Index for Red Fruit Sauce recipe. **Serves 4.**

Traditional 17th of May Dessert (Eggedosis)

There is no good translation for *eggedosis*. Eggs and sugar whipped until fluffy and velvety smooth. There are many recipes for *eggedosis*, I believe this recipe, using just the egg yolks, is the best in the world! Save the egg whites to use in other recipes.

Try serving the eggedosis on top of sweetened currants. The tangy berries and eggedosis is a delightful taste combination.

12 egg yolks	**1 tbsp. cold water**
¾ cup (1¾ dl) confectioners' sugar	

Place all ingredients in a medium size bowl and whip until thick and velvety smooth. The friend who shared this recipe said the *eggedosis* should be so thick one could write ones name in it. Place in your best crystal dessert bowl. Berlin wreaths and sand tarts are the proper accompaniment. **Serves 6.**

Aulestad, home of the beloved Norwegian poet Bjørnstjerne Bjørnson in Gaustad, Norway.

A Heavenly Mouthful (En himmelsriks munnfull)

3 eggs	**½ cup (1¼ dl) orange juice**
½ cup, scant (1 dl) sugar	**3 tbsp. hazelnuts, chopped**
1¹⁄₃ cup (3 dl) whipping cream	**3 tbsp. maraschino cherries, chopped**
1 pkg. Knox gelatine, unflavored	**3 tbsp. chocolate, grated**

Beat egg and sugar until of *eggedosis* consistency, light and fluffy. Whip cream and add. Sprinkle gelatin over ¼ cup cold water; let stand 3 minutes. Heat in double boiler until completely dissolved. In a thin stream, while stirring continuously, pour into the egg/cream mixture. Add orange juice, nuts, and cherries, saving out a few for decoration. Pour into a pretty dessert bowl and decorate. **Serves 8.**

Veiled Peasant Girls (Tilslørte bondepiker)

1½ lb. (675 g) apples	**³⁄₈ cup (1 dl) sugar**
½ cup (1¼ dl) water	**1½-2 cups (4¾-5 dl) heavy cream**
³⁄₈ cup (1 dl) approx. sugar	**½ tsp. pure vanilla extract**
2 ½ tbsp. butter	
2 cups (5 dl) white bread, dried and ground	

A true classic! So simple, and simply delicious.

Peel and core apples, and cut in wedges. Cook in the water until tender. Be careful not to scorch. Add sugar to taste. Stir to the consistency of applesauce, but leave a few whole bits of apples. Cool. Melt the butter or margarine in a frying pan. Add the bread crumbs and sugar. Mix and brown over medium heat. Turn constantly with a spatula as they brown. The bread can easily be burnt if it is not stirred all the time. The crumbs should be a light caramel color. When done spread on platter to cool. Whip cream until firm and glossy, adding a little vanilla if desired. Layer bread crumbs, applesauce and whipped cream in a beautiful glass bowl. Place a layer of cream on top. Sprinkle a few crumbs on top for garnish. **Serves 4.**

Cream of Wheat Pudding (Semulepudding)

Traditionally served with apricot or red fruit sauce. In our home, as in many others, it was a Sunday treat.

Cream of Wheat, uncooked
  enough for 4 servings
1 tbsp. sugar
½ cup (1¼ dl) raisins

1 egg, slightly beaten
¾ tsp. almond extract

Cook Cream of Wheat following directions on package, using milk, not water. When cooked, add sugar. Remove from heat and stir in raisins; add egg and mix well. Return to heat, stirring constantly until it approaches the boiling point. Remove and add flavoring. Rinse an appropriate size bowl with cold water before pouring in the pudding. Sprinkle sugar on surface to prevent film from forming. Chill. To loosen the pudding slip a thin knife down around the sides to let air in around the edges. Invert on a platter and decorate as desired. See Index for Apricot or Red Fruit Sauce recipes. **Serves 4.**

Cloudberry Ice Cream Parfait (Molteisparfait)

½ cup plus 1 tbsp. (100 g) sugar
¼cup, scant (½ dl) water
1 vanilla bean or
½ tbsp. vanilla sugar

5 egg yolks
1²/₃ cups (4 dl) whipping cream
1 cup (2½ dl) stirred cloudberries
Extra whip cream and berries for
  decoration

Bring sugar, water and vanilla bean to a boil. (Split vanilla bean in half lengthwise and scrape out the seeds and add). Let simmer 5 minutes. Slightly beat egg yolks. Add the warm vanilla liquid, (with the vanilla bean removed) into the eggs in a thin stream, while beating the eggs until light and fluffy, *eggedosis* consistency, about 10 minutes. Whip the cream until stiff, but not dry, and blend lightly with the egg mixture. Fold in the cloudberries, and freeze in a nice, appropriate size container, at least until the next day. Invert onto a deep platter and encircle with cloudberries (see picture). Decorate top with whipped cream and a few cloudberries.

Almond Brittle Ice Cream (Krokanis)

Ice cream was reserved for special occasions only, it was truly party time when this was served. You do not need an ice cream maker to make this ice cream.

1¾ cup (4½ dl) almonds
1 tbsp. water

1 cup (2½ dl) sugar
3 cups (7½ dl) whipping cream

Scald and chop the almonds. Add water and sprinkle the sugar over the bottom of a small, heavy skillet, and let it melt over low heat. Do not stir until the sugar is completely melted or lumps may form which are difficult to reduce. Watch carefully so the sugar on the bottom does not brown before that on top has melted. When completely melted stir constantly with a long-handled wooden spoon until the sugar has turned light brown. Add the chopped almonds and pour onto a greased cookie sheet. Cool and crush.

Chill bowl, beaters and cream at least two hours before whipping. This way the milk fat will stay firm during whipping process rather than becoming oily from the friction. Whip cream at medium high speed until it begins to thicken, then lower the speed and continue beating until cream is firm and glossy, but not dry. Carefully blend in the crushed almond mixture. Pour into mold and freeze.

Whipped Berry Pudding (Russedessert)

It may be served with milk, cream or vanilla sauce. Currant juice is a favorite, but you can use other tart juice like lingonberry or cranberry. If you use raspberry, strawberry or other non-tart juices, add a tablespoon of lemon juice.

3 cups (7½ dl) currant juice	**½ cup (1¼ dl) Cream-of-Wheat,**
6 tbsp. sugar	**non-instant, uncooked**

In a heavy bottomed pan bring the currant juice to a boil over moderate heat. Sprinkle in the sugar, a little at a time, while stirring. Add Cream-of-Wheat in a thin stream, stirring briskly. Turn heat to low, and simmer for about 8 minutes, stirring occasionally to prevent it sticking to the pan. It should be the consistency of thick pureé. Pour the pudding into a large mixing bowl, beat with your electric mixer on high speed for about 15 minutes or until the pudding has tripled in volume, and is a light pink color. Pour into a large dessert bowl. Decorate with fresh currants if available. Serve at room temperature within a few hours. **Serves 6 to 8.**

Too often we think tasty food has to be expensive and time-consuming to make. In days past it took the Norwegian homemaker a good hour to whip this pudding, but not so today. With our modern equipment, like magic it will triple in volume in no time.

Banana Cream (Banankrem)

1 cup (2½ dl) whipping cream	**3 tbsp. sugar**
¾ tsp. banana extract	**2 bananas**
1 tsp. vanilla sugar	**Lemon juice**
3 egg yolks	**Strawberries for decoration**

Whip the cream until firm and glossy. Add banana extract and vanilla sugar. Beat the egg yolks with sugar until light and fluffy. Mash bananas with fork. Add a few drops of lemon juice to prevent darkening. Add to egg mixture together with the whipped cream. Pour into dessert glasses. Just before serving decorate with fresh strawberries and possibly banana slices. **Serves 8**.

Note: This recipe may also be used for filling cakes.

Sweet Fondue (Søt fondue)

3 cups (7½ dl) Ski-Queen Gjetost	**Touch of cardamon, ginger,**
2 cups (5 dl) liquid, or more,	**Cinnamon or nutmeg**
milk, cream, apple cider or	**Fresh fruit**
orange juice	**Bread sticks**

Over moderate heat, melt the cheese while stirring continually. If sauce is too thin let sauce cook until liquid is reduced, or add a little cornstarch which has been dissolved in a little water. Add your choice of spice (cardamon is a favorite in our home). Keep

Friendships grow closer, and talk livelier around a fondue pot. This delightfully sweet, smooth sauce served with fresh fruits is great for dessert or an evening snack.

a low heat under the fondue pot. Arrange a tray of fruit and bread sticks for dipping. Be sure each person has a long fondue fork. **Serves 6-8.**

Thick Rice Pancakes (Rislapper)

When you make rice porridge plan to make enough so you have left-overs to make these rislapper. Mamma often managed to have left-over porridge to make them as a treat when we listened to Saturday barnetimen (Children's Hour) on the radio - no less!

Once the batter is made, fry the pancakes immediately. Amounts will depend on how thick the porridge is. The batter will liquify if it stands and the pancakes will loose their shapes. Fry a sample cake, and add more flour if needed.

2 cups (5 dl) rice porridge	**3 eggs**
2-3 tbsp. sugar	**¼ tsp. salt (optional)**
1¼ cups (3 dl) flour	**Butter or margarine**
¼ tsp. cinnamon or cardamom	

Mix the rice porridge with sugar, most of the flour, cinnamon or cardamom, and the lightly beaten eggs. Brown a little butter or margarine in a frying pan, and ladle enough batter into the pan to make about a 3 inch size pancake and smooth the surface to make the pancakes equally large. Fry until golden brown on both sides. Serve rice pancakes right from the frying pan with sugar or spread with jam. **Serves 5-6.**

Telemark Gomme (Telemarkgomme)

Gomme has a long history in Norway. This unique gomme from Telemark requires a lot of stirring, but with our electric beaters it is well worth the effort. The finished gomme will have a delicious and unusually creamy consistency.

6 qts. (6 liter) milk, whole	**½ cup brown sugar**
6 eggs	

In a heavy bottom pan bring the milk, over moderate heat, to the boiling point while stirring continually. Pour into a separate casserole with a heavy bottom and let it simmer uncovered for approximately 5 hours. Gently shake the pan periodically. Do not remove the coating, *snerken,* which will form on top of the milk. The *gomme* will now have the consistency of a thick sauce and have a light golden color. Beat eggs and sugar together in a bowl. Add the boiled milk, a few tablespoons at a time, while continually beating at high speed. When all milk is added, continue to beat on low until the *gomme* is lukewarm. Enjoy with waffles and lefse. There is plenty here to share as well.

Summer Cold Dish (Summerkoldtskål)

Desserts made with milk, soured milk or cream, have been popular in Norway for ages. Some of the most popular are included here.

²/₃ cup (1½ dl) whipping cream	**Lemon, sliced thin**
1 qt. (liter) cultured milk or kefir	**3 tbsp. almonds, coarsely**
Juice of ½ lemon	**chopped**
3 tbsp. sugar	**Strawberries, fresh**
1 tsp. vanilla sugar	**Rusks**

Whip cream. Carefully stir in cultured milk or kefir. Add lemon juice, sugar and vanilla sugar. Pour into a large bowl. Cover and chill thoroughly - possibly in the freezer for awhile. When ready to be served, decorate with lemon slices and serve with almonds, strawberries and rusks. **Serves 6.**

Crumbled Flatbread in Kefir Milk (Flatbrødsoll)

Flatbread   **Brown sugar**
Kefir

Break up desired amount of crisp flatbread in a wide mouthed dessert or soup bowl. Pour a generous amount of kefir milk over the flatbread, and sprinkle with brown sugar.

Cool and refreshing on a hot summer's day!

Kefir Milk Dessert (Melkeringer)

1 qt. (liter) milk, whole   **Cinnamon and sugar**
½ cup (1¼ dl) kefir   **Crushed zwieback**
½ cup (1¼ dl) sour cream

Bring milk to boiling point. Remove from heat and cool until lukewarm. Divide into 4 dessert bowls and add 2 tablespoons each of kefir and sour cream to each bowl. Let stand covered at room temperature until firm. Refrigerate until serving time. Serve with cinnamon, sugar and crushed zwieback. **Serves 4.**

An old summertime treat still used by those who love it's refreshing taste.

Candies

Coconut Balls I (Kokosboller I)

Goodies like these coconut balls were so undescribably delicious to the youth growing up after World War II. Possibly because they were a "once in awhile treat." Yet, after these many years nostalgia sets in for most of us, when we bite into a coconut ball. Freia cooking chocolate may be substituted with semi-sweet chocolate or milk chocolate.

¼ cup (1¼ dl) water   1 Freia cooking chocolate, 4¼ oz. (125 g)
2½ cups (6½ dl, scant)) sugar   4 tbsp. cocoa fat
2 tbsp. Knox unflavored gelatine   2 tbsp. canning wax
2 tsp. vanilla sugar   1¼ cup (3 dl) coconut, finely grated
½ cup (1 dl, scant) water, boiling

Boil water and sugar 14 minutes. Cool. Soften gelatine 2 minutes in as little water as possible, and add to the ½ cup of boiling water. Cool. Combine the two mixtures, add vanilla sugar and beat until a firm mass. Spoon this cream unto lightly buttered wax paper or foil and let stand 30 to 40 minutes or until firm. Melt chocolate, cocoa-fat, and wax in top of double boiler. Using two spoons, gently dip the 24 creams into the chocolate mixture and roll in coconut. Leave the coconut balls on paper to set.

Coconut Balls II (Kokosboller II)

A quick version of coconut balls without the creamy filling. They may be rolled in ground nuts or in coconut.

4¼ oz. (125 g) cooking chocolate,
  unsweetened
1 large or 2 small eggs

4 cups (10 dl) coconut, or more
Ground hazelnuts or almonds

Melt chocolate in double boiler. Cool slightly, and beat in egg(s). Add enough coconut until there is more coconut than chocolate. Shape into little balls, and roll in more coconut or in ground nuts. Leave on wax paper to set. **Makes 32.**

Marzipan with Chocolate Truffle (Marsipan med sjokolade trøffel)

9 oz. (250 gr) marzipan

Truffle:
½ cup scant (1 dl) canned milk
1 bar 4 oz. (125 g) Freia light,
  cooking chocolate
2⅓ tbsp. water

1 tsp. rum extract
⅔ cup (50 g) cocoa
1 tbsp. confectioners' sugar

Use marzipan recipe in this book or buy almond paste. Roll into balls and press flat like a peppermint patty. Set aside.
Truffle: Bring the milk to a boil. Break up chocolate and add. Stir until chocolate is melted, add water and rum extract. Cool quickly and stir thoroughly. When lukewarm add the cocoa. Beat until thick and smooth. Add confectioners' sugar to taste. Cool completely. Fill decorating tube with truffle and decorate the marzipan patties. Top with a small colored candy.

Chocolate Spheres (Sjokoladekuler)

⅝ cup (150 g) butter
½ cup, scant (1 dl) canned milk
3⅓ cups (350 g) confectioners' sugar

⅔ cup (50 g) cocoa
¾ cup (50 g) coconut

Add butter and canned milk to a heavy bottomed sauce pan. Sift in confectioners' sugar and cocoa. Over low heat stir thoroughly until a solid, smooth mass. Remove from heat, form 1 incg (2½ cm) balls and roll in coconut. Wrap in cellophane paper or place into paper candy cups. Keep cool.

Cocoa-Balls (Kakaokuler)

An easy and traditional candy children like to make.

¾ cup (2 dl) sugar
5 tbsp. cocoa
2¾ cups (7 dl) barely cooked oats
4 tbsp. vanilla sugar

2 tbsp. soft butter, scant
2 tbsp. Pero (coffee substitute)
Shredded coconut

Mix sugar, cocoa, oatmeal and vanilla sugar. Cut in butter and add Pero or coffee and mix well. Shape into balls the size of walnuts and roll in coconut. Place on a platter, then cover with foil and chill until set. Keep cool.

Breads, Flatbread, Lefse and More

Our Daily Bread (*Vårt daglige brød*)

In Norway, homemade bread, hot out of the oven, is a favorite treat anytime. Today we do not have to fire up the old wood stove, so set aside an afternoon, or an evening to make some delicious breads, rolls, lefser or flatbread to keep for those times when you wish for something nourishing and tasty. Breads, rolls and lefser freeze well, and flatbread keeps well in airtight containers.

Surely one of the happiest memories of home is the tantalizing aroma of freshly baked bread. I have seen many persons butter a thick slice of homemade bread with such a gleam of anticipation in their eyes that it defies description.

Many shy away from making bread because they think it is a difficult process, when actually it is rather easy. It does take a little time and muscle, unless you have a food processor with a kneading hook (I love my Braun). But one efforts are richly rewarded as soon as the heavenly aroma begins to seep out of the oven. You can make your breads plain or do what is popular in Norway - try out a fancy design. (see picture and Else Rønnevig's Coarse Bread recipe).

I realize there are several good bread making machines on the market, which obviously are great time savers. But they do take away the joy of making the bread. But if a bread machine is the only way you have time to enjoy homemade bread, by all means, use one.

No matter what type of bread you make, it is an undisputed fact that homemade bread benefits our families greatly, since we choose the ingredients and do not add chemical stabilizers or preservatives. Homemade bread is an excellent source of dietary fiber and provides protein and carbohydrates. And when we bake with whole grains, we ensure our families are supplied with one of the richest sources of vitamin B and iron.

Natural food stores usually carry a large selection of varied grains and flour, and they are often willing to take special orders. Once your grain or flour is purchased, maintain its food value by storing it in a cool, dry place. Freezing or plastic containers with tight fitting lids are perfect for this.

Successful Bread Making (*Vellykket brødbakst*)

All ingredients should be at room temperature. Assemble in advance all ingredients and any needed equipment and utensils. Prepare the baking pans.

The proper flour is important. Bread flour is best for all types of bread, or use unbleached flour.

Handle the yeast with care for its complete cooperation. Dry yeast should be dissolved in a temperature of approximately 110-115°F (43-46°C), whereas 85°F (30°C) is just right for compressed yeast. To hasten this action you may add a little

Use the best ingredients you can afford. It is of no avail to exert the effort of bread making only to see your endeavor fail or fall short of your expectation because you cheated on the ingredients.

sugar, but no more than specified in the recipe. Fresh yeast will activate within a few minutes.

The dough must be workable, neither too stiff nor sticky. Allow it to rise in a warm, draft-free area, giving it enough time to double in bulk. If desired, the dough may be allowed to rise and fall a number of times during the dough-making process to improve texture, but do not allow it to over-expand.

Do not cheat on your kneading. Gluten develops through prolonged kneading and results in a smoother, more elastic dough. A food processor with a dough hook is ideal (see Special Help Chapter).

Oven temperature must be accurate. Be sure bread is thoroughly baked. Do invest in a **Commercial-Grade Instant-Read Test Thermometer**, it takes the guessing out of bread baking. The internal temperature of perfectly baked bread is 190-205°F (88-96°C). The Instant-Read Test Thermometer can tell you the internal temperature in seconds. If you do not have one, tap the bottom of the bread, when it sounds hollow, it is done.

Failure causes in bread making:

Porous bread: usually stems from insufficient kneading, thus not giving the gluten a chance to develop. This in turn causes bubbles of gas to be distributed unevenly throughout the loaf. It is of utmost importance to knead thoroughly. Allowing the dough to overexpand may also result in porous bread. Do not allow dough to exceed double in bulk before punching down.

Sour or yeast flavor: is caused by too much yeast, allowing the dough to over-expand, or not keeping dough warm enough during rising process. By placing dough in a closed draft-free area, such as an oven, this problem will be eliminated.

Water-streaked, soggy or heavy bread: may be caused by poor quality flour, inferior quality yeast and thus slow rising, lack of thorough baking, or rough handling of the freshly baked bread before it was completely cooled.

Broken or separated crust: could be caused by pour quality flour or adding too much flour, or not allowing dough to rise properly. To give each loaf a shiny surface, brush with water, milk or butter before you bake. However, loaves will get a rougher surface and a more homemade look, which many prefer, if you do not brush the dough. Whatever you do, find the time to make homemade bread. *Lykke til*, Good luck!

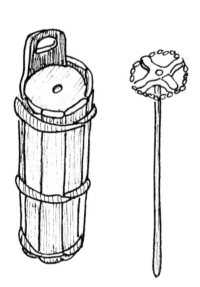

On Baking Breads and Cookies *(Slik baker vi brød og småkaker)*

Keep in mind, as a general rule, that the longer the item needs to bake, the lower it should be in the oven.

- ♥ Breads - pound cakes - loaf cakes - on the lowest rack.
- ♥ Hard rolls - dinner rolls - sponge cakes - on the middle rack.
- ♥ Crackers - cookies on the middle rack, or slightly above.

Herb Bread (Urteloff)

1 pkg. active dry yeast	4 cups (500 g) bread flour	*Excellent with hot*
1¼ cups (3 dl) water, warm	¼ cup (50 g) butter, softened	*soups or salads.*
½ tsp. salt	¾ cup (1¾ dl) mixed fresh herbs, such as;	
½ tsp. sugar	chives, dill, parsley and basil	
¼ cup, scant (50 g) butter	Egg	

Dissolve yeast in warm water and add to a large bowl. Add salt and sugar. Work ¼ cup butter into 3 cups flour as for pie crust, add to yeast mixture. Knead 7 minutes until dough is pliable and smooth. Cover and let rise in refrigerator overnight. Remove to a floured surface and work in as much of the remaining flour as needed to make a smooth dough. Roll the dough out to 10x20 inches (25x50 cm). Spread softened butter across the dough. Sprinkle with finely chopped herbs. Beginning with the long edge, roll the bread up jelly roll fashion, and place seam down on a parchment covered baking sheet. With a sharp knife make diagonal cuts, on top of the bread's surface, about 1-inch (2½ cm) apart. Cover and rise 20 minutes. Brush with egg and bake in preheated 435°F (225°C) oven for 20 minutes.

Else's Coarse Bread (Else's Grovbrød)

As Mistress of Snøringsmoen she favors her guests with meals spiced with cultural history. To visit Snøringsmoen is "a journey for the senses". It is to enjoy the tastes, sounds, aromas and atmosphere of the past. Now you can make her delicious and beautifully decorated bread. Make the dough in the evening and set in refrigerator overnight.

2½ cup (6¼ dl) water 115°F (45°C)	¾ cup (1¾ dl) dark rye flour
2 pkgs. active dry yeast	1½-2 cups (4-5 dl) bread flour
1 tbsp. dark syrup	¼ cup (20 g) wheat bran
2 tbsp. margarine, melted	¾ cup (80 g) oat bran
and cooled	1 tbsp. salt
2½ cups (5 dl) graham flour	

Else Rønnevig is the vivacious and talented Mistress of Snøringsmoen, the first Swiss Chalet build in 1867, in Lillesand. Else has a deep love and concern for the Norwegian cultural history and food traditions. She has won many prizes for her delicious and fancy breads (see picture).

In a large bowl, add warm water, yeast and syrup. Let stand 5 minutes until yeast dissolves. Melt margarine and cool. When yeast has dissolved, add all remaining ingredients. Mix with a wooden spoon until the dough leaves the sides of the bowl. Turn out onto a lightly floured surface and knead 5-8 minutes. Place in a lightly greased bowl, turn once. Cover tightly with lightly greased plastic wrap and set to cool overnight. Remove to a lightly floured surface and knead 2-3 minutes and shape into a round loaf. Place on parchment covered baking sheet.

Dough for decorations:

½ cup (1¼ dl) water, warm	1¼ cups (150 g) bread flour
½ tbsp. active dry yeast	Egg yolk
¾ cup (100 g) light rye flour	Water

In a medium sized bowl, add warm water and yeast. Let stand 5 minutes until yeast dissolves. Stir in enough flour to make a fairly firm dough. Do not begin to knead before as much water as possible has carefully been worked into the flour. If the dough is too firm a *little* additional water may be added. Cover tightly with lightly greased plastic wrap, and set to cool overnight. To make spike of grain, roll into two ropes pointed at one end. Cut along the edges to form a spike (see picture). Or shape into desired decoration, and fasten to the round loaf with water. Set bread to rise 30 minutes. Preheat oven to 390°F (200°C). Just before baking brush the decoration only, with a slightly beaten egg yolk to which has been added 1 tablespoon of water. Bake on lowest rack 30-40 minutes. Bread is done when internal temperature is 190-205°F (88-96°C). Or tap bread on the bottom, when it sounds hollow, it is done. Watch the decoration so it does not become too dark. Cover with aluminum foil if necessary. **Makes 1 large round loaf.**

   Tips: If you would like to display your beautiful creation, leave the bread to dry for 48 hours, with oven doors ajar, and temperature between 140-210°F (60-100°C). The breads must be completely dry, or they could explode. If desired spray with non-glossy lacquer.

Else's White Bread *(Else's hvetebrød)*

7 cups (1 kg) bread flour	**1 tbsp. salt**
1 pkg. active dry yeast	**1½ tbsp. margarine**
1 tbsp. sugar	**2¼ cups (5½ dl) water or milk**

Follow directions for Else's Coarse Bread. It is important to dissolve yeast at 104-122°F (40-50C)° water or milk.

Multi-Grain Bread *(Kneipploff)*

Triticale, the first man-made hybrid grain, combines the nutrition of wheat, the taste of rye, and a protein/gluten content right in between the two. It also has a better balance of amino acids than either rye or wheat alone.

A wonderfully satisfying bread made with either triticale or wheat kernels, easily attainable at natural food markets.

1 cup (180 g) triticale or wheat kernels	**1 tbsp. molasses or honey**
¾ cup (1¾ dl) water, boiling	**2½ cups (300 g) whole wheat flour**
2 tbsp. active dry yeast	**1 tsp. salt**
2 cups (5 dl) kefir or soured skim milk	**2 tbsp. sunflower seed oil**
	3^1/$_3$ cups (450 g) bread flour

In a small bowl, pour the boiling water over the triticale or wheat kernels, and let stand 1 hour. In a large bowl, add the yeast to a little of the kefir or sour skim milk, which has been slightly warmed. Add molasses or honey. When yeast is dissolved, add the remaining milk. Beat in the whole wheat flour, salt, and oil. Add the whole kernels and bread flour. Turn dough out on a floured board and knead the dough until glossy and elastic, about 10 minutes. Return to bowl which has been lightly greased, turn once, and cover. Set to rise in a draft-free, warm place until double in bulk. Remove onto a lightly floured board. Shape into a large round loaf and place in a 10-inch (25 cm) greased springform pan. Cover and let rise approximately 20 minutes. Brush with water and bake in preheated oven, 355-390°F (180-200°C), about 1 hour. The loaf is done when internal temperature is 190-205°F (88-96°C), or the bread sounds hollow when tapped on the bottom. Let cool slightly in the pan before removing to a rack. Cool completely. **Makes 1 large round loaf.**

Sweet Cardamom Bread (Hvetekake)

2 pkgs. active dry yeast
2½ cups (6 dl) milk, warmed
3 tbsp. margarine, melted
4¾ cups (11¾ dl) unbleached
   all-purpose flour

¹/₃ cup (65 g) sugar
1½ tsp. salt
1½ tsp. cardamom, freshly ground
Butter, melted

Traditionally this bread is formed into round loaves, so flavorful they are called hvetekake, *wheat cake. Norwegians enjoy this bread, with the heavenly cardamom aroma and flavor topped with the ever popular sweet caramel-colored* gjetost, *goat cheese. It also tastes good with other mild cheeses or preserves.*

In a large bowl, add yeast, milk, and margarine and stir until yeast is dissolved. Sift in 3½-3¾ cups (8¾-9¼ dl) of the flour, sugar, salt and cardamom. Beat batter until glossy. Add 1 cup more flour. The dough will be very soft. Cover and let rest 15 minutes. Turn dough out on a lightly floured surface and knead until elastic and glossy, 8-10 minutes, adding additional flour if needed. Lightly grease the bowl, and return dough to the bowl, turning once. Let rise in a draft free, warm place until double in bulk, about 1 hour. Punch down. Turn dough out on a lightly floured board, using as little flour as possible. Divide into 2 parts, and shape into round loaves. Place on baking sheets covered with parchment paper, or dust lightly with flour, but do not grease the sheets. Set to rise in a draft-free, warm place until almost double in bulk. Preheat oven to 375°F (190°C). Brush with melted butter and bake until done and a golden color, about 40-45 minutes. Remove to racks and brush with butter once more. Breads are done when they sound hollow when tapped on the bottom. **Makes 2 round loaves.**

Mother Selland's Bread (Mor Selland's brød)

Place the following ingredients in a bowl:

3 cups (7½ dl) whole wheat flour
½ cup (1¼ dl) brown sugar
½ cup (1¼ dl) molasses

½ cup (1¼ dl) shortening
4 tsp. salt

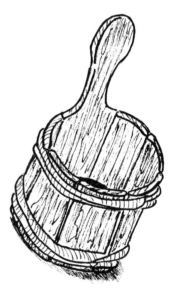

Pour over 4 cups hot water. Stir and cool to lukewarm. Add:

2 cups bread flour

Mix well and add:

2 pkgs. active dry yeast dissolved in ¹/₃ cup lukewarm water
Add 7-8 additional cups bread flour.

Mix well and knead 10 minutes. Put in greased, large bowl; turn over once. Rise in a warm place until double in bulk, about two hours. Punch down and let rise a second time. Knead lightly, shape into 4 loaves and when they have risen to almost double in bulk. Bake in 400°F (205°C) oven for 10 minutes, reduce to 350°F (175°C) and bake 30 minutes longer. **Makes 4 loaves.**

Rye Bread (Rugbrød)

1½ pkg. active dry yeast	¾ cup (1¾ dl) margarine
½ cup (1¼ dl) water, warm	2 tsp. salt
2 cups (5 dl) rye flour, sifted	2 cups (5 dl) water, boiling
¾ cup (1¾ dl) molasses	6-6½ cups (15-16¼ dl) bread flour

In a small bowl add water and yeast, let yeast dissolve. In a large bowl add rye flour, molasses, margarine and salt. Pour the boiling water over this flour mixture and stir well. Cool to lukewarm. Add yeast mixture. Gradually stir in enough bread flour to make a soft dough. Mix thoroughly. Turn out on a well-floured surface. Cover dough and let rest 10 minutes. Knead until dough becomes satiny and pliant, approximately 10 minutes. Place in a lightly greased bowl, turn it over once to grease surface. Cover and let rise until double in bulk. Punch down and let rise again until almost double. Punch down and divide into three parts. Then shape into rounds. Place on greased or parchment covered cookie sheet and let rise again until almost double in bulk, approximately 35-40 minutes. Bake in 350°F (175°C) oven, 35 to 40 minutes. Cool on rack, and brush with butter while still hot. **Makes 3 round loaves.**

Sigrid's Best Rusks (Sigrid's beste skonroker)

A rusk is kind of a large round biscuit, sliced in two, and toasted in the oven after baking. The people of Selbu, where Sigrid Juul Røset lives, use a lot of tettemelk, a Norwegian type yogurt, during the summer. Traditionally tettemelk is served with crushed rusks and brown sugar.

With a little variation in the recipe, you can serve these rusks with butter and cheese, particularly Norwegian goat cheese. That is how I remember enjoying the rusks as a child. Delicious!

3½ tbsp. (50 g) margarine	1½ cups (100 g) wheat bran
7 tbsp. (100 g) lard	⅓ cup (75 g) sugar
3¼ cups (8 dl) water or milk	½ tsp. salt
2 pkg. yeast	1¼ tbsp. crushed anise
5⅓ cups (700 g) flour, unbleached	1 tsp. salt of hartshorn
1⅝ cup (200 g) whole wheat flour	

In a heavy pan melt the margarine and lard and add water or milk, heat to lukewarm. Use a small amount of the liquid to dissolve the yeast, let stand 5 minutes, return to the milk mixture. In a large bowl add remaining ingredients, but save out ⅓ of the unbleached flour. Pour in the milk and fat mixture. Add additional flour if needed. The dough should be very soft and pliable. Set to rise in a lightly greased bowl until it doubles in bulk. Turn dough out on lightly oiled working surface. Knead lightly. Divide dough into 30 pieces and roll into balls. Place on greased baking sheet, and let rise until almost double in bulk. Preheat oven to 480°F (250°C) and bake 10-12 minutes, or until they barely get color. Cool on rack. Divide the buns with a saw-toothed knife (it makes a smooth surface) and continue baking for 45-60 minutes in 175-210°F (80-100°C) with oven door ajar. Dry until crisp. These rusks are best used crushed for toppings. If you desire to use the rusks with butter and cheese use 3½ tbsp. (50 g) lard and 7 tbsp. (100 g) margarine, and use half milk (not 2%) and half water. **Makes 60 rusks.**

Hard Rolls (Korpsrundstykker)

This recipe is rather large, but the rolls keep well in the freezer. So why not gather some friends and have a fun baking day together, or cut the recipe to fill your needs.

½ cup, scant (100 g) margarine,
   melted
6¾ cups (17 dl) milk, skim
2 pkgs. active dry yeast
3⁷/₈ lbs (1¾ kg) flour

6 cups (250 g) wheat bran
4 tsp. salt
4 tbsp. sugar
Egg

Sigrid Juul Røset is a home economics teacher. She created this recipe for a junior music band rally held in South-Trøndelag. She gathered 21 of her friends in Selbu and made 5000 of these hard rolls for the delighted musicians.

In a heavy saucepan combine margarine and milk, heat just until margarine has melted. Cool to lukewarm. Dissolve the yeast in a little of the milk, stir until dissolved. In a large bowl mix the remaining ingredients, except egg, and leave out a little of the flour. Add the milk and yeast mixture. With a large wooden spoon stir until well mixed adding enough flour to make a fairly firm dough. Cover with a towel and let rise in a warm, draft-free place. Punch down. Remove to a lightly floured board and divide into equal portions. Shape into round or oval rolls, and place on greased baking sheet. Brush with lightly beaten egg. Bake in 480°F (250°C) degree oven. Bake about 12-15 minutes or until done. Cool on rack. **Makes 48 large or 65 medium rolls.**

Bergen Pretzels *(Bergenskringler)*

⁷/₈ cup (2 dl) skim milk, lukewarm
1 pkg. active dry yeast
3 tbsp. margarine, melted

½ tsp. salt
2½ cups, scant (6 dl) flour

A kringle is usually a pretzel-shaped pastry or coffee bread. These individually sized kringler are dry and crisp, and are also known as water-kringler. I first tasted these kringler while attending Fana Folklore in Bergen. They served them as an accompaniment to sour cream porridge and cured meats.

In a medium bowl dissolve yeast in lukewarm milk. Add melted margarine, salt, and enough flour to make a firm dough. Remove to a board and knead the dough until smooth and elastic, about 10 minutes. Divide into 14-16 equal parts. Do not use flour while shaping into *kringler* but dip your fingers in lukewarm water. Roll into sausages about the size of your little finger and shape into pretzels. Be careful not to make the center part too thick. Cook in a large kettle with lots of boiling water, as soon as made They will sink to the bottom soon after added to the water, and then rise to the surface when they have raised. Remove from water and place on greased cookie sheet and bake in 350°F (175°C) until a light golden brown, about 30 minutes. Lower heat to 250°F (120°C) and continue to bake until crisp. Cool on rack. **Makes 14-16 large pretzels.**

Christmas Bread I *(Julekake I)*

¾ cup (1¾ dl) milk
½ cup (1¼ dl) sugar
¼ cup (½ dl) butter
1½ tsp. salt
2 pkg. active dry yeast
½ cup (1¼ dl) water

2 eggs, beaten
5 cups (12½ dl) flour, sifted
1 tsp. cardamom seeds, pulverized
1½ cups (3½ dl) raisins
½ cup (1¼ dl) citron
Egg or water

A traditional bread with raisins, citron and cardamon. Delicious eaten plain or with butter and the brown sweet goat cheese, or orange marmalade. However it is eaten, it is a must in every home during the Christmas holidays.

In a small heavy bottom pan, heat the milk until bubbles form around the edges of pan; remove from heat. Add sugar, butter and salt. Stir until butter is melted. Cool to lukewarm. Sprinkle yeast over water in large bowl, stir until dissolved. Stir in milk mixture. Add eggs, 2 cups flour and cardamon; beat with wooden spoon until smooth. Add raisins and citron. Stir in enough of remaining flour (2½ to 3 cups) to make a soft dough. Cover with towel. Let rest 10 minutes. Turn out dough unto lightly floured surface; knead until smooth and elastic about 8 minutes. Place in lightly greased, large bowl. Turn once to bring up greased side. Cover with towel; let rise in warm place until double in bulk - about 1½-2 hours. Punch down, divide in half. Shape each half into a ball. Cover, let rest 10 minutes. Pat each ball into a round loaf, place on greased baking sheet and let rise until double in bulk - about 1½-2 hours. Preheat oven to 350°F (175°C). Brush loaves with slightly beaten egg or water. Bake 20 minutes; cover with foil, and bake an additional 25 minutes, or until deep golden brown. Cool on wire racks. **Makes 2 rounds.**

Christmas Bread II (Julekake II)

This julekake, *more like a cake, diffes from Christmas Bread I in that baking powder is used in place of yeast. It can be made in a jiffy and is absolutely delicious.*

1⅛ cups (250 g) butter	4 tsp. vanilla sugar
2 cups (425 g) sugar	4 tsp. baking powder
3 eggs	2 cups (5 dl) coffee cream
4 cups (900 g) flour	⅞ cup (100 g) citron, finely chopped
1 tsp. cardamom	1⅛ cup (250 g) raisins

Cream butter and sugar until light and fluffy. Add the eggs, one at a time. Mix flour (save out a little to mix with fruit to prevent it from sinking to the bottom of pan), cardamom, baking powder and vanilla sugar and add to butter mixture alternately with cream. Add fruit and stir well. Preheat oven to 350°F (175°C). Grease two loaf pans and line the bottoms with wax paper. Pour batter into pans and bake 1 hour. Cool on rack. **Makes 2 loaves.**

Orange Loaf Cake (Appelsinformkake)

Quickly and easily made with a rich orange taste. Keeps well in airtight container or in freezer.

2 eggs	½ cup, scant (1 dl) milk
⅔ cup (125 g) sugar	¾ cup (100 g) raisins
½ cup, scant (100 g) butter	2 cups, scant (250 g) flour
1 cup (2½ dl) orange marmalade	2 tsp. baking powder

Beat eggs and sugar until light and fluffy. Melt butter, cool slightly and whip together with the egg mixture. Add marmalade, milk and raisins. Mix well. Sift in flour and baking powder and mix thoroughly. Grease a large bread pan and pour the batter into the pan. Bake in 350° (175°C) oven on the *lowest* rack 55-60 minutes. **Makes 1 large loaf.**

Cardamom Buns (Kardemommeboller)

2 cups (5 dl) milk	¾ cup (1¾ dl) sugar
¼ cup (55 g) butter	1 tbsp. sugar
¼ cup (55 g) margarine	½ tsp. salt
1 pkg. active dry yeast	6 whole cardamom seeds, crushed
¼ cup (½ dl) water, warm	7 cups flour

Scald milk. Add butter and margarine and let stand until melted, and milk is slightly cooled. Soften yeast in warm water with 1 tablespoon of sugar added. In a large bowl add remaining sugar, salt and cardamom. Pour in lukewarm milk mixture. Add yeast, and enough flour to make a stiff dough. Work thoroughly. Place in a greased bowl. Cover and let rise until double in bulk. Punch down and shape into balls, the size of ping pong balls. Place 1 inch (2½ cm) apart on greased baking sheet. Cover with tea towel and let rise until double in bulk. Bake in 450°F (230°C) oven for 5 minutes. (Yes, 5 minutes is right). Brush with butter while still hot.

Saffron Buns (Safranbrød)

These buns are traditionally made at Christmas time (see illustrations). In times past the different motifs had symbolic or magical meanings. Many believed that the cross had the power to protect.

1 cup (2½ dl) milk	1 pkg. active dry yeast
½ cup, scant (1 dl) sugar	¼ cup (½ dl) water, warm
1 tsp. salt	1 egg, small
½ cup, scant (100 g) butter	4 cups (10 dl) unbleached flour
½ tsp. saffron threads, crushed	⅓ cup (¾ dl) raisins, optional
	Egg and pearl sugar

In a heavy saucepan combine milk, sugar, salt, butter, and saffron and bring to the boiling point. Stir. Remove from heat and let cool to lukewarm. Pour into food processor bowl equipped with a dough hook, or a large bowl. Dissolve yeast in luke warm water and add. Add egg, and about half of the flour, and mix thoroughly. Add remaining flour, to avoid a heavy bread use as little flour as possible. The dough will be sticky. Using the dough hook beat for 1½ minutes, or use your electric mixer for about 5 minutes. Place in a greased bowl, cover with lightly greased plastic wrap, and set to cool in a warm place for 1 hour, or until double in bulk.

Shape into saffron buns pictured, or make into braided breads. Raisins used for decorations needs to be added before the second rising. Set to raise in a warm place for 30 minutes, covered with greased plastic wrap. Brush with beaten egg, and sprinkle with pearl sugar. Bake at 425°F (220°C) until a golden brown, about 15 to 20 minutes. Cool slightly then remove to rack to cool completely. **Makes 10 large buns, or 16 medium.**

School Buns with Vanilla Custard (Skoleboller)

1½ cups (3½ dl) milk, lukewarm	Topping:
1 pkg. active dry yeast	
½ cup, scant (100 g) butter, melted	Vanilla Egg Custard
½ cup, scant (1 dl) sugar	Vanilla Glaze
½ tsp. cardamom	Shredded coconut
4 cups, approx. (10 dl) unbleached flour	

Norwegian children love these buns with a center of vanilla custard. Use the recipe for vanilla custard in this book or use vanilla pudding, but then use only half the milk the recipe calls for.

Heat the milk to 110°F (43°C), and dissolve the yeast in the milk. Add melted and cooled butter. Add the sugar and cardamom, and enough flour to make a soft dough. Knead until smooth and elastic, up to 10 minutes. Place in greased bowl, turn once, and let rise to almost double in bulk. Remove once during the rising period and knead slightly. When risen, roll into 12-14 balls and place on parchment covered cookie sheet. Make a deep indentation in the center and let the balls raise until light and smooth.

Generously fill the indentation with 1 recipe of Vanilla Egg Custard (see index). Bake in 480°F (250°C) 10-12 minutes. Cool on racks. When cool, encircle the egg custard with a thick band of confectioners' sugar glaze (see index). Dip in shredded coconut, it will adhere to the glaze. And uhm, uhm, you will have contented children. **Makes 16 school buns.**

Lefse

Lefse is gjestebudkost! That is to say, party fare. In the last century flatbread was everyday fare, lefse belonged to the banquets and special celebrations. Almost every district had, and still has, its own favorite recipe for lefse, although it goes by different names in the different districts.

Most lefse recipes do not require yeast, a few do, such as *krotakaker* from Hardanger. It used to be that some women would go from farm to farm and make enough lefse for the families to last a year. It does take a little time to make lefse, however, when it tastes that good it is worth the effort. So go to work to keep this long, enjoyed Norwegian tradition alive.

Most likely your first lefse will not be a paper-thin tasty creation, yet, if you will keep at it, you will triumph. Today, we have so many tools to help us succeed, and if you are serious about learning how to make lefse, make a few investments to ensure success.

- ♥ Potato ricer
- ♥ A grooved lefse rolling pin.
- ♥ A cotton-polyester "sock". I bless the day, years ago, when my sister Gro gave me my first one.
- ♥ Cotton-polyester pastry cloth, a must! The excellent Original All Purpose Pastry Board with pastry cloth is available from Jacobs of Wilmar. See Sources.
- ♥ Lefse stick with beveled tips. (You can get fancy and rosemal the top part.)
- ♥ Lefse grill.

Not all the above tools are a must, but they do save time, and make the job pleasant. However, a lefse grill is expensive, and many have started out with a skillet or electric frying pan. Your lefse will not be as large, but it will taste just as good, and then, when you have become more efficient you can make the investment in the grill. You can get by with a regular rolling pin, but I highly recommend you invest in a grooved rolling pin which helps with heat distribution, and pulverizes any lumps, and experts agree, prevent tearing.

Quick Potato Lefse *(Snøgg potet lefse)*

This is a great recipe for beginners, or those stressed for time. A no-fail recipe. The water content of instant potatoes is always the same. You will feel good about your efforts from your very first try. I promise!

2 cups (5 dl) water
2 cups (5 dl) instant potatoes
   (shake to settle)
3 tbsp. shortening

3 tbsp. butter
2 tsp. salt
1 tbsp. sugar

Bring water to a boil, remove from heat and stir in instant potatoes, shortening, butter, salt, and sugar. Cool. For each measuring cup of this mixture add ½ cup flour and divide in four portions. Keep remainder of potato mixture refrigerated until ready to use. Roll each portion to dinner-plate size, as thin as possible, using additional flour, (as little as possible, too much flour makes a tough *lefse*) a pastry cloth and a grooved rolling pin with sock. To prevent sticking, turn the dough with the *lefse* stick as needed. When *lefse* is desired thickness, flip one end of lefse over *lefse* stick and roll up to center. Place lefse on grill and unroll. When bubbles appear turn and bake other side. If needed, turn over once more till the brown spots appear. Do not overbake as it will make the *lefse* dry and it will loose its flavor. It is traditionally served with butter and sugar.

I am not sure how the Norwegian homemaker of yesteryear would feel about using instant potatoes for lefse making. Maybe they would have welcomed it in lives filled mostly with toil.

Potato Lefse I (Potet lefse I)

3 large baking potatoes	½ teaspoon sugar
2 tbsp. butter	1 tsp. salt
¼ cup (½ dl) heavy cream	1 cup (2½ dl) flour, or more

Boil the potatoes without peeling, peel and mash while still warm and put through ricer. To get the lumps out, you might have to put them through ricer more than once. Add the remaining ingredients, mix well, cover and chill for eight hours or overnight. Mix in ½ cup (1¼ dl) flour. Divide into 15-16 balls if you want dinner-plate size. Using a grooved rolling pin with sock, (sock optional), and pastry canvas, roll each ball out as thin as possible. Use flour as needed (but not too much), and keep balance of dough in the refrigerator. Bake each *lefse* on medium to hot griddle, turning until both sides are flecked with brown. Do not overbake.

Potato Lefse II (Potet lefser II)

4 cups (9½ dl) potatoes cooked	½ cup (1¼ dl) Crisco oil
1 tsp. salt	2 tbsp. sugar
½ cup (1¼ dl) whipping cream	1½ cups (3½ dl) flour

Boil and rice potatoes, add salt, cream and oil to *warm* potatoes. Completely cool the potatoes before adding flour. You can cut down a little on the cream and oil. Making them too rich will make them hard to handle. Mix sugar with flour and add, kneading as you roll them out with a grooved rolling pin. Bake on *takke*, round griddle.

You can almost see through these delectable lefser. But it is the taste that will cause you to make them often.

Tender Nordland's Lefse (Mørlefse fra Nordland)

1¾ cups (4½ dl) sour cream or ⁷/₈ cup each buttermilk and sour cream	2 tsp. hartshorn salt Unbleached flour
¼ cup (½ dl) sugar	Barley flour, optional
¼ cup (½ dl) syrup, Lyle's golden	

Whip together sour cream and sugar. Stir in syrup. Sift salt of hartshorn with flour and stir into the sour cream mixture until it forms a fairly soft dough. Substituting some barley flour for the unbleached flour will make *lefse* darker but very tender and delicious. Allow to rest for an hour for easier rolling. Handle the dough as little as possible. Divide dough into six or seven parts and roll out a little thicker than flatbread. Place on a greased cookie sheet. Prick entire surface with a fork and bake until golden in hot oven 400-425°F (205-220°C), the lefse will rise somewhat. Be sure it is thoroughly baked but tender and pliable. When baking is completed, stack on a clean cloth and keep covered. When cool, butter generously and sprinkle with sugar. Place together like a sandwich and cut in wedges.

Small Potato Cake (Lumpe - potetkake - hellekake)

Lumpe *tastes delicious with cured meats. Many enjoy these potato cakes with Norwegian goat cheese, or butter and sugar.*

However, the *lumpe* I remember best from my childhood in Oslo, is when we ate *pølse med lumpe*. A thin sausage, smothered in Idun mustard and wrapped in *lumpe*. In those days they were sold at *bua* - an enclosed market-cart where they also sold drinks and confectioneries. And it would be unthinkable in those days not to find *pølse med lumpe* at athletic events such as Holmenkolldagen, or when at the beach or even children's parties.

During one of my first return visits to Norway, after several years absence, nostalgia washed over me when, one sub zero day in February, my sister Eva and I entered Stortorget, a market place in downtown Oslo. Where we hurriedly purchased, at a market cart, our *pølse med lumpe*. Just as we remembered they were delicious. We exchanged glances, and agreed we must have one more!

Lumpe is easy to make; with just potatoes, flour and a little salt. They are made like lefse, smaller, but a little thicker. They can be served in a variety of ways.

Before potatoes were cultivated in 18th century Norway the *lumpe* were made from barley, oat flour and water. Later the potato replaced the water. *Lumpe* was as a rule eaten dry, except on Sundays when butter was added, and thus on that day became referred to as butter-*lumpe*. (Many now enjoy new-baked *lumpe* with butter and sugar with their hot beverage). All types of flour can be used, either all of one, or several mixed, but the tastiest and softest result when only potatoes and barley flour is used. A mixture of all-purpose and barley flour also give good result.

2 lbs. (900 g) potatoes   **1¼ cups (3 dl), approx. barley flour**
1 tsp. salt

Boil unpeeled potatoes. Peel, and twice grind, rice, or mash while still warm, until potatoes are smooth and elastic, thus requiring less flour. Add salt during this process, rather than adding it to the water, it increases the elasticity of the potatoes. The more elastic the potatoes the better the *lumpe*. Cool. Add flour to a small portion of potatoes at a time, stir just enough to make a firm, easily-handled dough. Making a lot of dough at once and leaving it stand may cause the dough to become sticky. Cut off slices with a sharp knife. Press these down lightly with the back of your hand, and finish rolling out with grooved rolling pin into 6-8-inch (15-17½ cm) flaps. Doing it this way one needs less flour. Brush off all excess flour before baking.

Place lumpe on medium hot *lefse* or other griddle and turn often with a pliable spatula. Prick any blisters that form while baking. When done they should be light in color with large, light brown spots. If the griddle is too hot they will remain raw inside; if too low, they will be hard and tough. Allow them to dry out for a few minutes, then wrap in a clean towel and cover until ready to be served. They are tastiest when used immediately. They can be served with butter and sugar, or with sharp cheese. As for me it will always be *pølse with lumpe*.

Flatbread (Flatbrød)

Gunnar Askeland in his book *Norsk Mat*, talks about the history and the art of making flatbread. He says there were many reasons why the homemakers clung to the use of flatbread. One was its exceptional keeping quality. It would keep for years in a *stabbur* - a storehouse built on stilts. Another reason was that it suited itself to the available Norwegian flour, such as barley and oats. Finally, it was the type of bread which made many variations possible, from a paper-thin to a thick, coarse type; the latter being very filling and satisfying.

For years flatbread almost disappeared, but has now regained its popular place in the Norwegian diet. There are only a few places where flatbread is baked at home. It is now made in factories.

Flatbread is a tie with the old-home cooking, Gunnar explains, and we should not allow it to be forgotten. It takes practice to learn this art, but the reward is great for those who make the attempt. A more delightful addition to a meal than freshly baked, crisp, fragrant flatbread is hard to find. Flatbread should be just as much a mainstay to the Norwegian as French bread is to the French.

Years ago *flatbrød bakedagen* - the day for making flatbread - was a hard day's work on the farms. Often the day was set aside to make enough to last through the winter. Because it was such a tedious, back-breaking job the men of the household were often called upon to assist. The liquid ingredients were basically water and sour whey, thus making flatbread, with its coarse flour, a good addition to the nutritional needs of the family.

Any kind of flour may be used for flatbread, but oat and barley flour have been the most widely used, either together or separately. They are also preferred by the factories. It does make a most delicious bread but is rather difficult to work with. For this reason, a little white or rye flour was added in the preparation of the flatbread, making it not only delicious but much easier to handle. Water is the most widely used for a finer, lighter type flatbread. The usual proportion is about 1¼ cup (3 dl) liquid to 2.2 lbs (1 kg) of flour.

It is important to mix flatbread in a large utensil allowing ample room for kneading. Experienced flatbread makers usually let the dough rest a period of time before rolling out.

The art of rolling out flatbread is not easily acquired-but persevere! The first requirement is a large, sturdy table and a good, medium weight, grooved rolling pin. It is quite fascinating to watch an experienced flatbread maker at work. The round of dough seems to slide almost by itself underneath the rolling pin until suddenly it lies there as an almost transparent flap of bread of uniform shape. One won't become that experienced after only a few tries, of course, but if we start by handling smaller portions of dough and bake it on a smaller surface such as a griddle, complications are minimized, and confidence is established. If, in early rolling attempts, the outside edges become frayed, do not despair - they can be trimmed off. It is of greater importance to roll the dough thin enough as this insures crisp, delicate finished product. The dough should be turned often during the rolling out period, using a long, straight carving knife or spatula. When the dough is rolled out to the proper thickness, it must, according to custom, *vippes* - in the old days' a clean linen cloth was tied to the end of a stick, dipped in water, and then used to beat the dough. A wooden whisk dipped in water may also be used. To dampen is important.

Before rolling out the dough it must be kneaded well, without additional flour, until it becomes smooth and elastic. Press flat, place in middle of the table with plenty of flour underneath and on top, and begin to roll. While rolling, stretch the dough

Flatbread, Norway's most frequently used and most loved bread, was at one time considered a mainstay. In Western Norway, a homemaker was not considered to be a good manager if she did not keep a supply of flatbread at all times. A young girl who couldn't weave, spin, or make flatbread, wasn't considered much of a catch by eligible bachelors.

often and make certain it does not stick to the table as this will result in flatbread with holes and irregular shape. An even, moderate griddle temperature for baking the flatbread is essential; if it is too hot the bread will bubble. To test, spread a little flour on the griddle and if it turns brown within a couple of minutes it is proper temperature. Bake until crisp and light brown on both sides.

When the bread is baked, put it on a rack or large piece of paper on the table to cool. Stack the flatbread, one on top of the other, and cover with a weight to help maintain a uniform flatness after they have cooled

If you wish, you can complete rolling out all the dough before beginning the baking process. It is not easy for an inexperienced person to accomplish both the rolling out and baking in one operation. If all the rolling is done at once, stack the rolled out flaps, one on top of the other, and sprinkle with a little flour between each piece and on the bottom of the stack. Do not allow them to remain like this for very long, especially if the room is warm, because they will all adhere to one another.

Years ago the Norwegian home-maker stacked rocks on top of the flatbread pile to prevent the mice from gnawing their way through.

Potato Flatbread *(Flatbrød med poteter)*

If you are making flatbread with potatoes, boil the unpeeled potatoes, then peel and rice or grind twice. Cool potatoes completely before adding flour. It is difficult to give an exact measurement for flour as potatoes differ widely in moisture content, therefore, one must add flour accordingly. The kind of flour most satisfactorily used with potatoes is barley, oat, or pea flour (available at natural food stores), wholewheat, wheat, or rye. Place the riced or ground potatoes in a bowl with a little flour on the bottom and add a little salt (optional) and flour as you knead a little at a time, until the dough becomes smooth and elastic. It is not necessary to add liquid to potato flatbread. It is best to work in a cool room as the dough has a tendency to become soft when it is warm. The potato dough should be prepared the night before baking, covered with a piece of cloth, and put in a cool place. Knead a little more flour into the dough just before rolling, using the same type of flour as was incorporated into the dough. Potato bread is very crisp and delicious.

Barley Flatbread *(Flatbrød med byggmel)*

To 3½ cup (8½ dl) barley flour and ½ cup (1½ dl) rye flour use approximately ¾ cup (1¾ dl) liquid and ½ teaspoon salt. This makes a dough which is very easy to handle.

Oat Flour Flatbread *(Flatbrød med havremel)*

Use same measurements as for barley flatbread. This dough is very soft and should be put through a potato ricer or meat grinder at least twice before beginning to knead. Make these rather thick and bake as soon as they are rolled out. Use low heat.

Flatbread I *(Flatbrød I)*

½ cup (1¼ dl) lard, melted
¼ cup (½ dl) sugar
½ cup (1¼ dl) oatmeal flour
1 cup (2½ dl) graham flour
¾ tsp. baking soda

¾ tsp. baking soda
1 tsp. salt
1½ cups (3½ dl) buttermilk
Unbleached flour as needed

Combine ingredients, adding just enough white flour to make dough workable, but not sticky. Roll out into rounds using grooved rolling pin and a pastry cloth. Cut into pieces and bake on cookie sheet in a 350°F (175°C) oven for about 8 minutes or until crisp.

Flatbread II (Flatbrød II)

1 cup (2½ dl) buttermilk   3 tbsp. sugar
½ cup (1¼ dl) Karo syrup, dark   1 tsp. baking soda
½ cup (1¼ dl) shortening, melted   2 cups graham flour, or
1 tsp. salt   2½-3 cups (6¼-7½ dl) whole wheat flour

Mix all ingredients together. Roll out paper thin. Place in a big sheet on ungreased baking sheet sprinkled with a little corn meal, and bake in 350°F (175°C) oven for about 8 minutes. If desired, once you have placed the dough on the baking sheet you may use a *fattigman* cutter or a pizza wheel to mark the desired size. This will make it easy to separate the flatbread into even pieces when baked.

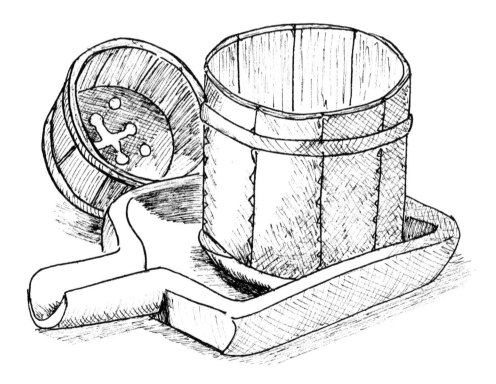

Wedding Couple

Weddings (Bryllup)

Weddings are among the most tradition-rich of all Norwegian observances. During the middle ages, in addition to the church wedding ceremony, there was always a financial settlement ceremony performed at home. The church at that time insisted that the minister take part in the financial settlement ritual at home, it being very similar to the wedding ritual performed earlier in the church. During the financial arrangement ceremony a determination was made as to type of gifts and the necessary financial arrangements. Five witnesses were required. Following this ritual the couple exchanged gifts as did their parents on both sides as well as other members of the family.

The marriage was not sanctioned until the bridegroom had paid kjøpesum (a price) for his bride. Before leaving for the church the bridegroom presented his bride-to-be with a *benkegave* (special gift), and on the day following the wedding he was expected to give her a *morgengave* (morning gift). Both these gifts were very elaborate and were hers to keep in case of her husband's death.

Generally, weddings were performed at certain times of the year - usually spring or early summer, or in the fall following the harvest.

As a rule weddings were performed on the farm where the couples planned to live, which in many cases were the bridegroom's home. The wedding would last from 2 to 3 days or as long as a week, with the more prosperous families celebrating the longest. Food was plentiful at these wedding banquets as family and friends participated in *matsendinga* (food contributions), which was sent either the day before or brought along to the wedding celebration.

Everyone pitched in and helped to make it a feast to remember with plenty of food and drink - especially drink - as this was the measuring stick by which the success of the wedding was judged.

Both bride and groom had their own officials, *embetsfolk. Brudekonene* (women assisting the bride) never left her side from dressing time prior to the ceremony until she was konekledd (dressed as a married woman). Likewise the *brurmennene* (bridegroom's attendants) remained with and assisted the bridegroom. Each "official" had his duty to perform from the time the music began for ushering in the bride until the fiddler played *reiselåten* (farewell tune) on the last day.

These wedding traditions were in use throughout the 19th century and partly into the 20th. Rules were strictly followed but there was also an abundance of fun and frolic on this joyous occasion. The betrothed couple had many fond memories to reminisce over in the years to come.

Food at today's weddings are quite varied as each couple selects special delights from favorite dinner menus; however, luscious cream cakes and festive *kransekake* (tall almond wreath cake) seem to remain the favored choice of dessert.

Stave Church

Cakes and Pastries

Golden Spice Cake *(Sirupskake)*

½ cup, scant (100 g) butter
2 eggs
¾ cup (1¾ dl) syrup, Golden Lyle
¼ cup (½ dl) orange marmalade

¾ tsp. ginger
2 tsp. baking powder
1½ cup flour
²⁄₃ cup (1½ dl) cream, light

Cream butter until soft, add eggs, syrup and orange marmalade and blend well. Add ginger and baking powder to the flour. Add to butter mixture alternately with cream. Mix thoroughly. Pour into a greased, 1½ quart (liter) loaf pan and bake in 350°F (175°C) oven about 30 minutes. **Makes 1 loaf cake.**

Honey Loaf Cake *(Honningkake)*

4 eggs, separated
1¹⁄₈ cup (250 g) sugar
7 tbsp. (100 g) butter
⁷⁄₈ cup (250 g) honey
¼ tsp. cloves

¼ tsp. pepper
½ tsp. ginger
1 tsp. baking powder
1²⁄₃ cup (250 g) flour

Beat egg yolks and sugar until well mixed. Melt the butter and mix with fluid honey and add to egg mixture. Combine dry ingredients and add, blending fully. Whip egg whites until stiff peaks form, and fold into batter. Pour the batter into a greased 1½ quart (liter) paper lined loaf pan. Bake in preheated 300°F (150°C) about 50 minutes. Decorate with chocolate glace and almonds if desired. **Makes 1 loaf cake.**

> **TIPS: ALL CREAM CAKES REACH THE PEAK OF THEIR FLAVOR IF REFRIGERATED UP TO 24 HOURS BEFORE SERVING.**

Cream Cake *(Bløtekake)*

6 eggs
1 cup (2½ dl) sugar
1 tbsp. water
1 cup (2½ dl) flour
1½ tsp. baking powder
1 tbsp. potato starch flour or
   cornstarch

Filling:
1 cup (2½ dl) whipping cream
6 oz. (170 g) raspberry jam
2 bananas, sliced
1 orange
Frosting:
1½ cups (3¾ dl) whipping cream

My sister Eva's favorite standby for many years. Easily altered by using fruit of your choice. Apricots or apricot jam is excellent.

Preheat oven to 325°F (160°C). Beat eggs and sugar until light and fluffy. Add the water. Sift dry ingredients together and fold into the egg mixture, mixing well. Pour into a 10-inch (25 cm) greased spring-form pan. Bake 40 minutes. Cool on cake rack. When completely cool, divide horizontally into 2 layers. Sprinkle layers with freshly squeezed orange juice. Place the bottom layer on a platter, baked side down. Whip 1 cup (2½ dl) cream until thick and glossy, and fold in raspberry jam and chopped bananas. Spread evenly over the bottom layer. Top with second layer baked side up. Whip 1½ cups (3¾ dl) cream and sweeten to taste. Spread over cake and decorate as desired. **Serves 10 to 12.**

Autumn Cake (Høstkake)

This cake has become very popular in Norway, and serving it is a great way to welcome the autumn. You will receive accolades every time you serve it.

Although it may be enjoyed for singular occasions, it may also be enjoyed any time of the year by substituting blueberries and strawberries for lingon and cloudberries. It reaches the peak of its flavor if refrigerated up to 24 hours before serving. See Index for Marzipan Topping.

6 eggs
1 cup sugar (2½ dl) sugar
1¼ cup (3 dl) flour
1 tsp. baking powder

Filling:
2 cups (5 dl) lingonberries
3 cups (7½ dl) cloudberries
Confectioners' sugar to taste
3 cups (7½ dl) whipping cream

Garnish:
1²/₃ lbs. (750 g) marzipan
Yellow food coloring

Wine jelly:
1 tbsp. Knox gelatine
¾ cup (1¾ dl) white wine or
    white grape juice
Juice of ½ lemon
Sugar to taste

Preheat oven to 340°F (170°C). Beat eggs and sugar until light and fluffy. Combine flour and baking powder and sift over the egg mixture, and carefully fold in. Pour into a 10-inch (25 cm) springform pan. Bake on lowest rack in the oven about 45 minutes. Remove from oven and cool on rack. When completely cold, divide horizontally into 3 layers. Reserve a small amount of each berry for decoration. Mash the remaining berries separately. Sweeten to taste with confectioners' sugar.

Whip the cream. Reserve a small amount of whipped cream for decoration. Mix half the cream with the lingonberry purée, the remaining half with the cloudberry purée. Place the bottom layer of the cake, baked side down, on a platter. Spread with lingonberry cream. Top with the middle layer of cake and spread with cloudberry cream. End with the top layer baked side up. Spread with a thin layer of whipped cream.

Cut a circle of parchment paper slightly smaller than the cake and place on top of the cake. Roll out most of the marzipan to a round sheet, big enough to cover top and sides, and place over the cake. In the center cut the marzipan into twelve pie shaped wedges, but do not cut all the way out to the edge of the cake. Starting with the tip roll one wedge at a time away from the center point, forming a scroll. Remove the parchment paper with a fork. Spoon the reserved lingonberries into the center, surround them with the cloudberries and spread to the marzipan scrolls.

Sprinkle 3 tablespoons cold water over the gelatin. Let stand 2 minutes to soften, then heat until thoroughly dissolved. Combine wine or grape juice and lemon juice and sweeten to taste. Stir in the gelatin. Strain. Refrigerate until just beginning to set. Spoon carefully over the berries. Smooth out with a knife dipped in boiling water. Color the remaining marzipan yellow. Roll into a strip and place around the bottom of the cake. Refrigerate until ready to serve. Just before serving sprinkle lightly with sifted confectioners' sugar. **Serves 12 to 14.**

Strawberry Cream Cake *(Jordbærkake)*

1½-2 qts. (liters) fresh strawberries	2 cups (5 dl) whipping cream
1 sponge cake	2 tbsp. sugar
Orange juice or milk	1 banana
	6 oz. pkg. strawberry jello

Wash and hull strawberries, set aside to dry on paper towel. Use sponge cake recipe for Cream Cake or Autumn Cake, and divide horizontally into two layers. Moisten each layer with a little orange juice or milk. Whip the cream, and add sugar. Reserve ⅓ cream for decoration. Slice banana very thin and mix with a few berries, add to cream and mix fully. Place the bottom layer of sponge cake on a platter, baked side down, and spread evenly with whipped cream mixture.

Top with second layer, baked side up. Cover top layer of cake with the whole strawberries facing point up. Fasten a strip of foil around the cake, extending above the berries. Dissolve gelatin according to directions, but use ⅓ cup less water than called for. Refrigerate jello until it begins to jell slightly, and spoon carefully over the berries. Smooth out with a knife dipped in boiling water. When jello is completely congealed remove foil and frost sides of cake with whipped cream. **Serves 12.**

Juicy, rich red strawberries make this cake perfect for enjoying balmy summer evenings with good friends on the patio. It's beautiful looks are only rivaled by its luscious taste. The best strawberries appear on the market in May or June, but frozen strawberries may also be used.

Almond Mocha Cake *(Mandelmokkakake)*

4 eggs	Filling and topping:
1 cup (2½ dl) sugar	2 cups (5 dl) whipping cream
¾ cup (1¾ dl) flour	2 tbsp. sugar
1 tbsp. potato flour or cornstarch	2 tsp. instant coffee
Dash of salt	or Pero
3 tbsp. cold coffee or Pero	1 tsp. mocha flavoring
1 tsp. mocha flavoring	2 tbsp. almonds, slivered
Milk for moistening	

Beat eggs and sugar until light and fluffy. Sift dry ingredients over egg mixture and fold in, blending fully. Stir in cold coffee or Pero. Pour into greased and floured 9-inch (23 cm) round, springform pan, and bake in 350°F (175°C) oven for 25 to 30 minutes. Remove to rack and cool completely. When completely cold divide horizontally into two or three layers, and sprinkle with a little milk. Whip cream, sugar, instant coffee or Pero until thick and glossy. Add mocha flavoring. Stir. Place bottom layer of cake on a platter, bottom side down. Spread some of the cream over the layer. Top with second layer baked side up. Use remaining cream to decorate the top and sides. Toast the almonds and sprinkle on top. **Serves 10-12.**

If you love mocha flavoring, this cake is for you. Pero is a good substitute for coffee. It is made from whole grains, and is available at most grocery stores. See Sources.

Cherry Cream Cake *(Kirsebærkremkake)*

2 cups (5 dl) almonds or other nuts	8 egg whites
2 cups (5 dl) confectioners' sugar	

Grind almonds twice, the second time with the confectioners' sugar. The almonds should have the consistency of flour. Whip the egg whites until stiff but not dry, and blend with the nuts. Divide and spread batter in two greased 9-inch (23 cm) springform pans, and bake at 320°F (160°C) 25-30 minutes. Cool slightly in pan before removing to rack to cool completely. **Makes two 9-inch layers.**

Cherry Cream:

1¼ cup (3 dl) whipping cream
2 egg yolks
2 tbsp. confectioners' sugar

3½ tbsp. chocolate sauce or syrup
3½ tbsp. cherry juice

Beat the cream until firm and glossy. Add eggs and confectioners' sugar which have been whipped together until light and fluffy. Stir in the chocolate sauce or syrup, and add cherry juice to taste. Place one cake layer on platter, baked side down, and cover with half of the cream mixture. Add second layer, baked side up, and top with remaining cream. Keep refrigerated until serving time. See picture. **Serves 12.**

Marzipan Cake (Aprikose/ananas marsipankake)

Sponge Cake:
6 eggs
¾ cup (1¾ dl) sugar

1⅝ cup (3¾ dl) flour
1 tsp. baking powder

Beat eggs and sugar to *eggedosis* consistency, light and fluffy. Sift baking powder with the flour and carefully fold into the eggs. Pour into a greased 8-9½-inch (20-24 cm) round springform pan and bake at 320°F (160°C) about 45 minutes. Cool on cake rack and divide horizontally into two layers. **Makes 1 8 or 9½-inch cake.**

Almond layer:
¼ cup (½ dl) almonds
¼ cup (½ dl) zwieback, crushed

½ cup (1¼ dl) confectioners' sugar
2 egg whites

Grind almonds twice, the second time with the confectioners' sugar and zwieback. Beat egg whites until stiff but not dry, and carefully blend with the almond mixture. Spread batter in an 8 to 9½ inch (20 to 24 cm) round springform pan and bake at 320°F (160°C) for 20-30 minutes.

½ of a 15 oz. can (425 g) pineapple, crushed and drained
½ of a 16 oz. can (450 g) apricots drained and chopped
2½ cup (6 dl) whipping cream

3 tbsp. apricot juice
1 lb. 6½ oz. (750 g) marzipan
Bridge and heart, purchased, or use other desired decorations

Save juice from the drained fruit. Sprinkle both layers of sponge cake and almond layer with juice from the canned fruit. On a platter, place the bottom layer of the sponge cake, baked side down. Whip cream until thick and glossy. Add 3 tablespoons of apricot juice to about half of the cream. Cover the bottom layer with chopped apricots and half of the whipped cream with the added juice. Top with almond layer, crushed pineapple, and remainder of cream with the added juice. Add 2nd layer of sponge cake. Spread a thin layer of whipped cream on top and sides of cake saving out enough for decoration. Prepare marzipan topping (see Index) and cover the cake, top and sides, with the marzipan, saving out enough marzipan for roses and leaves. See Wedding Cake for directions on how to make roses. With a decorator tube add whipped cream around the edge of cake and decorate with marzipan roses and leaves. See picture. **Makes one 8 to 9½-inch (20 to 24 cm) cake.**

The Queen's Sweet Secret *(Dronningens søte hemmelighet)*

2 jelly rolls (see Index)
1 Freia semi-sweet cooking
 chocolate, 4½ oz (125 g)
2-2½ cups (5-6 dl) lingonberry jam
³/₈ cup (1 dl) currant juice

Decoration:
1¾ cup (4 dl) whipping cream
Lemon balm or peppermint leaves

Make two recipes of jelly rolls. Grate and add chocolate with the flour before blending with the eggs. (The chocolate may be doubled if desired). Spread lingonberry jam evenly across the cakes. Cut each cake in 2¾-inch (7 cm) wide strips. Roll the first strip together tightly. Add the next strip on the outside of the first one, continuing to roll snugly until the last strip from both cakes is used up (snowball principle). Place on a large platter, sprinkle the cake with currant juice. Whip the cream until thick and glossy. Use a decorating tube to decorate the cake with the whipped cream, and add some lemon balm or mint leaves around the lower edge. See picture. **Serves 12-14.**

Jelly Roll with Caramel Topping *(Karamelrulade)*

4 eggs
½ cup (1¼ dl) sugar
1 cup (2½ dl) flour
¼ tsp. baking powder

Filling:
1¼-1²/₃ cup (2-4 dl) whipping cream

Caramel topping:
2 cups (5 dl) sugar
2 tbsp. water
1 cup (225 g) butter, melted
1 cup (2½ dl) whipping cream
1 tbsp. flour
½ cup (1¼ dl) milk
Nuts coarsely chopped, optional

A thin sheet of sponge cake spread with whipped cream and rolled to form layers, then topped with caramel. The caramel may be substituted with whipped cream, and served with berries on the side.

Beat the eggs and sugar to firm *eggedosis* consistency, thick. Sift together the flour and baking powder and blend thoroughly with the eggs. Grease a jelly roll pan in 2 or 3 spots, line with parchment or wax paper and spread the batter evenly over it. Preheat oven to 390°F (200°C) and bake the cake in the middle of the oven for 8-10 minutes. Place a large piece of wax paper on the counter or rack and sprinkle with a little sugar. Invert the cake onto the paper and cover the cake with the inverted pan, forming a lid, until cool. Whip the cream and spread over the cake, and roll it up with the help of the paper. Trim ends. Wrap it firmly in the wax paper and set to cool in refrigerator with the seam down. **Makes 1 jelly roll.**

 Caramel topping: Carefully brown sugar and water in a heavy saucepan. Melt the butter and add with the cream to the sugar. Add the flour to the milk, blend and add to the sugar mixture in the saucepan and continue to stir while mixture comes to a boil. Remove from heat. Cool. Unwrap the cake and place on platter. Pour the caramel sauce over the cake. Sprinkle with chopped nuts if desired.

Meringue Cake *(Marengskake)*

A great way to use up extra egg whites. Cake freezes well. Fill with vanilla cream, or whipped cream, top with your favorite berries. You can use fresh or frozen, or add scoops of ice cream topped with chocolate or caramel sauce. The variations are limited only by your imagination.

4 egg whites	1 tsp. potato flour
1 cup (2½ dl) sugar	1 tsp. vanilla sugar

Draw a 9 inch (23 cm) circle on parchment paper or a brown paper bag. Beat the egg whites until frothy. Mix sugar, potato flour and vanilla sugar, and add a spoonful at a time to the egg whites. Mix well after each addition. Spread within the circle and pull up at the edges to form a small crater. Bake at 200°F (90°C) for 2 hours. Turn off the oven and leave the cake in the oven until cold. Cool completely before freezing. Fill as desired. **Serves 10.**

Filling and Decoration:

1¼ cups (3 dl) whipping cream	Cloudberries or other berries
1-2 tsp. vanilla sugar	

Whip cream. Add vanilla sugar and add to the center of cake. Top with berries.

Daim Cake (Daimkake)

This recipe originated at Freia, Norway's oldest and most celebrated chocolate factory. While visiting Freia in Oslo, Bodil Bergan, Freia's head guide, gave me this recipe. Now it is among our favorite desserts (see picture). Simply delectable!

Meringue:	⅓ tsp. cream of tartar
2 egg whites	½ cup (1¼ dl) sugar

Ice cream:	Decorations:
2 egg yolks	½ cup (1¼ dl) whipping cream
½ cup, scant (1 dl) sugar	Daim chocolate
1¼ cup (3 dl) whipping cream	Candied orange peel, shredded
4 Freia Daim chocolate bars,	
or substitute 7 Heath bars	

Beat egg whites until frothy. Add cream of tartar and beat until soft peaks. Add sugar one tablespoon at a time, beat well after each addition, until stiff peaks form. Pour into 9-inch (23 cm) paper-lined and well greased springform pan. Spread meringue evenly and bake on middle rack at 275°F (135°C) for 45 minutes. Turn oven off. Leave in oven another 45 minutes. Cool on rack 10 minutes, carefully peel off paper, then cool thoroughly.

Ice cream: Whip egg yolks and sugar until, light and fluffy. In a separate, chilled bowl, whip cream until firm and carefully fold into eggs. Coarsely chop chocolate (Slightly freezing the candy bars makes them easier to chop) and add, saving some for decoration. Return cake to pan and pour cream mixture on top, smoothing it out evenly. Freeze at least two hours.

Decoration: Whip cream, decorate with decorating tube. Sprinkle with Daim chocolate and candied orange peel.

Frozen Chocolate Torte *(Frossen sjokoladeterte)*

3 egg whites
½ tsp. cream of tartar
¾ cup (1¾ dl) sugar
¾ cup (1¾ dl) hazelnuts
   or pecans, finely chopped

Filling:
2 cups (5 dl) whipping cream
¾ cup (1¾ dl) chocolate syrup
1 tsp. pure vanilla extract
Milk chocolate, shaved

Delectable ready to eat dessert right from the freezer. Remove 10 minutes before serving time.

Beat egg whites until frothy. Add cream of tartar and beat until soft peaks form. Add sugar, 1 tablespoon at a time, and beat until very stiff peaks, but not dry, form. Fold in nuts. Draw 2, 9-inch (23 cm) circles on a brown paper sack, spread mixture, evenly divided within the circles. Bake in preheated 275°F (135°) oven for 45 minutes. Turn off oven and leave door closed for 45 minutes longer. Remove to rack and cool completely.

Filling: Whip cream until firm. Stir in chocolate sauce and vanilla extract. Divide between layers and top. Sprinkle with shaved chocolate. Freeze until firm. **Serves 10-12.**

Mother Monson *(Mor Monsen)*

1 cup ((2½ dl) plus 1 tbsp.
  butter or margarine
1¼ cup (3 dl) sugar
6 eggs
Peel of 1 lemon, grated
1¾ cups (4½ dl) flour
1 tsp. baking powder

Garnish:
½ cup (1¼ dl) scalded almonds, slivered
½ cup (1¼ dl) currants
3-4 tbsp. granulated or
  Pearl sugar

This moist delicious cake is a must for Christmas, but its origin is a mystery to all.

Cream butter or margarine with sugar until creamy. Add eggs, one at a time, and blend thoroughly after each addition. Stir in the lemon peel. Mix flour and baking powder and add. Pour the batter into a 16x8-1 inch pan, lined with parchment or wax paper and heavily greased. Smooth batter out evenly. Sprinkle with almonds, currants and sugar. Press the garnish *lightly* into the batter so it does not fall off when cake is done. Bake on middle rack of the oven at 375°F (190°C) for 20-25 minutes. The cake should be light golden and baked through, but not dry. Remove it from oven as soon as no batter sticks to an inserted cake tester. Cool slightly on a cake rack. Cover cake with waxed paper and a cookie sheet and turn the cake pan upside down on the sheet. Place a wire rack on the upturned cake and turn again so the cake rests right side up on the rack. Cool the cake on the wire rack. When the cake is cold, cut in diamond shapes with a very sharp knife.

Almond Cake (Fyrstekake)

Fyrste means prince or sovereign. This insignificant looking cake has a delectable almond macaroon filling. It is a traditional favorite for all memorable occasions in Norway. It is very rich and should be served in small portions as is, or with a dab of whipped cream or a spoonful of vanilla ice cream.

⅝ cup (140 g) butter or margarine
½ cup (1¼ dl) sugar
2 egg yolks
2 tbsp. water
1 tsp. baking powder
1¾ cup (4¼ dl) flour

Filling:
2 cups (5 dl) almonds, unblanched
2 cups (5 dl) confectioners' sugar
3-4 egg whites, slightly beaten
2 tbsp. water, approx.
1 tsp. almond or rum extract
Egg to brush cake with

Cream butter and sugar until light and fluffy. Add egg yolks and water. Mix well. Add baking powder to flour and stir into butter mixture. Chill. In the meantime prepare filling by grinding the almonds twice, the second time together with confectioners' sugar. Blend thoroughly with egg whites, water, and extract. Press ⅔ of the chilled dough into a 9-inch (23 cm) ungreased, spring-form pan having dough cover up the sides about 1¼ inch (3 cm). Spread almond mixture evenly over dough. Roll remainder of dough out to ⅛ inch (2 mm) thickness and cut 8 strips ½ inch (1¼ cm) in width. Lay 4 of the strips parallel to each other across the top of the filling. Arrange the remaining 4 strips at right angles, weaving to form a lattice pattern. Cut out another ½ inch (1¼ cm) wide strip and press around the edge of the cake. Brush with slightly beaten egg. Bake at 375°F (190°°C) for 25 to 30 minutes, or until golden brown and thoroughly baked. Leave cake on the rack for a few minutes before carefully removing from pan onto platter. Cut in wedges. **Serves 10-12.**

Apple Cake (Eplekake)

Nothing tastes much better than a good apple cake. It was a welcome treat when guests arrived in our home, or served as Sunday evening treat. To make it extra special top it with a lightly sweetened whipped cream or vanilla sauce.

2 cups (5 dl) flour
2 tsp. baking powder
1 cup (2½ dl) butter
1 cup (2½ dl) sugar
2 eggs
2 tsp. vanilla sugar

3-5 Granny Smith apples
Lemon juice
Frosting:
½ cup (1¼ dl) confectioners' sugar
Coffee cream
1 tsp. rum extra

Mix flour and baking powder. Add to butter and mix as for pie crust. Add remaining ingredients, except apples and lemon juice. Work into a pliable dough. Divide in two unequal portions. Pat the largest portion into 8-inch (20 cm) springform pan, covering the bottom and 1½ inch (4 cm) up side of pan. Wash, peel, core and slice apples and sprinkle with a little lemon juice to prevent discoloration. Cover dough with apples and top with remaining dough. Bake in preheated 350°F (175°), 40 to 50 minutes. When cool remove from pan onto platter. Mix ingredients for frosting, and spread over cake. **Serves 8-10.**

Birthday Kringle (*Fødselsdagskringle*)

1 pkg. active dry yeast	**Filling:**
1 tbsp. water, lukewarm	5 tbsp. (75 g) butter
2 eggs, slightly beaten	$^1/_3$ cup (50 g) sugar
2$^1/_8$ (300 g) flour	½ cup (50 g) raisins
$^1/_3$ cup, (50 g) sugar	½ cup (50 g) citron, finely chopped
¼ tsp. salt	½ cup (50 g) almonds, chopped
7 oz. (200 g) butter	

The perfect substitute for those who do not want a cake on their birthday. Also pleasing any time a good delicacy is called for. You need to have a little room to prepare as the dough needs to be rolled out to a length of 34 inches. It will take 4-5 hours to raise twice.

Dissolve yeast in water, and beat into eggs. Sift together flour, sugar and salt and cut in the butter. Mix with eggs and work until you have a smooth and elastic dough. Cover, and let rise in a warm place until double in bulk. Punch down dough and turn out onto floured board. Knead adding flour as needed, to prevent sticking, until dough is soft and elastic. Roll out to a 6x34-inch (15x86 cm) long ribbon.
Filling: Cream butter and sugar until light, and spread over the dough. Sprinkle with raisins, citron and almonds. Fold the long sides toward the center overlapping slightly. Form into kringle shape on large cookie sheet. Cover and set to raise until double in bulk. Brush with egg and sprinkle with sugar. Bake on middle rack in 375°F (190°C) preheated oven for 25 minutes.

Oslo Kringle (*Oslo Kringle*)

1 cup (2 ½ dl) flour	2 tbsp. water
½ cup (1¼ dl) butter	

Mix flour and butter; add cold water and mix as for pie crust. Divide dough in two and roll out in two ropes 16 inches (40½ cm) long. Place on ungreased cookie sheet, and with your hands, flatten each portion out to 4 inches (10 cm) wide.

Cream puff paste:

1 cup (2½ dl) water	3 eggs
½ cup (1¼ dl) butter	1 tsp. almond extract
1 cup (2½ dl) flour	

Bring water and butter to a boil. Remove from stove and immediately add all flour; beat until smooth. Add one egg at a time, beating well after each addition. Add flavoring. Spread on the above strips covering dough completely. Bake at 350°F (175°C) for 45 minutes. **Makes 2 pastries, 30 pieces when cut.**

"Sister sweeps the cottage clean, decorates with birches, across the floor she sprinkles small Lilies of the Valley, and rosebuds many: A flawless place for a child."

Frost when cool with the following icing:

1 cup (2½ dl) confectioners' sugar	½ tsp. almond extract
1 tbsp. butter, soft	Cream

Mix confectioners' sugar, butter and almond. Add just enough cream for spreading consistency. Spread, or push through a decorating tube onto pastries. They are best eaten the same day, but freezes well.

Danish Pastry (Wienerbrød)

I dislike the name "Danish" because what Americans think of as "Danish" is a sad imitation, not comparable to the delectable *wienerbrød* made in Scandinavia. Wiener means Viennese (man), and brød means bread. Which does not explain the flaky heavenly pastry Scandinavians call *wienerbrød*, however, once you have tasted *wienerbrød*, it does not matter. But knowing what true "Danish" is, you likely will share them with friends repeatedly.

1⅞ cup (250 g) flour
2 tbsp. sugar
1 tbsp. margarine
1 pkg. active dry yeast

½ cup (1¼ dl) milk, cold
1 egg
1⅞ cup (200 g) margarine

Sift together flour and sugar. Cut in 1 tablespoon margarine, it will prevent dough from becoming leathery. Add yeast to cold milk and let it dissolve. Add yeast mixture and egg to the flour. *Lightly mix the ingredients. The dough will be extremely soft.* Chill 15 minutes. In a cool place, quickly roll the dough out to a large square, ¼-inch (½ cm) thick, using as little flour as possible. Use a cheese knife to thinly slice butter and place on ⅔ of the dough, approx. ¾-inch (2 cm) from the edge. Fold the ⅓ unbuttered part over ⅓ of the buttered dough, and the remaining ⅓ over on top. Repeat crosswise. Roll the dough out and repeat the folding 2 or more times or until the margarine is distributed evenly. This gives you a flaky pastry. It is important that the margarine does not ooze out. If it does the dough will become sticky and difficult to roll out, and the finished product will be a disappointment. Bake in preheated 475°F (245°C) for 15 min.

Wienerbrød filling: You can use the same basic dough for all *wienerbrød*. By varying the shapes and fillings you come up with the delectable pastries so much in demand. In addition to the fillings which follow, prunes, apricots, and thick applesauce are popular.

Vanilla Cream Filling:
½ cup, scant (1 dl) milk
1 tbsp. flour
1 egg yolk

1 tbsp. sugar
1 tsp. vanilla sugar

Add all the ingredients except the vanilla sugar to a heavy bottomed saucepan. Beat vigorously until the cream is thickened and reaches the boiling point. Do not let it boil, but remove from the heat. Beat now and then while it is cooling. Add vanilla sugar to taste.

Almond fruit filling:
2 tbsp. almonds
2 tbsp. currants
2 tbsp. citron

2 tbsp. sugar
Enough egg whites to make a
   firm mass which does not run

Garnish:
2 tbsp. (30 g) almonds, chopped

2 tbsp. pearl sugar, coarsely crushed

Shaping Wienerbrød:

Cocks Comb: Roll the dough in a square 20x20 inches (50x50 cm). Cut into squares 8x8 inches (20x20 cm). Place a teaspoonful of the filling of your choice in the center. Fold in half. Press the edges together with a fork dipped in water. Cut 3 to 4 slits along the pressed edge. Bend to resemble a cock's comb. Place on baking sheet to rise in a warm place, for 1 hour. Brush with beaten egg and sprinkle with almonds and pearl sugar. Preheat oven to 480°F (250°C). Bake from 8 to 10 minutes.

Envelopes and triangles: Cut the dough up like for cock's comb. Place 1 teaspoonful filling of your choice in the center. Fold all four corner in towards the center. Press down firmly so they do not open too much during the baking. Or fold diagonally so as to form a triangle. Follow remainder of recipe for cock's comb.

Cream Puffs with Raspberry (Vannbakkels med bringebær)

Vannbakkels:
1 cup (2½ dl) water
½ cup (125 g) butter
½ cup (125 g) flour
4 eggs

Bringebærfromasj:
4 eggs
²/₃ cup (1½ dl) sugar
1²/₃ cup (4 dl) whipping cream
1 pkg. unflavored Knox gelatine
¾ cup (1¾ dl) raspberries, fresh or frozen

Versatile vannbakkels are ever popular. They are easy to make and always a success. The traditional fillings are whipping cream, egg custard, or ice cream, but now try this raspberry mousse filling.

Combine water and butter (cut into pieces) in a heavy sauce pan and bring to a full boil. When butter is melted move from heat and add flour all at once and stir vigorously with a wooden spoon until it forms a ball. Beat in 1 egg at a time, beating well after each addition. Cover a cookie sheet with parchment paper, or leave ungreased, and drop dough by tablespoonful onto the paper, (about the size of golf balls) 3 inches (8 cm) apart. Bake at 390°F 200°C) 20-25 minutes. Do not peek during baking as this will cause the puffs to fall. After baking is finished, leave them in the oven for about 1 hour with heat cut off and oven door open halfway. They need to cool slowly and to be fully dry. **Makes 14-16.**

Bringebærfromasj: Beat eggs and sugar until of *eggedosis* consistency, light and fluffy. Whip cream. In a small saucepan sprinkle ¼ cup (½ dl) scant, water over gelatin. Let stand 1 minute. Stir over low heat until gelatine is completely dissolved, about 3 minutes. Drizzle gelatine into whipped cream stirring constantly until blended, and add to egg mixture. Carefully fold in cleaned raspberries. They maybe frozen, thawed and well drained. Cut off the tops of the cream puffs. As soon as the mousse begins to gel fill the puffs, and replace the tops. Set to chill. Just before serving sift a little confectioners' sugar over the cream puffs.

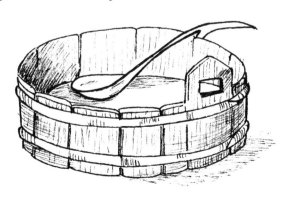

Cream Cornets (Fløteruller)

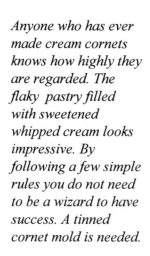

It is beneficial to use margarine for these tarts. The dough is more difficult to handle when butter is used. Work in a cool kitchen or by an open window if it is cooler outside. The dough will turn sticky if it gets warm. It is best to make the dough the day before, or even a few days before it is needed, and wrap securely in foil.

2 cups (250 g) flour	½ cup (1¼ dl) water, ice cold
1⅛ cup (250 g) margarine, chilled	1 tsp. white vinegar
	Whipped cream

Rinse your cleaned hands in lukewarm water and squeeze the salt from the margarine under cold running water. Then squeeze out excess water in a clean cloth or paper towel. Divide margarine into thirds. Sift the flour on baking surface and make a well. Dice ⅓ of the margarine and add to the well. Cut the margarine into the flour with a pastry blender. Add water and vinegar and form into a ball. Handle dough lightly. Chill at least 15 minutes but not directly on ice. Remove dough from the refrigerator and roll out to a thick square. Blend one half of the remaining margarine with a little flour and spread over ⅔ of the dough. Fold the ungreased part toward the center (brush any flour from its surface) and the other third over it. Roll out lightly and quickly with as little flour as possible. Now fold the dough into thirds without buttering. Chill 15 minutes. Roll out to a large square and continue as before, using the remainder of the butter. Chill 20 minutes. Preheat the oven to 400°F (205°C). Roll the dough very thin, and cut into 1x18-inches (2½x46 cm) long ribbons. Wet the ribbons with cold water on one side. Take one ribbon and squeeze one end of it at the tip of the mold to secure it. Wrap the "ribbon" around the mold, the wet side toward the mold, and overlapping slightly as you keep wrapping it around until you reach the end of the mold. Trim the extra dough off at the end of the mold. Place standing up on a cookie sheet. Bake 15-18 minutes. Cool slightly before separating cornet from mold. To loosen pastry run a thin, sharp knife between the dough and the mold. Use a cookie press or pastry tube to fill with whipped cream, sweetened with a little honey or sugar.

Napoleons (Napoleonskaker)

Use the pastry recipe for Cornets and follow the directions up to the dough having been chilled the third time. Roll the dough out ⅛ inch (5 mm) thick. With the help of a ruler and pastry cutter cut out 2x3 inches (5x8 cm) cakes. Place on ungreased cookie sheet, rinsed with cold water and chill for 10 minutes before baking. Prick the dough with a fork before baking. Bake at 445°F (230°C) 25 to 30 minutes until golden yellow. Cool on a rack. When cold fill between layers (saving the prettiest ones for the top) with vanilla egg custard. **Makes 30.**

Vanilla Egg Custard; Double the recipe for Vanilla Egg Custard (see Index). In a small saucepan sprinkle the gelatine over ¼ cup (½ dl) water and let stand 1 minute. Stir over low heat until gelatine is completely dissolved, about 3 minutes. Drizzle gelatine mixture into vanilla egg custard and stir until well blended. Divide the custard between half of the pastries.

Glace: is made from confectioners' sugar and water. Add rum extract to taste. Use a warm knife to spread the glace over the remaining pastries and place on top of the vanilla custard. Press slightly.

Shrovetide Buns (Fastelavnsboller)

1¹/₃ cup (3 dl) milk	½ cup (115 g) butter or margarine
1 pkg. active dry yeast	melted and slightly cooled
¼ cup (½ dl) sugar	1 qt. (liter) flour or enough
½ tsp. salt	flour to make a smooth, pliant
1½ tsp. cardamom	dough
1 egg, slightly beaten	Egg for brushing

Heat milk until lukewarm. Pour into mixing bowl and stir in remaining ingredients except flour. Stir in a little flour at a time until the dough is smooth and elastic. Place in greased bowl, cover and set aside to rise in a warm place until double in bulk. On well floured pastry cloth, turn dough out and knead very lightly. Divide into 18 portions. Form each portion into a ball by placing your hand in cupping shape over the ball pressing down while making a large circle with your hand. As you roll the ball let up on the weight little by little allowing the dough to form into a smooth ball. Slit a pocket. With a spoon dipped in water, fill each pocket with almond filling, then seal back up. Place apart on greased cookie sheet, cover and let rise 15 minutes. Preheat oven to 350°F (175°C). Brush buns with beaten egg, which allows them to rise without cracking, and gives them a smooth finish. Bake for 15 minutes. Cool on wire rack. To leave plain read the directions but ignore filling instructions. Or add other suggested fillings. **Makes 18 buns.**

Almond-filled buns:

1 cup (2½ dl) almonds, ground	2-4 tbsp. water
1 cup (2½ dl) confectioners' sugar	Egg white

Blend almonds and powdered sugar well. Add water and enough egg white needed to mix thoroughly.

Cream-Filled Buns:

This is the traditional filling for the Shrovetide buns. A gentle reminder of happy days spent in Norway with siblings and parents. Shrovetide without these cream-filled buns would not be Shrovetide.

Cut baked, cooled buns in two horizontally. Whip 2 cups (5 dl) of whipping cream, and add sugar to taste. Cover bottom part of the bun with a large spoonful of whipped cream. Replace top and sprinkle with confectioners' sugar.

Raisin-Citron filled buns:

Work 1 cup (2½ dl) raisins and ²/₃ cups (1½ dl) chopped citron into dough. Divide into 18 pieces, form into balls and place on greased baking sheet. Follow previous directions on baking.

The World's Best (Verdens beste)

This cake is also known as the Kvæfjord cake. When I think of Kvæfjord close to Tromsø, fresh fish, lefse and game comes to mind. A little curious such a celebrated cake should originate in rugged Northern Norway. There are numerous versions of

The week before Shrovetide Sunday, (7th Sunday before Easter) the bakeries in Norway begin to fill up with Shrovetide buns. Many homemakers, however, still prepare their own treasured family recipes.

this recipe. This is my favorite. The Norwegians call it *vidunderlig!* - Wonderful! You be the judge.

⁵/₈ cup, generous (150 g) butter or margarine	1 tsp. baking powder
¾ cup (150 g) sugar	1¹/₈ cup (150 g) flour
5 egg yolks	4 tbsp. milk
	1 tsp. baking powder

Meringue:	**Filling:**
5 egg whites	Vanilla custard
1 cup (200 g) sugar	1¼ cup (3 dl) whipping cream
(50 g) almonds	1 tsp. rum extract

Cream butter and sugar until light and fluffy. Beat in the egg yolks one at a time. Sift the baking powder with the flour and add alternately with the milk. Line a 8x12 inch (20x30 cm) pan with parchment or wax paper and grease well. Pour in batter and smooth the top. Beat the egg whites until stiff but not dry. Gradually add the sugar and beat until stiff and glossy. Spread meringue over the cake batter. Sprinkle with almonds. Bake in preheated 355°F (180°C) oven until golden. Prepare double recipe of vanilla custard (See Index). Add rum flavoring, and carefully fold the whipped cream into cold custard. Cut cake in two horizontally and spread with filling. Replace the top. Keep chilled until serving time. **Makes 1 8x12-inch cake.**

Almond Tower Cake (Kransekake)

Kransekake reigns supreme in Norway. Weddings, birthdays, promotions, holidays, it is always there. Don't shy away from making this delicacy. It is not difficult - honestly - just a little time consuming. Follow the directions, do exactly what it says, and soon you can sparkle with pride, knowing you have made the most traditional of Norwegian cakes!

Kransekake is just plain fun to make and decorate. Here are two tips; almonds used must be of the best quality. Many prefer to blanch them, which makes the cake lighter in appearance. Leaving the almonds unblanced will make a darker cake, though richer in flavor. I prefer unblanched almonds, but you might like to try half and half.

Decorations: Norwegian flags are a must. The traditional *knallbonboner*, party crackers - frilly party favors, are very expensive and hard to find. You can decorate the cake in another beautiful way, with marzipan flowers (see picture). Make them from the same *kransekake* dough, omitting flour and not baking, or use fancy wrapped *konfekt*, chocolates. Secure all decorations with a light caramel. Decorations on the cake should be rather uniform. The cake should not be loaded down, but simple and elegant.

Many think of *kransekake* only in its traditional form - the tower shape - but one can make varied shapes such as baskets, logs, or horns of plenty. *Kransekake* keeps well in an airtight container. Adding a raw, peeled potato or a fresh piece of bread to the container will result in a chewy cake. The cake may also be frozen; when defrosted, the cake will be chewy from the moisture. Prepare and bake the kransekake rings in advance and freeze. Remove from freezer in time to defrost and decorate before serving.

Please read all directions before proceeding. This recipe makes a 16-ring cake. If you do not have kransekake pans, don't despair. Prepare dough according to directions. Cut into proper sizes and form rings - the smallest should be 5½ inches (14 cm) with each additional ring a scant ¾-inch (2 cm) larger. Cover cookie sheet with aluminum foil, grease well and place rings on top.

5½ cup (13½ dl) almonds, ground,   4 egg whites, slightly beaten
  left as is or blanched   2 tbsp. flour
5½ cup (13½ dl) confectioners' sugar

Grind the thoroughly washed and dried almonds. (If you choose to blanch the almonds, pour boiling water over them, then place in a steamer over simmering water until the hulls loosen and become easy to remove. Do not let almonds boil, they will loose their flavor and become leathery.) For good results, it is important to work with thoroughly dry almonds. Let them stand covered for at least 24 hours or dry them in a medium-hot oven, being careful not to overdo.

Grind almonds a second time with the confectioners' sugar. Add slightly beaten egg whites a little at a time and mix well. Take care that the mixture does not become too moist, it will rise to excess, become porous and, as a result, be difficult to remove from the pan. This can be remedied by the addition of a little flour and confectioners' sugar. On the other hand, if the cake is not moist enough, the cake will not rise and will turn hard and dry. In this case, add a little egg white. It is advisable to test by first baking a small sample.

Before you begin, let the dough rest, preferably covered, at least 10 minutes or even until the next day. This will make working with it easier. Grease ring-shaped pans with unsalted butter or cooking oil, and sprinkle with a little Cream of Wheat. Roll out small portions (finger thickness) to fit the rings. Cut the edges with a knife and butt edges to form a perfect circle. This will ensure a balanced finished product. Bake rings on a cookie sheet in the middle of the oven at 300°F (150°C). *Do not* over bake. Cool quickly, preferably in a draft. When almost cool, carefully slide cake from the pans. With a pastry brush, remove excess Cream of Wheat.

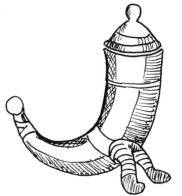

Frosting:

1 cup (2½ dl) confectioners' sugar   ½ tsp. white vinegar
1 egg white, slightly beaten

Stir vinegar and egg white into confectioners' sugar until frosting is thick enough to be used in a cake decorator. Decorate one ring at a time with a zigzag pattern, making sure the pattern reaches well over the edge of each ring. When the rings are stacked, one over the other, the extra icing serves as an adhesive. Make leaves and roses, or other flowers, from marzipan, or decorate *kransekake* with party crackers or fancy wrapped chocolates. Attach decorations with caramel. Add small flags. When serving *kransekake*, remove the lower rings and break into serving-size pieces.

Caramel: The amount you need to make depends on how many decorations you are adding to your *kransekake*. Two to four tablespoons of sugar should be sufficient. It is easiest to make caramel in a frying pan. Warm the pan over low heat, then add the sugar. It is best not to stir until sugar is melted because lumps form easily and are difficult to melt. When melted, keep caramel warm while attaching decorations. The candy hardens almost instantly when cooled.

Wedding Cake (Bryllupskake)

Times change, and today many use this type of contemporary wedding cake. Though not an old traditional cake, it will please the most discriminating wedding couples and all their guests. The horse shoes topping the cake are made from white chocolate. They stand for good luck in Norway.

When you want something superbly delicious, just cut the recipe in half, or thirds, and you will have a cake which will bring memorable moments to any occasion. This cake is baked in 7-8½ and 11-inch (18-22 and 28 cm) round springform pans. It is best to make the cake in two batches. Divide the dough in two. One portion will fit the two smallest pans, and the other half the largest pan. The almonds are weighed after they have been scalded. Read the recipe through before beginning to make this cake.

16 eggs
2 cups (5 dl) sugar
1½ cups (200 g) almonds,
    blanched and ground

1⅓ cups (200 g) flour
2 tsp. baking powder

Grease the pans and cover bottom with parchment paper. Whip eggs and sugar to *eggedosis* consistency, light and fluffy. Carefully fold in the thoroughly ground almonds, add flour which has been sifted with the baking powder. Divide batter into proper size pans. The smallest pans takes about 30 minutes, medium 35-40 minutes, and large, from 50-60 minutes. When baked cool on rack.

Filling and decoration:

¾-1¼ cup (2-3 dl) sparkling apple
    juice, such as Martinelli

2 cups (5 dl) thick apricot jam,
    lightly sweetened
4-5 Freia Daim chocolates, or
    substitute 7-8 Heath bars

2 qts.(liters) whipping cream
3 tbsp. sugar

4⅜ lbs. (2 kg) marzipan approx.
Red and green food coloring
Bridal couple or white chocolate decoration

See Index for Marzipan Topping, or purchase almond paste and follow direction on package. Divide all the cakes horizontally in two or three layers. It is easier to divide the cakes if they are partially frozen. Sprinkle sparkling apple cider on all the layers and spread with a thin layer of jam. Chill the bowl and the beaters before whipping cream. Whip about 2 cups of cream at a time (adding a little sugar to each batch). Add coarsely chopped chocolates to half of the whipped cream. Fill the cakes with the chocolate cream, spreading it evenly over 1 layer of each of the three different sizes of cakes. Top with the second layer of cake, bottom side up, and cover all three cakes on top and sides with the remaining whipped cream.

Marzipan cover: Keep marzipan at room temperature and roll out enough marzipan to cover the top and side of one cake at a time, about (5 mm) thick. If needed, use a little confectioners' sugar to help with the rolling out. The sugar can be easily brushed off with a pastry brush.

Place cakes on a three tier cake stand, beginning with the largest on the bottom. Fill a decorator tube with whipped cream and decorate the three cakes with stars (See Wedding Cake photograph). Make marzipan roses (in different sizes) and leaves and finish decorating the cake according to the picture. Top the cake with desired decoration.

Roses and leaves: (See picture). Color approximately ¼ of the marzipan with red and green food coloring (mostly red for the roses). Do not add too much food coloring at a time, you want a soft pink color. You can always add more if needed. To obtain a more natural green add 1 drop of blue for every two drops of green. Again add a little at a time, you cannot remove the color once it is added. Roll green marzipan out and cut out leaves and mark veins with candy tools, a toothpick or knife. It is a good idea to at least make the roses and leaves a couple of days ahead of time. They keep well in airtight tins.

Roll pink marzipan out as thin as possible. Cut into 5-6-inch (13-15 cm) long ribbons, the width depends on how big you want the rose to be. At one end start rolling up the ribbon, a little tight at the beginning and loosing it up as you go, allowing the center portion to protrude slightly in some roses, and recess in others. Bend the outer layer outward to resemble the configuration of a rose.

Norway's Grand Fruit Pie (Norges storartet fruktpie)

For inspiration see colored photo. Follow the easy steps to make this mouth-watering fruit pie. Large enough to serve 12 people.

Pie Dough:

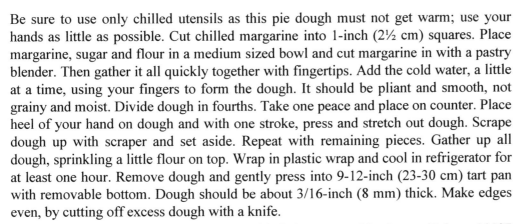

½-⅝ cup (120-160 g) margarine
1½-2 tbsp. sugar
1¹⁄₈-1½ cup (150-200 g) flour
3-5 tbsp. water, cold

Be sure to use only chilled utensils as this pie dough must not get warm; use your hands as little as possible. Cut chilled margarine into 1-inch (2½ cm) squares. Place margarine, sugar and flour in a medium sized bowl and cut margarine in with a pastry blender. Then gather it all quickly together with fingertips. Add the cold water, a little at a time, using your fingers to form the dough. It should be pliant and smooth, not grainy and moist. Divide dough in fourths. Take one peace and place on counter. Place heel of your hand on dough and with one stroke, press and stretch out dough. Scrape dough up with scraper and set aside. Repeat with remaining pieces. Gather up all dough, sprinkling a little flour on top. Wrap in plastic wrap and cool in refrigerator for at least one hour. Remove dough and gently press into 9-12-inch (23-30 cm) tart pan with removable bottom. Dough should be about 3/16-inch (8 mm) thick. Make edges even, by cutting off excess dough with a knife.

To prevent dough from rising, prick with fork. Let rest 15 minutes. Bake at 395°F (200°C) in middle of the oven for 10-12 minutes. It is ready when it begins to leave edge and has a light, golden color. Air circulation makes pie crust crisp. Cool on rack. If finished pie will stand more than two hours before eaten, "seal" bottom with currant or apricot glaze. If you want to keep it longer brush with melted chocolate. (The glace recipe makes enough to seal the crust and to brush on the berries.) Before berries are added, cover bottom of pie shell with vanilla cream.

Vanilla Cream:

4 egg yolks
⅔ cup (1½ dl) sugar
1½ tbsp. vanilla sugar
1¾ cup (4 dl) whole milk, boiling
½ cup (50 g) flour

Beat egg yolks, sugar and vanilla sugar until light and fluffy. It should be stiff enough that when it falls back into itself, the drips lay on top. Beat in the flour. While beating add the boiling milk, drop by drop at first, then in a *thin* stream. Pour mixture into a heavy bottomed pan and place over medium heat. Stir vigorously while it is being brought to a boil. Lower heat and simmer 2 to 3 minutes after boiling has begun. Remove from heat and cool.

Add berries of your choice, see photo for suggestion. Quickly rinse berries and remove all foreign objects. Drain well on a paper towel while you prepare glace.

Glaze:
2 tbsp. sugar
¼ cup, scant (1 dl) currant jelly or apricot marmalade

Stir sugar and jelly or marmalade together in sauce pan. Place over medium heat and warm 2 to 3 minutes. Glace should thicken to the point that drippings from a spoon are viscous. Do not simmer too long, it may turn to caramel. Brush the glace over the pie crust to prevent it from becoming soggy.

Spread vanilla cream in bottom of pie crust. Place berries closely together, forming a decorative pattern. Brush a thin layer of glace over berries. Serve as is with vanilla ice cream or whipped cream. **Serves 10-12.**

Creams, Frosting and Glazes

Vanilla or Rum Egg Custard (Eggekrem)

There are many ways to use egg custard as filling for cakes. One can vary the taste by adding flavorings such as rum extract, vanilla or almond, or by adding tart jams, jellies or fruit.

The custard may be thickened with all-purpose flour or potato starch flour. However, it will have a shinier and smoother appearance if potato starch flour is used. When making large amounts of egg cream it will be creamier if the sugar and eggs are whipped separately to *eggedosis* consistency, light and fluffy.

1²/₃ cup (4 dl) milk	4 egg yolks
¼ cup (½ dl) sugar	1 tbsp. potato starch flour
1 tsp. vanilla sugar or	
1 tsp. rum flavoring	

In a heavy saucepan bring the milk to a boil. Set aside. In a bowl, beat eggs and sugars until *eggedosis* consistency, light and fluffy. Add the hot milk, a few drops at a time, blending well after each addition. Return to saucepan and place over medium heat. Dissolve potato starch flour in a little water and add in a thin stream while stirring constantly until the it thickens to proper consistency. It *must not* boil. (Add rum flavoring if used). Cool by placing pan in cold water.

Egg Custard with Gelatine (Eggekrem med gelatin)

This custard is good for Napoleon cakes or cream cakes.

1¾ cup milk or coffee cream	2 pkg. Knox gelatine, unflavored
3 tbsp. flour	1 cup (2½ dl) whipping cream
4 egg yolks	Flavoring
2 tbsp. sugar, heaping	

In a heavy saucepan combine milk and flour and bring to a boil. Let simmer a couple of minutes. Remove from heat and cool slightly. Beat egg yolks and sugar until light and fluffy and carefully stir into milk mixture. Return to medium heat and stir constantly until it thickens. Do not let it boil. Remove from heat. Soften gelatine with small amount of water, and heat until thoroughly dissolved. While stirring pour in a thin stream into the hot mixture. Pour custard into a bowl and stir now and then as it cools and begins to thicken. When cool, whip cream and fold it into the custard. Add choice of flavorings. **Makes 3 cups.**

Vanilla or Rum Cream (Vaniljekrem)

2 egg yolks, large
½ cup (1¼ dl) sugar
1½ tsp. vanilla sugar

1 tbsp. potato starch flour
2 cups (5 dl) coffee cream or milk

Add all ingredients to a cold saucepan and blend fully. Set pan over medium heat and stir continually while bringing it to the boiling point. It *must not* boil. Place saucepan in cold water and beat cream until cold. Chill before using.

Mandarin Orange/Chocolate Cream
(Mandarinsjokoladekrem)

1 pkg. 4 oz. (125 g) Freia
  semisweet cooking chocolate
2 cups (5 dl) whipping cream
½ tsp. grated orange peel

1 pkg. Knox gelatin, unflavored
1 11 oz. can (310 g) mandarin
  orange segments, drained well

Delicious filling for cream cakes.

In a heavy pan, melt the chocolate in the cream. Chill. Whip until firm and add orange peel. In a small saucepan, sprinkle gelatine over a little water and let stand two minutes. Heat and stir until fully dissolved. Cool slightly, and while stirring add to chocolate cream in a thin stream. Stir in mandarin orange segments.

Butter Cream (Smørkrem)

½ cup (1¼ dl) butter, unsalted
1 cup (2½ dl) confectioners' sugar

Flavorings of your choice

Butter cream is quick and easy to make. It is excellent to fill or frost cakes with, and flavorings may be varied.

Have butter at room temperature. Beat until light and fluffy. Gradually add confectioners' sugar and beat until well blended, and cream is light and white in color. Leave as is or add flavorings. **Makes ¾ cup (2 dl).**

Butter Cream II (Smørkrem II)

½ cup, scant (100 g) butter
1 cup (2½ dl) confectioners' sugar
2 egg yolks

1 tbsp. cocoa, unsweetened
¾ tsp. vanilla sugar, or
½ tsp. vanilla extract

Have butter at room temperature. Beat until light and fluffy. Gradually add confectioners' sugar and beat until well blended, and cream is light and white in color. Thoroughly blend in egg yolks, cocoa, and flavoring. **Makes about ¾ cup (2 dl).**

Flavorings for Butter Cream (Smakstilsetning av smørkrem)

1 tsp. mocha extract
1-2 tbsp. cocoa, unsweetened
2 oz. (60 g) chocolate, melted

2 tbsp. orange peel, grated
  and lightly sweetened, or
½ tbsp. orange juice and touch

1 tsp. vanilla sugar
½ tsp. vanilla extract, pure

of grated orange peel
2 tbsp. lemon peel, grated
   and lightly sweetened

Do not use lemon or orange peel if you are planning to use a decorator tube.

Marzipan for Cake Toppings (Marsipanlokk)

1½ cups (200 g) almonds, blanched
2¾ cups (300 g) confectioners'
   sugar, approx.

1 egg white, approx.
1 tbsp. water, approx.

Enough to cover top and bottom of a 10-inch (25 cm) cake.

Blanch the almonds, and dry well. Grind almonds twice, the second time with confectioners' sugar. They should be like flour. Add slightly beaten egg white and water, work the mass together until viscous. Form into a ball. On a marble slab or on top of a white plastic bag roll the marzipan out on a little sifted confectioners' sugar. Making the marzipan "lid" is simplified by rolling out the marzipan between 2 large plastic sheets, or use a plain, large plastic bag, a carrying size bag. Place the marzipan inside the bag on a counter and roll on the outside of the bag until desired size. Cut the bag to open. Place your hand underneath the plastic and begin placing from the edge of the cake, removing the bag carefully as you go. Trim the "lid" to even edges.

Imitation Marzipan Topping (Falsk marsipan)

Excellent as toppings for cream or other cakes.

3½ tbsp. (½ dl) water
2 tbsp. (30 g) butter
1 tbsp. scant (25 g) flour

1 cup, good measure (350 g)
   confectioners' sugar
1 egg white
Few drops almond oil or extract

In a heavy saucepan over low heat make a thick porridge of water, butter and flour, stirring constantly. Cool slightly and add the remainder of the ingredients. Follow roll out direction in preceding recipe.

Confectioners' Sugar or Chocolate Glaze (Melisglasur)

1 cup confectioners' sugar
2 tbsp. milk or cream rum, or
   2 tbsp. cocoa

Flavorings such as vanilla, almond,

Sift confectioners' sugar (and cocoa if used), add milk or cream and blend until smooth and glossy. Add desired flavoring such as almond, rum, vanilla etc.

Cookies and Waffles

Crisp Diamond Cookies (Sirupsnitter)

9 oz. (¼ kg) syrup, Golden Lyle
1⅓ cup (3¼ dl) sugar
¼ cup (½ dl) butter, melted
⅔ cup (1½ dl) whipping cream
1 qt. (liter) flour approx.
½ tsp. pepper
1 tsp. ginger

⅛ tsp. nutmeg, freshly grated
1 tsp. anise
½ tsp. baking soda

Decoration:
Almonds, scalded
Egg white

Thin, crisp and traditionally a welcome Christmas cookie. Cut into diamond shape with a pastry wheel and add a scalded almond in the center.

Warm syrup, sugar and butter in a heavy sauce pan. Cool and add most of the cream, leaving out 2 tablespoons. Blend spices with half of the flour and add. Stir baking soda into the 2 tablespoons of cream, and add with remaining flour to cookies. You do not want the dough to be too dry, it is therefore advisable to leave out a little flour which may be added if needed. Work the dough well and leave refrigerated until the next day. On lightly floured surface, roll out very thin, a portion at the time, and cut into diamond shapes with a fluted pastry wheel. Gently press a half of a scalded almond in the center and brush with egg white. Bake at 355-365°F (180-185°C) for 5-6 minutes. Watch carefully they will burn easily.

Cookie Stacks (Bordstabelbakkels)

Stabel means pile or stacks. They are served by placing two cookies a few inches apart, with the next two crossing, ½ inch (1¼ cm) from the ends of the first two. Continue stacking until desired height.

3 egg yolks
1⅓ cup (1¼ dl) sugar
2 tbsp. whipping cream
1⅛ cup (250 g) butter, softened
3½ - 3⅞ cups (500 g) flour, approx.
Grated peel of 1 lemon

Almond Meringue:
1⅞ cups (4½ dl) almonds, ground
2⅓ cups (250 g) confectioners' sugar
Grated peel of 1 lemon
4 egg whites, beaten

An old traditional, superb tasting cookie, better known on the farms than in the cities. Yet now it has become quite popular all around.

Beat egg yolks and sugar until light and fluffy. Stir in whipping cream. Mix grated lemon peel with flour and add to mixture alternately with the soft butter. Mix fully. Let dough rest 1 hour. On lightly floured surface roll out a thin dough, (many say the thickness of a blade of straw), and cut out lengths 6x1_inch (15cmx3cm). Grease or cover cookie sheet with parchment paper and bake cookies in the middle of 355°F (180°C) oven for 6 minutes.

Almond meringue: Grind almonds twice, second time with confectioners' sugar. Add lemon peel and egg whites and mix well. Add almond meringue in a stripe down the center of the cookie. The meringue swells so do not put it all the way to the edge. Return to the oven to dry at 160°F (70°C), leaving the oven door ajar. The cookies are finished when the meringue is set yet still white.

Oatmeal-Lace Cookies (Havrekniplekaker)

1 cup (225 g) butter	½ tsp. salt
1 cup (2½ dl) sugar	2 cups (5 dl) oats, quick cooking
⅔ cup (1½ dl) flour, sifted	¼ cup milk

Heat oven to 375°F (190°C). Melt butter in saucepan. Stir in remaining ingredients, mixing well. Drop by ½ teaspoon about 3 inches (8 cm) apart on greased and floured cookie sheet. Spread thinly. Bake for 5 to 7 minutes. Watch carefully. Let stand a few minutes before removing from pan.

Dalesmen (Døler)

Unpretentious looking and undescribably delicious.

¾ cup plus 1 tbsp. (1¾ dl) butter	⅜ cup (½ dl) whipping cream
⅔ cup (1½ dl) sugar	1 tsp. vanilla sugar or
5 tbsp. potato flour	pure extract
1 cup (2½ dl) flour	1 cup (2½ dl) hazelnuts or almonds

Cream butter and sugar until light fluffy. Mix potato flour with flour and vanilla sugar, if used. Sift a little into the butter mixture and stir. Add cream, vanilla extract if used, the remaining flour, and coarsely chopped nuts. Drop by teaspoonful onto greased or parchment covered cookie sheet and bake for 10 to 12 minutes in preheated 350°F (175°C) oven for 10 to 12 minutes or until light golden in color.

Serina Cookies (Serinakaker)

3¼ cup (8 dl) flour	1¼ cup (3 dl) butter
1½ cup ((3½ dl) sugar	2 eggs, separated
1½ tsp. baking powder	1 cup (2½ dl) almonds, blanched
½ tsp. salt of hartshorn, finely chopped	Pearl sugar
1 tsp. vanilla sugar or pure vanilla extract	

In a large bowl combine flour, 1¼ cups (3 dl) of the sugar, baking powder, salt of hartshorn, and vanilla sugar, if used. Cut in butter with pastry blender till pieces are the size of small peas. Set aside. Beat 1 egg white until firm. Gradually add remaining ¼ cup (½ dl) sugar, beating until stiff and glossy. Combine egg yolks with vanilla extract if used, fold into beaten egg white. Blend with flour mixture, then work with fingers until well mixed. Do not overwork the dough, this will cause the cookies to loose some of their crispness. Shape dough into 1-inch (2½ cm) balls. Place on well-greased cookie sheet, press down with fork in a criss-cross pattern. Brush with remaining slightly beaten egg white and sprinkle with chopped almonds and pearl sugar, press the garnish lightly into the cookies so they do not fall off. Preheat oven to 350°F (175°C). Bake 15 minutes or until golden brown. Cool slightly before removing to racks. **Makes 7 dozen.**

Marianne's Cookies (Marianne's Specier)

Be sure to make these cookies with real butter.

3½ cups (450 g) flour	1⅝ cups (375 g) butter
1¾ cups (200 g) confectioners' sugar	

Else Rønnevig and her Prize-Winning Breads.

Britt Kåsen, a Promoter of
Health, Office of Information
for Fruits and Vegetables ↓

Nisser and Fruit make a Healthy
and Happy Holiday. ↑

Sand Tarts - Strull - Goro ↓

Chocolate (Sjokolade)

Delightful, delectable, delicious Freia chocolate! We seem to be encircled about by chocolate, from the darkest to the purest white. However, not all chocolates are equal, and using an inferior chocolate can ruin an otherwise delicious recipe.

In recipes calling for chocolate in this book I have used Freia, the world renowned Norwegian chocolate. Both Freia Dronning and Selskapssjokolade, semi-sweet cooking chocolate, comes in 4.38 ounces (125 g) bars. Freia cooking and eating chocolates are available in Scandinavian Delicatessens or by mail. See Sources.

Freia Chocolate Boy ↑

The Dairy Maid's Wafers and Lefse ↓

Norway's Grand Fruit Pie

A Celebration: Back row left: Chocolate Pudding, Queens Sweet Secret, Cloudberry Ice-cream Parfait, Napoleons, Cherry Cream Cake, Marzipan Cake.↑

Daim Cake↓

Almond Tower Cake, *Kransekake* ↑

Shrovetide Buns ↓

Marzipan Wedding Cake

Else Rønnevig's Beautiful Party Table at Snøringsmoen, Lillesand, Norway.

Mix all ingredients together in a food processor. It makes a firm dough. Roll into long ropes about 2 inches (5 cm) thick, and slice in 1/8 inch (½ cm) thick slices. Bake at 350°F (175°C) oven until light golden.

Knepp Cookies (Kneppkaker)

3 eggs	1 tsp. salt of hartshorn
1 cup (2½ dl) sugar	¼ tsp. pepper
1 cup (2½ dl) syrup, Golden Lyle	As much unbleached flour
¼ cup (½ dl) milk	as needed

Preheat oven to 350°F (175°C). Beat eggs and sugar well. Heat the honey or syrup until lukewarm and add to egg mixture. Add milk. Sift together spices and flour, and fold in. Drop by teaspoonsful on greased cookie sheet. Bake until golden brown, about 10-12 minutes. **Makes 3 dozen.**

Tiny Doughnuts (Smultringer)

Smultringer tops the list of the "7 must" cookies on the Norwegian homemaker's Christmas baking list. It is important to deep fry them quickly in hot lard or Crisco. They keep well in airtight containers as well as in the freezer.

These are small cookie-doughnuts, not what we in America think of as doughnuts.

¹/₃ cup (75 g) margarine or butter	3 tsp. cardamon
2 eggs	3¾ cups (500 g) flour
1 cup (200 g) sugar	2 tsp. salt of hartshorn
1¹/₃ cups (3 dl) canned milk, whipped	

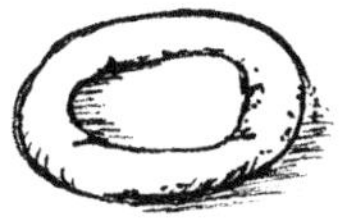

Melt and cool margarine or butter. Beat eggs and sugar until light and fluffy. Beat the canned milk until stiff and fold in. Mix and stir dry ingredients into egg/milk mixture, being careful not to add too much flour, dough should be soft. Use just enough flour to be able to roll the dough out to ³/₈-inch (1 cm) thickness. Cut out with a small doughnut cutter or 2 graduated glasses. Deep fry in hot lard or Crisco until golden brown. Drain on paper towels. Store in airtight containers.

Traditional Crests (Potetmeltopper)

½ cup (100 g) margarine	¼ cup (½ dl) almonds, chopped
³/₈ cup, scant (75 g) sugar	¾ cup (180 g) potato starch flour
1 egg, seperated	

This recipe brings memories of the distant past, of visits to bestemors, grandma's kitchen and several cookie cans stacked neatly in the pantry.

Cream margarine until light. Add sugar ¼ at a time and continue beating until light and creamy. Separate egg and blend the yolk fully with butter mixture. Add almonds and sift in the flour. Mix well. Beat the egg white until stiff but not dry, fold in. Preheat oven to 390°F (200°C) and place dough by teaspoonfuls on parchment covered baking sheet. Bake 10 minutes or until light golden. **Makes 1½ dozens.**

Mazarin Tarts (Mazariner)

1¼ cups (3 dl) flour	**Filling:**
½ tsp. baking powder	¹/₃ cup (¾ dl) butter

¼ cup (½ dl) sugar
½ cup (1¼ dl) butter
1 tbsp. ice water

½ cup (1½ dl) sugar
¾ cup (1¾ dl) almonds, ground
2 eggs
½ tsp. almond extract

Almond lovers will relish these traditional tarts filled with a delectable almond filling.

Mix flour, baking powder and sugar. Cut in butter and add ice water. Shape into a ball and chill thoroughly. Remove dough from the refrigerator. With thumb, press a little dough into buttered muffin or *sandkake* tins. Prepare filling by creaming butter and sugar until light. Add ground almonds and extract. Add eggs, one at a time and beat well. Put 2 teaspoons almond filling in each. Roll a little of the dough out and cut a thin, ⅓ inch (8 mm) strips and crisscross over the filling. Tuck the ends between the filling and the crust. Bake on baking sheet, on the lowest rack, in 350°F (175°C) oven for 20-25 minutes. **Makes about 1½ dozen tarts.**

Sand Nuts (Sandnøtter)

Sometimes one cannot explain the names of old traditional cookies like these, but they are enjoyed all over Norway.

½ cup (1¼ dl) margarine or
   butter, half of it unsalted
⅔ cup (1½ dl) sugar
1 egg, small

1¼ cups (200 g) potato starch flour
½ cup (60 g) unbleached flour
2 tsp. vanilla sugar
1 tsp. baking powder

Cream margarine or butter with sugar until light and fluffy. Add the egg and mix. Mix remaining ingredients and add to the mixture a little at a time, blending well. Chill in the refrigerator for a couple of hours. Shape into small balls about 1⅛-inch (3 cm) diameter. Place on greased cookie sheet and gently press down with a fork. Bake in very hot oven 410°F (210°C) until golden. Watch carefully so they do not burn.

Rosettes (Rosetter)

A delightful, always welcome traditional cookie which looks beautiful.

They keep for 6 months in a freezer or airtight container. You do need a rosette iron, now available in most stores that carry kitchen utensils. Look for the ones that have two rosette molds, it will cut your baking time in half.

2 eggs
1 tbsp. sugar
½ tsp. salt
½ tsp. cardamom

1½ cups (3½ dl) flour
1 cup (2½ dl) milk
Safflower oil

Beat eggs lightly. Add sugar, salt, and cardamom to the flour and mix well. Add to eggs alternately with milk and mix thoroughly. The batter should be like thick cream. It may be made the night before and refrigerated. Or allow the batter to stand 30 minutes to alleviate air bubbles. Use an electric controlled pan. Heat oil to 365°F (185°C) before dipping iron in the oil for 10 seconds (making sure the pan is deep enough to allow mold to be completely submerged). Drain slightly on paper towels. Keep the temperature between 350-375°F (175-190°C). Dip hot iron into batter being careful not to get batter on top of the rim, it will make it impossible to remove the rosette. Submerge in heated oil thoroughly covering the mold and cook until lightly browned. If rosette does not leave iron when cooked, release it with a fork. Drain well before storing. Serve plain or sprinkled with confectioners' sugar. **Makes 40.**

Monks I (Munker I)

In America they are often known by their Danish name, Aebleskiver. Monk pans are available from most Scandinavian Delicatessens and kitchenware import stores.

3 eggs
2 cups (5 dl) buttermilk
1 tbsp. sugar
½ tsp salt

1 tsp. baking powder
2½ cups (6 dl) flour
Fruit or jelly

These delicate ball-shaped monks have a batter which resembles pancakes. They were often served in our grandparents' day, but originated in Denmark.

Beat eggs and blend with milk. In separate bowl sift the dry ingredients. Make a large indentation in the center of the dry mixture and slowly stir in the liquid, stirring as you pour. Let the batter rest a few minutes. Heat the monk pan. Add a little shortening to each compartment and when the shortening begins to smoke fill each half full with batter. When cooked on one side add some fruit or jelly. Turn using two forks, one on either side. When thoroughly baked sprinkle with confectioners' sugar.

Monks II (Munker II)

Apples
6 eggs, seperated
2 qts. (liter) buttermilk
6 cups (15 dl) flour
6 tsp. baking powder

1½ tsp. baking soda
1½ tsp. salt
6 tbsp. sugar
Confectioners' sugar
Jam

Wash, peel and slice apples. Boil until barely tender, set aside. Separate eggs. Mix egg yolks with buttermilk. In a separate bowl add dry ingredients, and stir in buttermilk mixture. Beat egg whites until stiff, but not dry, and gently fold into batter. Heat the monk pan. Add a little oil, shortening or margarine to each compartment, when very hot fill each half full with batter. When cooked on one side add a small piece of apple or jam. Turn using two forks, one on either side. When thoroughly baked, remove and sprinkle with confectioners' sugar. Serve warm with jam or applesauce. The recipe may be halved.

The Dairymaid's Wafers (Seterjentas rømmebrød)

1 cup (2½ dl) sour cream
⅞ cup (200 g) butter
¼ cup (½ dl) water
¼ tsp. salt

½ tsp. cardamon
4 tbsp. sugar
1 qt. (liter) flour, approx.

This cookie is rolled out very thin and baked in a krumkake iron, but not rolled up into a cone like krumkaker. It is an old traditional recipe.

Have butter at room temperature, stir together with sour cream. Add remaining ingredients, leaving out a little flour for rolling out the dough. Knead into a fairly firm dough. Chill for 2 hours. Sprinkle a little sugar on top and roll into the dough. Cut out a cardboard template the size of *krumkake* iron; trace and cut wafers from the pattern. Bake in heated *krumkake* iron until a nice golden color.

Cardamom Cone-Shaped Wafers (Krumkaker)

Egg (1 egg makes 9 wafers)   **Flour**
Sugar   **Cardamon**
Butter or margarine

Weigh the egg(s) with shell on. To the weight of each egg add the same weight each of sugar, butter and flour, mixed with a little cardamom. Mix it all together. Heat *krumkake* iron, ungreased, until a drop of water sputters when sprinkled on its surface. Butter iron slightly for the first two cakes. Place a generous tablespoon of batter in the middle of the iron and close. Bake over medium heat until golden. Remove cake with a fork and immediately roll up into cone or cylinder shape.

Variation: Quickly place *krumkake* in or over a small dessert cup or bowl and serve as dessert filled with whipped cream and fruit or berries of your choice.

Goro (Goro)

To make *goro* takes time. Enlist a family member or friend. Keep paper towels handy to wipe up the fat which oozes out of the iron.

3 egg yolks   **1 tsp. cardamom**
²/₃ cup (1½ dl) sugar   **6 cups (15 dl) unbleached flour**
1 cup (2½) whipping cream   **3 cups (7½) butter, lightly salted**

Beat together egg yolks, sugar and cream. Add cardamom to flour and sift half of the flour, a little at a time, into the egg mixture and mix well. Put the remainder of the flour on counter and place dough on top. Roll dough out to a thick flap, and spread butter in thin layers across the dough. Fold over and roll once more. Roll up and chill for 24 hours. Roll out thin. Cut a cardboard template the size of *goro* iron; trace and cut cookies from the pattern. Bake in hot, ungreased *goro* iron until a light golden color. Wipe fat off as it trickles out. Remove from iron with a spatula onto a cutting board. Cut off the frayed edges and cut apart while still hot. Cool completely. May be frozen. **Makes about 12 dozen.**

Poor Man's Cookies (Fattigman)

However, the authenticated reason is that cream, eggs, butter and such were easy to come by on the Norwegian farms where the recipes originated. These diamond-crullers go back to the mid 19th century, and is a must at Christmas time in most Norwegian homes. Keeps well in airtight containers.

7 egg yolks   **2 tbsp. cognac**
½ cup (1¼ dl) sugar   **2²/₃ cups (350 g) flour, approx.**
1 cup (2½ dl) whipping cream   **¼ tsp. cardamon**
¼ tsp. lemon peel, grated   **Lard or shortening**

Beat egg yolks and sugar until light and fluffy. Whip cream until firm and add to eggs together with lemon peel and cognac. Add cardamon to flour and sift into mixture, keeping out a little flour to sprinkle over dough, and some to roll dough out with. Cover and chill until next day. Remove a small portion, place on lightly floured surface and roll out to a thin dough. Cut into diamond shapes with a *fattigman* cutter or use a pastry wheel and ruler. Make a slit about 1¹/₈-inch (3 cm) long in the middle and carefully slip one corner through. Place on a board or baking sheet sprinkled lightly with flour. Fry in hot lard or shortening. They swell and develop air bubbles during the cooking. Remove when golden brown and drain well on paper towels. Sprinkle with confectioners' sugar if desired. Store in airtight containers. **Makes 7½ dozen.**

Berlin Wreaths (Berlinerkranser)

3 egg yolks, hard boiled
4 egg yolks, raw
⁷/₈ cup (200 g) sugar
½ tsp. vanilla sugar

2 cups (5 dl) butter
3¹/₈ cups (7½ dl) flour
Egg white
Pearl sugar

These cookies are among the most favorite in Norwegian holiday baking. However they are a little tricky to make, but if you persevere you will be rewarded with delicate little tidbits.

Mash the hard boiled, cold egg yolks and combine with the raw. Add sugars and beat well. Wash out the butter to remove most of the salt. Add alternately to the egg mixture with the flour. Chill. Roll into thin "ropes" about ¹/₃ inch (8 mm) thick. Cut into 4 inch (10 cm) lengths and form small wreaths, overlapping ends. Press down lightly to make ends stick together. Dip first in beaten egg white, then in pearl sugar. Preheat oven to 375°F (190°C) and bake on greased cookie sheet about 10 minutes. **Makes about 7 dozen.**

Hartshorn (Hjortetakk)

4 egg yolks and 2 egg whites
1¾ cup (4½ dl) sugar
¹/₃ cup (¾ dl) whipping cream
¾ cup (170 g) butter, melted

4 cups (450 g) flour
½ tsp. cardamom
1 tsp. salt of hartshorn

Cream egg yolks, egg whites and sugar together until light and fluffy. Stir in whipped cream and cooled, melted, butter. Add half the flour which has been mixed with cardamom and salt of hartshorn. Cover and let stand overnight. Next day add enough flour to make a medium firm dough. Roll into pencil thick lengths, cut, butt edges and roll to make even. Make 3-4 diagonal slits on outer edge rings with a sharp knife. Deep fry in hot fat. Cool and drain on absorbent paper. Store in airtight containers. **Makes about 6 dozen.**

Custard Cream Tartlet (Linser)

2 cups (5 dl) flour
¾ cup (170 g) butter
2 egg yolks
2½ tbsp. sugar

Custard Cream:
1 cup (2½ dl) milk or coffee cream
1 vanilla bean, cut lengthwise
4 egg yolks
¼ cup (½ dl) sugar
1 tbsp. cornstarch

Linser bring back memories of many special family get-togethers at Nesodden. If you do not have heart shaped linse pans, muffin pans may be substituted.

Custard Cream: In a heavy pan make the custard by bringing the milk and the vanilla bean to a boil, let simmer 10 minutes. Remove vanilla bean. Beat eggs and sugar until of *eggedosis* consistency (light and fluffy). While stirring, add spoonfuls of the boiling milk to the egg mixture. Place it all, with the cornstarch, back into the pan over moderate heat, stirring constantly until thickened. It must not boil. Cool in cold water.

Pastry: Blend the butter into flour with pastry blender, or with your finger tips, until it resembles small peas. Add sugar and egg yolks and work together quickly into a soft dough. Form into a ball and chill. Roll out ²/₃ of the pastry and line greased *linse* pans, preferably heart-shaped. Divide the filling equally among the lined pans. Roll out remaining pastry and lay over filling, using unbeaten egg white on edges as a binding agent, and pressing gently around the edges. Place on cookie sheet and bake at 400°F (205°C) for approx. 15 minutes or until golden. Cool a few minutes before carefully removing from the pans, as they are quite fragile. These tartlet are usually frosted with sugar glaze or sprinkled with confectioners' sugar. **Makes 15 tartlet.**

Sand Tarts (Sandkaker)

Tarts are used all year round. Delicious eaten plain, or filled with whipped cream, decorated with grated chocolate or nuts, or berries and fruit, or fill with puddings and jello.

If you fill them, do so just before serving or they will become soggy. They keep well in airtight container and freezer. Recipe may be cut in half.

1 cup (2½ dl) sugar	**2 tsp. almond extract**
2 cups (450 g) butter	**4½ cups (11 dl) flour**
1 egg	

Cream butter and sugar white. Add egg, and blend in remaining ingredients. Chill dough overnight. Remove a small portion of the dough from the refrigerator. Put small amount of dough in fluted tart pan. Press a thin layer of dough on bottom and sides, turning the tart pan as you are working. Remove excess dough from edge. Place tart pan on cookie sheet and bake at 350°F (175°C) 12 to 15 minutes, or to a golden color. Cool slightly before turning tart pan over. The tart should slide out, but sometimes a tap with a spoon on the bottom of pan will loosen it. **Makes 7 dozen.**

Vanilla Wreaths (Smørkranser)

These cookies melt in your mouth like vanilla clouds. Especially good with vanilla ice cream, and fresh or frozen defrosted berries.

⁷/₈ cup less 1 tbsp. (185 g) butter	**1¾ cups (235 g) flour**
²/₃ cup (125 g) sugar	**½ tsp. baking powder**
1 egg	**1 tsp. vanilla sugar**

Cream butter and sugar until light and airy, and add remaining ingredients. Chill. Force through cookie-press about ½-inch (1¼ cm) wide and 4¾-inches (12 cm) long bars. Form into wreaths. Place on parchment covered cookie sheet. Bake in preheated 350°F (175°C) oven and bake until light golden. Cool on rack.

Waffles (Vafler)

Cakes and waffles baked in cast iron forms are among the oldest kind of Norwegian cakes. Some of the cake irons have been found with runic writings on them. The oldest waffle irons made one heart shaped or square waffle. Later three hearts in the same iron were popular. The heart-shaped waffle iron in use today traditionally has five hearts.

Waffles may be enjoyed in the morning, at lunch time, or in the evening. They are great when unexpected guests come to your door, because, generally, we all have the simple ingredients on hand. And it is a comfort to know that something so flavorful does not cost much.

There are innumerable recipes for waffles in Norway, inexpensive and healthy low-fat ones, made with barley flour and without butter and cream. Crisp delectable ones are high in calories but nevertheless irresistible. Try delicious waffles made with yeast.

Some waffles you can serve with a variety of sandwich meats, others, you can make into cream cakes, or serve them with ice cream and berries. Or maybe you still prefer the more traditional way; buttered and sprinkled with sugar, or topped with a thick slice of the sweet Norwegian goat cheese, or a spoonful of your favorite berry jam.

In earlier times *hverdagsvafler*, everyday waffles, were made with barley flour (now available at natural food stores). For guests the more refined flour was used with the addition of sour cream. The most commonly used waffle had a rather firm texture containing neither egg, yeast, nor baking powder, but boasted of better keeping qualities. The fancier waffle had fresh milk, cream, sour cream, butter, and sugar added which made a thicker and superior textured product. Try several of these waffle recipes, and maybe, just maybe, you too will become an avid fan of the Norwegian waffles.

Norwegians love waffles! They bake the waffles in heart shaped cast iron waffle irons. You can use an electric iron, but some of us, spellbound by the traditional heart shaped irons, who believe foolishly, maybe, that Norwegian waffles, to taste their best, must be baked in the heart shaped irons.

Cake Waffles *(Sprø vafler)*

4 eggs
1¹⁄₈ cups (250 g) sugar)
1¹⁄₈ cups (250 g) butter, melted

2¾ cups (500 g) potato starch flour
3 tsp. baking powder

Beat eggs and sugar to light and fluffy. Melt butter, cool slightly and add to egg mixture. Mix potato starch flour and baking powder and add. The batter will be rather firm. If you are using a non-electric heart shaped, Norwegian waffle iron, it is ready for baking when it is so hot that a drop of water splatters when flipped across its surface. Lightly butter its surface before the first waffle only. Bake a small test waffle. Drop batter by topped tablespoonful onto iron, and close tightly. Bake until golden and crisp. **Makes 12 waffles.**

These delicious waffles have no flour. They are at their very best when eaten warm. Marvelous topped with ice cream, sour or whipped cream and topped with fruit spreads.

Crisp Waffles with Cream *(Sprø kremvafler)*

1¹⁄₃ cup (3 dl) flour
½ tsp. salt
2 tbsp. sugar
1 tsp. vanilla sugar, or
    vanilla extract

¹⁄₃ cup (¾ dl) water
1 cup (2½ dl) sour cream
½ cup, scant (1¼ dl) butter
3 eggs

Mix all ingredients, except the egg whites, until you have a smooth batter. Let rest 25 - 30 minutes. Beat egg whites until they form peaks and gently fold into batter. (See Cake Waffles for baking instructions). Place on cake racks until cool. Serve with berry jam or sprinkle with confectioners' sugar.

Delicious and quick to make. You may beat the egg whites separately to make them extra light, but it is not necessary.

Everyday Waffles *(Hverdagsvafler)*

The recipe calls for cultured milk, (see Special Helps). Homogenized milk may be used but these waffles are tastier with cultured milk.

*Low in calories,
inexpensive, and tasty.
Bake in the afternoon,
place in Ziplock bag,
and enjoy as a treat
following dinner.*

2 eggs
1⅓ cup (3 dl) cultured milk
1⅓ cup (3 dl) flour

½ tsp. baking powder
2 tbsp. sugar
3 tbsp. margarine, melted

Beat the eggs with half the milk. Mix dry ingredients and add to eggs, stir until batter is smooth. Add remaining milk and melted butter and mix well. Let batter stand 10 minutes. (See Cake waffles for baking instructions). Serve with goat cheese or jam. Makes 8 heart-shaped waffles.

Waffles With Yeast (Vafler med gjær)

*If you are not in a
hurry, these low fat
waffles are incredibly
delicious. The batter
must be allowed to
rise ¾ of an hour. If
they are baked too
soon they will become
too hard.*

3 eggs
2-3 tbsp. sugar
2 cups scant (5 dl) milk
2 tbsp. margarine, melted

½ cup (1¼ dl) water
½ cup (1¼ dl) sour cream
1 tbsp. active dry yeast
2¼ cup, approx. (5½ dl) flour

Beat eggs with sugar until light and fluffy 7 to 10 minutes. Add milk and melted and cooled margarine. Stir yeast into a little sour cream, and add with ½ cup milk. Add enough flour to make the batter a proper consistency. Not too thin. Stir until well blended. Set aside to rise ¾ of an hour until bubbles form. Grease the iron well. Follow baking directions for Sour Cream Waffles I. Serve with butter and jam. These waffles taste just as good the next day if kept in an airtight plastic bag. They will loose their flavor somewhat if frozen.

Lemon Waffles (Vafler med sitronsmak)

*A rather unusual
flavor, but delicious
served hot or cold.*

5 eggs
¼ cup (½ dl) sugar
1 cup (2½ dl) flour
1 tsp. lemon juice, fresh

½ tsp. lemon peel (freshly
   grated)
1 cup (2½ dl) sour cream
¼ cup (½ dl) butter

Beat eggs and sugar until thick and fluffy, about 10 minutes. Alternately fold in the flour, which has been sifted with lemon peel, and sour cream. Stir in the butter and lemon juice. Set batter aside to rest 10 - 15 minutes. Heat heart-shaped waffle iron. It is hot enough when drops of water sprinkled on its surface sputter. Pour approximately ¾ cup batter in the center of the iron. Lower cover and bake until the steaming stops, 30 - 60 seconds on each side. Do not peek during baking period. **Makes 6 waffles.**

Parties

Giving a party can be an exhilarating experience if properly planned. Success is guaranteed if sufficient time is allowed for preparation and a few simple rules are followed.

Why give a party? We do not need an excuse for a party. Life is a celebration! So call your family or friends together and share your joy in living. And if you are Norwegian we have many fest days through the year, (see my book, Norway's Fest Days) themes just waiting for us to be enjoyed.

As a young girl in Norway, I learned much about party giving from my mother. She radiated happiness when she made her party preparations. She had fun both planning and preparing, knowing the enjoyment everyone, including her, would have. She did not have much money in her budget, but she utilized her imagination and talents. And she left a trail of happy guests after each get together. If you have a new idea on how to give a great party, use it. Our world would come to a standstill and be unbearably boring without our imaginations!

Make a list: Include on your list everything which needs to be done, then follow it. Invitations, decorations, food shopping, house cleaning etc. Plan your invitations, decorations, and menu around the chosen theme. The menu does not have to be elaborate, but do make it tasty and colorful. The food will have a lot to do with your party's success. Any food which can be prepared and frozen is to your advantage.

Decide on your guest list: You will succeed with the right planning, and by inviting the right people. At your own party you can invite whomever you please. We give parties for many reasons, one of them, should not be to invite people we feel "obligated" to. Your party should be to honor someone, to celebrate a special occasion, or just to give your friends and family a memorable good time. Invite only those whom you feel will socialize well with others, and whom you know will help others to enjoy themselves. That does not mean that everyone should have the same interests and professions, but it does mean people who enjoy people, and people who enjoy learning about others, and who enjoy life. People who not only will enjoy themselves, but who will through being themselves, help others to have a great time as well.

Make or buy special invitations. Mail out as much as three weeks in advance. Include telephone number for "regrets only." For most of us today, a telephone call will do, but do allow your guests plenty of advance notice.

Remember the flowers: If the occasion calls for special flowers, order in advance. Let the florist know you will pick them up as soon as the store opens, that way they will be ready for you. If it is a winter party, do not unwrap the flowers immediately upon arriving home. Remove some of the paper around the stems and place in water. This will get the blossoms accustomed to the temperature change and they will last longer.

Purchased flowers can be expensive. Hopefully, in the summer time, you have a few growing in your own garden, in window boxes or on the patio. If not, look around for wild flowers or greenery, they make beautiful decorations.

Put your house in order: Clean and vacuum the whole house, and polish the furniture. Wash and polish all tableware and dishes, iron table linen or place mats. The night before the party make another list reminding yourself of last-minute chores and check them off as you progress, thus assuring yourself that nothing is left undone.

The morning of your party: Food meant to be served fresh, such as relishes, salads and fruits should be purchased the morning of the party. Early in the morning

Do not hesitate to try something new and different just because it has never been done before. Use your talents - and your imagination. You can, of course, glean ideas from others, but a party is your coming out where you can plan and create for the enjoyment of others. Most people love parties. That is, everyone enjoys a party where the host and hostess have given some thought to the preparation of the party; the theme, food, decorations, timing, and whom to invite.

There is no party without candles. Today they come in every conceivable color and shape. You will have no problem finding the appropriate candles to complement your decor.

When the doorbell rings, swing open your door, and share with those lucky invited ones, the best that you are, the warmth of your home, your scrumptious food and the excitement of mingling with friends, or meeting new ones. Above all let them enjoy a relaxed, happy host and hostess who have learned the art of making others happy.

the stores are not crowded, and the produce is fresh. Select your needs, pick up your flowers and you will be home in no time.

Set your table: A beautifully dressed table will add immensely to the spirit of your party. Take time to make it beautiful. Your sparkling clean table ware, the polished silver, and the beautiful flowers you picked up, and candles will add that special touch.

The size of the party: The size of the party will determine whether or not it will be necessary to serve guests buffet style. If possible have enough card tables or other small tables set up so that your guests will be comfortable while dining. It would be helpful if the tables are set with needed tableware, glasses and cups. After the guests have served themselves and are seated you can pour the beverage. The secret of a successful buffet is that it looks tempting and tastes delicious. Utilize candles, flowers or special decorations. Place the meat, fish, vegetables, salad, relishes, fruits, and breads in groups. Making sure that each dish has its own serving piece.

The guests arrive: When on the day of your party, your home, table, and food are prepared or is cooking in the oven, then it is time for you to spruce up. You need to be at your best, and sparkle with enthusiasm. A droopy host or hostess has the same negative reaction on guests as droopy flowers. When you are ready, light the fire, if it is the season, start the background music, and lastly, light the candles strategically placed around your home.

Festive Occasions: The festive occasions of yesteryear were notable, I believe, not because they were extravagant, but because they were something out of the ordinary. Today, our lives are quite affluent compared with our parents times. Yet, those things we can purchase without giving much thought to the expense, does not necessarily make it a memorable occasion. Often it is the thoughtful, simple, and unique things we do for others that make them memorable.

An example is my 9th birthday, during World War II. Unbeknown to me, mamma had traded some of her beautiful hand embroidered work to secure red fruit jello, and some other special foods for that day. We had no refrigeration, but it was February, and plenty cold. She placed the jello outside on the veranda to set. I tingled throughout when I rubbed the morning frost off our kitchen window and discovered the bowl of jello. The hours stretched before evening tide when it could be enjoyed with family and friends. I remember nothing else about that birthday, but that gloriously red jello and the sacrifice made to make a little girl happy during very difficult times. Make your special occasions memorable by your thoughtful and imaginative deeds.

Table Setting with Norwegian Charm

It is an indisputable fact that food prepared with care and consideration, and served in beautiful surroundings brings indescribable pleasure, and instills nostalgia for years to come.

One of my most memorable supper evenings was spent dining in a living room in front of a cozy fireplace. The hostess had cleverly covered card tables with floor-length self-made tablecloths, and graced each table with a bud vase containing sweetheart roses. Each place setting had a small candle. With the crackling fire spreading its warmth throughout the room, a background of soft dinner music and glowing candles, the simple, but thoughtfully prepared meal tasted remarkably delicious.

Yet another occasion was breakfast in a mountain cottage. The table was set with a crisp colorful tablecloth and newly picked wild flowers for a centerpiece. It was not expensive and took only a little thought and caring on the part of the hostess.

Norwegians are very conscious of their surroundings and at no time are they more aware of them than mealtime. As far back as I can remember, special celebrations in our home always held foremost the anticipation of what was to come. Not just the preparation of the food, but the beautiful and imaginative decorations we watched mama make.

The tablecloth, be it lace, linen, the colorful permanent pressed ones, or an exquisitely hand-embroidered beauty, it tops the homemaker's "want" list. China, crystal, and silver is chosen with care and used with love and pride. Whatever the occasion, or the season, whatever the reason for a festive celebration, the Norwegian homemaker is always happy to display her talents in an exceptional table setting. To set an attractive table takes only a genuine desire to make the surroundings more pleasant and beautiful for the ones you love and associate with.

Centerpieces: There are many ways to make a memorable centerpiece. Place the flower arrangement on a mirror base, add crystal or silver candlesticks on either side. Or place two or three flowering plants down the center of the table, interspersed with complimentary or contrasting color candles.

Winter scene: A winter scene can also be created with a mirror as a base, fluffy cotton around the edges, a few skaters, a little tree and a bench on the side, floating candles in glass or crystal containers.

Shell fish dinner: For a shell fish dinner use a burlap tablecloth. Heavy pewter plates, or pottery and mugs would be great for such a party. No beautiful crystal and porcelain here. Place a container with sand, in a low, oblong wood box, down the center of the table. In the sand, wrap and bury special little favors. Around the sand place pretty shells, some small drift wood pieces, and floating-type candles, fastened into halved, cut out potato, covered with enough sand so only the candle will show. When dinner is through pass out tiny toy spades or spoons to each guest so they may dig for their special "treasure" you have buried for them. I promise you this center piece will start a lively conversation.

Fruit: Fruit always makes a beautiful centerpiece, if used as part of the dessert. Wash and polish fruit. Tuck fruit knives strategically around the fruit which has been arranged in a beautiful bowl. Remember color combinations and different textures of fruit.

A splendid cake: Another elegant, as well as popular Norwegian centerpiece is kransekake which has been decorated for the occasion. This too, may serve a dual purpose - as centerpiece and dessert. When serving, in order to preserve the original shape and beauty of the *kransekake*, begin by removing the bottom ring first and

I believe most Norwegians, like myself, are instilled with the idea that making their surroundings beautiful is an important and rewarding task. When it comes to table settings, most pride themselves in setting a colorful, beautifully coordinated table. Everything used for setting the table should be the best affordable. Since Norway abounds in many talented craftsmen and artists, who incidently, are second to none in the world, the homemaker may choose from a variety of styles in dishes, glassware and silverware.

cutting into suitable portions. Progress upward, until as the rings become small enough they may be served whole.

Setting the table: It seems so simple to set a table. I am not one for formalities and rules, though I like things to be gracious. I believe you make people happy when you care about them, and try to make pleasant surroundings. Yet, over the years I have been in places were the hosts have been uneasy, not being quite sure if they are "doing it right". It is for you I am adding these suggestions, that they might help you to feel more comfortable.

There are many ways of setting a table, but certain basic rules which are familiar to most, insure a pretty table. Make sure table overhang is even on all sides - 12 inches is about right.

Place setting: Place settings should be arranged immediately opposite each other and the same distance from the table edge. Tableware needs differ depending on the occasion, and we can add or take away accordingly. Place forks on left side of plate with dinner fork next to the plate, then salad fork. Place knives on right side with meat knife next to plate, then fish knife (if needed) and then soup spoon. In other words, arrange in order needed. In Norway the dessert spoon is placed above the plate with the handle facing right; the dessert fork likewise, with the handle facing left. A coffee or teaspoon is usually placed on the saucer. All stemware is centered above the plate, and to assure ease in serving, place the tallest glass to the left. The cup is placed on the right of the stemware and the salad plate to the left. Some meals require a finger bowl which is brought in at the end of the meal, filled three-fourth full with warm water, with a lemon wedge on the edge of the bowl.

Napkins: For a more formal party, fabric napkins are perhaps desirable, but in today's shops we find such a variety of quality paper napkins that you must use your judgement to fit the particular occasion. Napkins will add yet another dash to the table if they contrast in color from the tablecloth. They can be folded in many different and interesting shapes. A crowded table is neither relaxing nor pretty.

In days past, it was fashionable to fold the napkins in various shapes to add a festive air to the table. Today we try to simplify our busy lives. However, from time to time it is fun to add a little extra touch. A sampling of napkin folding follow. For honored guests, such as bride and groom, Norwegians on occasions fold their napkins differently from the rest.

Serving: All foods should be served from your guests' left side, and any plates or dishes should be removed from their right. Make certain that the same guests are not always served last. When soup is served, if it is supposed to be hot, be sure that it is piping hot. If it is to be cold, be sure it is thoroughly chilled. Soup should be served from the guest's right side. For self-service from a tray, it should be offered from the left. Serving pieces should be so placed on a platter or bowl as to eliminate the need for reaching. Throughout the meal the host or hostess should ascertain that her guests are well supplied with beverage at all times. When you are ready to serve dessert, remove all dishes from the table - everything except glasses, and cups if needed.

Flowers: Yes! You can say it with flowers. Their beautiful vivid colors when combined and properly arranged, will add beauty to any table, not only color but distinction as well. But use them properly.

For example, roses would clash with a crab feast, and daisies would not exactly compliment a formal table setting. Keep your flower arrangements low by utilizing flat bowls or small vases. It is frustrating to try and have a conversation across the table through peep holes in the foliage and flowers. Make the flower arrangement the proper size for table size.

Often during the freezing, dark, and dismal winter months in Norway, flowering potted plants or fresh cut flowers grace tables and window sills. Having been brought up in a home were flowers were as important a purchase on Friday as were the weekly groceries, I find flowers still an important part of my decorating scheme. Contrary to what many believe, they need not be expensive. It is not necessary to buy a pre-arranged centerpiece. Get the fresh cut flowers and arrange them yourself - you do not need a dozen of each. Just five, seven or nine flowers, depending on the occasion or type of flowers purchased. The florist will add a touch of green, or you possibly have all kinds of greenery growing in your own yard. Plant bulbs in pots each fall and they will bloom on your window sill in the middle of the winter. In the summer you need only a few square feet of soil to plant some seeds that will yield flowers all summer long. It takes such little effort and brings an abundance of delight in return.

Candles: Candles are available today in every conceivable color, size and shape. The type that floats on water; thin tapered ones which incorporate well with floral arrangements; tall slender ones for formal gatherings; short, squatty ones and more. And you do not just need to use one candle on each side of the flower arrangement. Use a mirror as a base and group several of one color or in different colors and shapes. It is dazzling.

Family Meals (Familie måltider)

Everyday family meals are the most meaningful, because they are spent with the most important people in the world to you - your family. There are numerous ways to make the table more attractive. First, be sure that the dishes and silverware are sparkling clean. Spread the table with a spotless, colorful tablecloth, or use place mats. For goodness sake, place mats are so unlimited (watch for sales) today, there is no reason one cannot have a variety of them. The plastic ones are excellent for families with small children. Place a few flowers or a bowl of fruit in the center of the table, or some favorite figurines, greens, leaves, or cones. Or make a special center piece for special days. Use candles often. Yes, of course for your family! They too enjoy beauty, and candles have such a soothing, quieting effect. You can make mealtime even more pleasant by folding the napkins in unusual ways.

I cannot resist telling you about another Norwegian person who was a great inspiration to me. Many years ago in Vermont, while I was serving with "Ski for Light" as a guide for the blind, I met Hjalmar Jensen then 78 years young. He was also a guide, accompanying the blind skiers from Norway. On my visit to Norway the following summer I had a lunch date with Hjalmar in downtown Oslo. He was rather distraught, saying his wife, also named Astrid, had been quite ill. And having suffered three heart attacks, he was quite concerned she would not make it this time. Her body was not producing marrow, nor its own blood. She was down to 80 pounds and had shrunk 5½ inches (14 cm). "But", he said, "if you could take the time, even a few minutes to come and meet her, it would mean a lot." I told him I must, and cancelled my next appointment. Within 20 minutes the train had brought us to Nordstrand, a suburb of Oslo, another 10 minute walk and we reached their home.

"Darling we are home," Hjalmar called, as he unlocked their front door. I was ill prepared for the greeting I received. A tiny figure nearly floated from the living room into the hallway. Stylishly dressed in a two piece outfit, with a vest, which minimized how frail she was. A string of pearls around her neck, beautiful well cared for silver gray hair, and a smile so warm and beautiful it would, I am convinced, brighten any gloomy day. She threw her arms out and gave me a hug. I had to double over to reach her cheek to cheek.

Astrid was aglow with enthusiasm and gratitude for life. On my short visit I learned many things from this remarkable 77 year old woman. And why am I telling you this? Because Astrid had learned how to live and make others happy. The home she had created by her sweet spirit, and actions, truly was a heaven on earth. Seven years earlier she had been hit by a street car and had spent several months in the hospital. Her right arm was totally useless yet she received joy from making bread and goodies for her husband, family and friends. And Hjalmar confided that it was Astrid that kept their home sparkling clean.

With pride she led me into her immaculate kitchen. On their small kitchen table was a hand embroidered table cloth, and fresh flowers. "It is all so beautiful!" I exclaimed. She squeezed my hand, "We believe in making it nice for each other," she confided. "We always use a tablecloth, fresh flowers and candles on the table when we share a meal." Her spirit warmed my heart. Let us follow her example and love, and make our homes and meals, a daily celebration for our families.

Napkin Folding

Palm Leaf (Palmeblad)

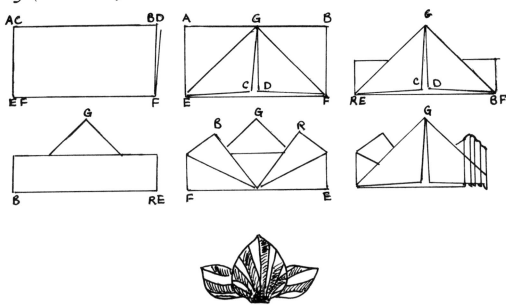

Fold the napkin in two. Fold the top corners C and D down and in toward the center. Fold the underneath half in double downward. Turn the napkin, and fold the corners A and B diagonally upwards. Pleat the whole napkin crosswise. Begin with the center and make equal size folds out to both sides. Fold the lower part of the pleats a little outward on both sides resembling a leaf. Stand by the plate or in a glass. See illustration.

Lily (Lilje)

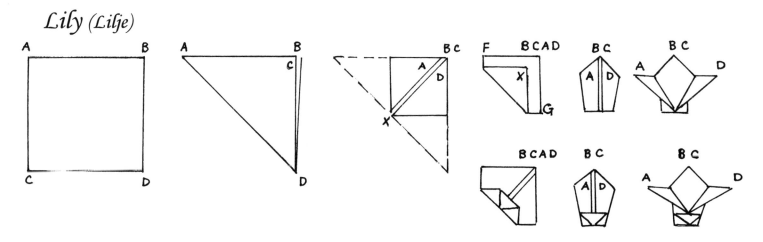

Fold the napkin doubled cornered - in between to make a triangle. Fold the corners A and B up to B and C. Turn the napkin and fold up the corner X. Fold the corners F and G inside each other so that corner X turns in. Slightly fold the corners A and D down, making 1 lily.

Variation:

Fold corner X to make a triple pleat. Follow remainder of directions as explained above.

Iris (Iris)

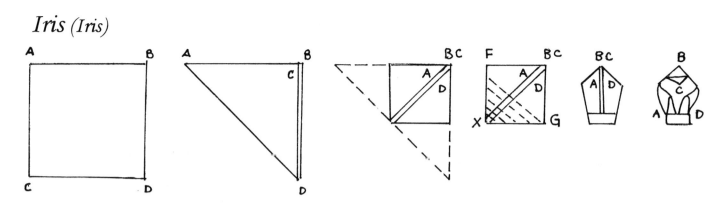

Fold the napkin corner - in between to form a triangle. Fold the corners A and D up to B and C. Fold corner X in, fold as shown in forth drawing. Fold corners F and G inside each other. Fold corners A and D down and in underneath the fold. Fold corner C slightly outward and down.

Fan (Vifte)

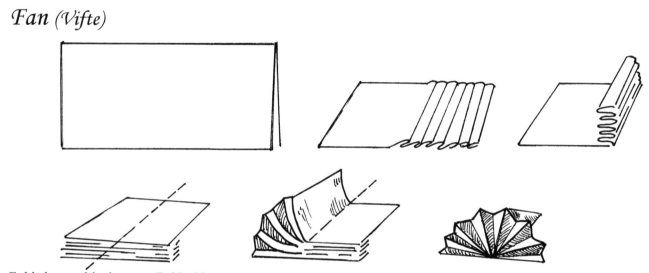

Fold the napkin in two. Fold side AB up, approximately 1¼-1½-inch (3-4 cm) from the double fold. Turn the napkin, and fold the other side up in the same manner. Pleat the whole napkin across, and press the folds tightly together. Carefully pull out both outer edges. Fold carefully out and down all the "in-folds" both on the outside and on the top, see illustration. Display the napkin to form a fan.

Candle *(Lys)*

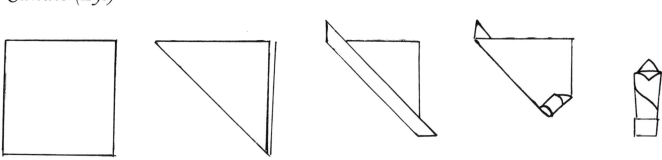

Place the napkin double corner in between, making a triangle. Fold one corner up along the long side of the triangle. Roll the triangle into a tight roll, so that the corner which was folded up is now on the outside of the roll. Fasten the tip in the fold, to help hold the roll in place. Fold one of the top tips slightly outward.

Slipper *(Tøffel)*

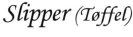

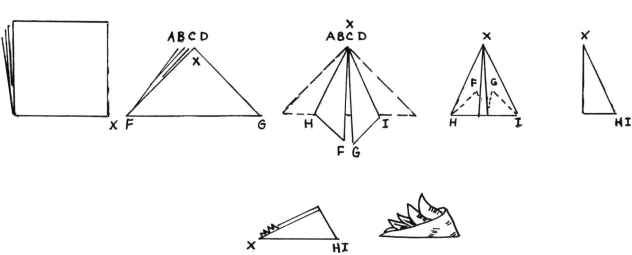

Fold the napkin in fourths. Fold corner X up to the opposite corner, forming a triangle. Turn the napkin so that the corners ABCD face upwards. Fold the corners F and G downward meeting in the center below the fold. Fold them down and up on the other side of the napkin, and fold the napkin double up over the folded corners, forming the slipper. Carefully pull up the folded corners.

Viking Ship (Vikingskip)

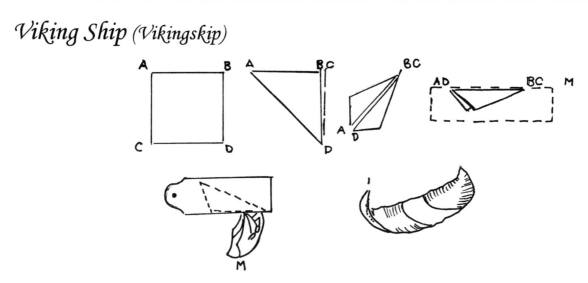

Make your own viking ship to serve crackers, cookies, nuts, and other treats in.

The napkins must be heavily starched. Place the napkin flat on the table. Place a piece of wax paper on top, the same size as the napkin. With the paper inside fold the napkin in two, forming a triangle. Fold the corners A and D toward each other, and double the napkin once more. Place the napkin in a towel which has been folded, with the whole fold turned inward. Place the towel with the napkin inside underneath a cutting board. Press down hard with your left hand, and with a jerk, pull the tip of the towel where the napkin lies, with your right hand, making it wrinkled.

Repeat with a second napkin. Fasten a thin steel thread, on the inside, in the tip of the napkin, enabling the tip to point upwards. Place the two napkins together, and cover the connection with another napkin if necessary.

Special Helps

Temperature Conversion Table *(Temperatur forvandling)*

Centigrade	Fahrenheit	Centigrade	Fahrenheit
63	145	180	356
71	160	190	375
93	200	200	392
100	212	205	401
107	225	210	410
110	230	218	424
121	250	220	428
135	275	225	437
140	284	232	450
149	300	246	475
160	320	260	500
163	325	274	525
177	350	288	550

To convert into centigrade into fahrenheit: multiply by 9, divide by 5, add 32.
To convert fahrenheit into centigrade: subtract 32, multiply by 5, divide by 9.

U.S. and Metric Measures *(U.S. og metersystem)*

SOLID MEASURES

U.S. Measures - Metric Measures

Ounces	Grams
1	28.35
2	56.70
3	85.05
4	113.40
5	141.75
6	170.10
7	198.45
8	226.80
9	255.15
10	283.50
11	311.85
12	340.20
13	368.55
14	396.90
15	425.25
16	453.60

LIQUID MEASURES

U.S. Measures - Metric Measures

Fluid Ounces	U.S. Measures		Milliliters
	1	tsp.	5
¼	2	tsp.	7
½	1	tbsp.	15
1	2	tbsp.	28
2	1/4	cup	56
3	3/8	cup	84
4	1/2	cup	112
5	5/8	cup	140
6	3/4	cup	170
7	7/8	cup	198
8	1	cup	225
9	1 1/8	cups	250
10	1 1/4	cups	280
11	1 3/8	cups	308
12	1 1/2	cups	336
13	1 5/8	cups	364
14	1 3/4	cups	392
15	1 7/8	cups	420
16	2	cups	448
17	2 1/8	cups	476
18	2 1/4	cups	504

Note: Measures are approximate.

U.S. and Metric Weights and Measures (U.S. og meter-system vekt og mål)

Conversion Formulas: Norwegian, American, Metric

To convert	Multiply	By
Grams to ounces	The grams	0.035
Ounces to gram	The ounces	28.35
Liters to quarts	The liters	0.95
Quarts to liters	The quarts	1.057

NOTE: The measurements used in this book follow the preceeding charts. However when converted they are rounded off to the nearest 0 or 5 degrees.

Common Kitchen Measures (Alminnelig vekt og mål)

1 tsp.	=	$^1/_3$ tbsp.	¼ cup	=	4 tbsp.
1 tbsp.	=	3 tsp.	$^3/_8$ cup	=	5 tbsp. or ¼ cup plus 2 tbsp.
2 tbsp.	=	$^1/_8$ cup or 1 fluid ounce	$^5/_8$ cup	=	10 tbsp. or ½ cup plus 2 tbsp.
4 tbsp.	=	¼ cup or 2 fluid ounces	$^7/_8$ cup	=	¾ cup plus 2 tbsp.
5$^1/_3$ tbsp.	=	$^1/_3$ cup or 2$^2/_3$ fluid ounces	1 cup	=	½ pint or 8 fluid ounces
8 tbsp.	=	½ cup or 4 fluid ounces	2 cups	=	1 pint or 16 fluid ounces
16 tbsp.	=	1 cup or 8 fluid ounces	2 pints	=	1 quart liquid, or 4 cups
			4 quarts	=	1 gallon, liquid

Boiling Milk (Koking av melk)

When you boil milk, use a heavy bottomed kettle. Avoid using an iron kettle unless it has a smooth bottom. Stir occasionally as the milk is brought to a boil. Watch carefully so it does not boil over. Try not to use milk for boiling direct from the refrigerator. It takes longer to boil and it tends to scorch easily. Never boil milk for a long period of time as too long of cooking period will reduce nutrients.

Whipping Cream (Visping av fløte)

Chill all equipment, or set the bowl in a larger bowl with water and lots of ice. Use a rounded-off bowl of proper size for the amount of cream needed. If you use an electric mixer leave part of the beaters above the cream as this helps to whip air into the cream and prevents it from turning to butter. The best way however, is to use those fun large, balloon-type whisks. I believe it gives the cream a better flavor. Underbeat the cream, rather than over-beat, the goal is a soft, flavorful cream.

Smorgasbord *(Smørgåsbord)*

A Norwegian food fare leaves an explicit and lasting impression on visitors to Norway. Especially so when it comes to the koldtbord, *or, the better known word,* Smørgåsbord, *pronounced Smur-gaws-boor. I have brought tourists to Norway, to the fjord hotels and mountain resorts, and when they were introduced to these culinary delicacies they were amazed. Tables arrayed with an abundance of Norway's best, and colorful foods make every guest excited to taste and enjoy.*

The *smørgåsbord* is a Scandinavian tradition. In Norway it goes back many centuries, having its start at the country weddings, baptisms, or other celebrations. Due to distances and rough travel these celebrations were not a common occurrence, and when people came together they celebrated for several days. The invited guests helped by contributing the best from their kitchens, allowing the hostess to keep her guests well fed. Accordingly the tables were weighed down with a sumptuous array of delicious foods. In the 17th century the custom was firmly established in private homes, and during the last century the tradition spread to restaurants and hotels.

To the novice the *smørgåsbord* at first glance is overwhelming. Many make the mistake of sampling each food the first time around, but this does not allow one to fully savor the different flavors of the great variety of foods.

But do not despair, there are certain procedures to the manifest plethora of the *smørgåsbord*. It will increase your enjoyment if you try to follow them.

Start with bread and butter, and some of the wide variety of herring dishes offered. You most likely will find pickled herring, mustard, tomato, curried, sour cream, and herring in cream sauce, as well as herring salads. Follow this with the other varieties of fish, trout, salmon, lobster, shrimp, eel, etc.

Next in turn are the egg dishes and salads, then different kinds of meat. A well planned *smørgåsbord* usually also offers an assortment of hot dishes, both meat and fish and finally, an assortment of cheeses and fruits for dessert. If you long for the delectable sweets you have read about, there will be more cakes, puddings and creams than you thought possible.

Aquavit *(Akevitt)*

In the early stages of the history of this drink (Norway's "Firewater") various spices and other plant matter was added to the liquor in order to improve its flavor. Later, when the producers learned to refine their products and to make neutral spirits, the same spices were still added; no longer to cover the bad taste, however, but simply in order to give the purer liquid any taste at all.

Caraway was a common spice and it grew wild in the district of Trøndelag north and south of Trondheim, and around lake Mjøsa in central Norway. These very same districts also had the country's largest potato production-which meant, of course, that it was here the early distilleries were founded. Thus, caraway was a natural choice for flavoring; not only was the local supply abundant, but it was also considered a particularly fresh and appetizing spice.

Caraway seeds in addition, seem to have a natural affinity to quite a number of Norwegian food specialties. This fact may be the main reason why the Norsemen have remained faithful to the *traditional* Norwegian *Akevitt* despite the fact that is hardly ever advertised. Potato is the base ingredient, but the caraway gives it its special flavor. It was the spread of the potato throughout Norway which led to the production of liquor on an industrial scale in Norway. Up to the time of the arrival of the potato in Norway, grain was more commonly used by private individuals who made their own liquor. But the potato was much less expensive and soon became the staple raw material. The necessary process became too complicated and called for much more elaborate equipment and thus the production of liquor on an industrial scale.

The line *akevitt* is a specialty which goes back to the days of the old sailing ships, when the Norwegian Akevitt sailed the seven seas. Today the Norwegian state monopoly still sticks with tradition. The Akevitt sails to Australia and back. The colorful labels with the old sailing ships on each bottle of Akevitt certify that the Akevitt has been to Australia and back, and has crossed the Equator.

There are many imported liquors for sale in Norway. Wine consumption has also had quite an increase, but Akevitt still is the overall favorite of the Norwegians. Any liquor that is yet lavished with the cost of a trip half way around the world is still the most unique and most highly prized by those who are "in the know."

To serve Akevitt the bottle must be cold enough to be frosty with dew, and experts say the glass should be small enough to make it possible for the dram to get lukewarm before it is finished. Akevitt has at times been called "firewater," and a warning is out to the newcomer not to overdo. It is a mighty powerful drink! On many old Norwegian drinking bowls this saying has been found:

Drik min ven, men drik med maade;
drik, men lad fornuften raade.

Drink, my friend, but drink with moderation;
drink, but let good judgement rule.

Kefir *(Kefir)*

Kefir is a cultured milk product used in some traditional recipes. If you are unable to obtain unflavored kefir in your area, (check with your Natural Food Stores) you can purchase kefir culture, which never needs to be replaced. If you cannot find it in your area, see Sources.

Tips for Freezing *(Tips om å fryse mat)*

Each year families loose valuable nutrition, not to mention the thousands, if not millions of dollars lost due to inadequate packaging of frozen food. It is a total waste to spend time, energy, and money on baking or preparing nutritious foods only to loose the flavor, color, and nutrition to freezer burns because time was not allowed to wrap the food properly.

Plastic wrap, plastic bags made for freezing, or aluminum foil is best. Be sure to squeeze out as much air as possible from the plastic bags. To prevent punctured plastic and light from getting to the food the final cover should be heavy brown paper (cut from paper sacks), tape and mark weight, date and contents correctly. (NO! You will not remember the date nor what it is).

It is nice to have fancy, and often expensive, food containers and wrapped packages in the freezer. But it is not necessary. You can have well wrapped foods without spending a lot of money. Rinsed out milk or juice cartons, cottage cheese or yogurt containers are excellent for storing soups, sauces, and casseroles. Mark and seal correctly.

Delfia Coco-Fat (Delfia kokosmatfett)

Delfia coco-fat is similar to margarine in consistency, but with a totally different flavor. It is made from the oil of the coco-nut. Imported from Norway, it is available in 8.8 oz. (250 g) packages. It can be purchased from most Scandinavian Delicatessens. If your store does not carry this product, see Sources.

Salt of Hartshorn - Ammonium Carbonate (Hjortetakk)

At one time hjortetakk was made from deer antlers, but today it is chemically produced and can be purchased at a drug store as Ammonium carbonate - Aqua ammoniae, or salt of hartshorn. It is also stocked by most Scandinavian Delicatessens.

Salt of hartshorn was the leavening agent used in cookies and crackers. It may leave a bitter taste in large cakes which contain a larger portion of moisture. However, Norwegian cookies, known for their crispness and delicate texture, owe some credit for these qualities to salt of hartshornt. It should be kept in a tightly covered glass jar or it will quickly loose its effectiveness. It has a characteristic potent odor of ammonia which disappears during the cooking process. You will find it in Scandinavian Delicatessens or see Sources.

Pearl Sugar (Pearl Sugar)

Pearl sugar is a coarse sugar used in Norway to sprinkle on cookies, pastries and coffee cakes before baking. It is sometimes called crystal sugar. You will find it in Scandinavian Delicatessens, or you may substitute coarsely crushed sugar cubes.
See Sources.

Syrup (Sirup)

The syrup recommended in all recipes throughout this book, unless otherwise stated, and which most closely resembles the syrup used in Norway, is a partially inverted refiner's syrup, such as Lyle's Golden Syrup from England, available at many supermarkets or at import delicatessens. See Sources.

Potato Starch Flour *(Potetmel)*

When potato starch flour is used in breads and cakes it acts as a preservative and also results in a more moist product. When used for baking, substitute _ cup (1½ dl) of potato starch flour for 1 cup (2½ dl) all-purpose flour.

Anything thickened with potato starch flour should be cooled quickly. Sprinkle with a little sugar to prevent film from forming. As a thickening agent, substitute 1½ teaspoons potato flour for 1 tablespoon all-purpose flour.

Using potato flour is quick and easy. But it is important to know how it works, so you will not end up with a leathery consistency from overcooking, or a floury taste from not bringing the food to a boil. There are a couple of methods you may use;

Thickening method 1: Mix potato flour with a little cold water. If left standing awhile, it settles on the bottom. Just give it a quick stir just before using. Bring the food to be thickened to a boil. Remove the pan from direct heat, and add the potato starch flour thickening in a thin stream, stirring *slowly*, but continually while adding. This will prevent lumping, but stirring too vigorously may cause lumping. Place pan back on the heat and bring to a boil while continuing to stir. Remove from heat. If boiled too long it may become watery or leathery.

Thickening method 2: The following method is best for small portions. Place the potato starch flour and food to be thickened together in a small sauce pan, bring to a boil and stir *slowly* until it begins to boil. Remove from heat. The starchy grains in potato starch flour are rather large and take a little while before they stick. When the foods and potato starch flour is mixed while cold it has time to expand and begin to stick during the heating process, and the consistency will be smooth. See Sources.

Potato starch flour, sometimes called potato flour, is available from most Scandinavian delicatessens, health food stores, and now in many supermarkets. It is an excellent thickening agent for fruit soups, compotes, sauces and creams, and is also used in cookies and cakes.

Vanilla Bean *(Vaniljestang)*

Some climbing tropical orchids produce a cylindrical, yellow-greenish colored bean or pod, from 5-10 inches (10-25 cm) long. These pods are cured and dried and during the process they shrink and turn to a mahogany brown color. These vanilla beans give the finest flavor and aroma of vanilla.

To get maximum flavor from the vanilla beans when purchased, they should be moist and soft, not stiff and dry. If you keep them wrapped with plastic wrap in an airtight jar, they will stay fresh for months. Some people freeze them. Either method works.

To scrape the seeds loose, place the bean on a hard surface, and cut lengthwise. Scrape down the length of the bean with a teaspoon, and place the beans in a mound with a little granulated sugar from the recipe. With the tip of your finger, work it back and forth and in circles until the seeds are totally separated from the sugar. Then steep up to 30 minutes in the liquid called for in the recipe.

To make vanilla sugar, split the vanilla bean in half, and place in a pound of confectioners' or granulated sugar in an air tight jar for one week. Use as directed in the recipes.

Vanilla Sugar *(Vaniljesukker)*

See Vanilla Bean on how to make your own, or purchase from Scandinavian Delicatessens, or other specialty shops. See Sources.

Saffron (Safran)

It is said that saffron is the world's most expensive spice. Keep in mind, however, you are not buying it by the pound. Recipes only call for minute quantities. And this spice is a traditional spice used in Norway.

One ounce of commercial saffron takes upward of 4000 flowers of the purple autumn crocus, which grows, and is harvested by hand in Spain. (Turkey and India also have choice saffron). It has a vibrant golden color. The long threads come packed in vials or you may purchase small packets in powder form. Heat the threads in a little liquid from the recipe, leave in, or strain if desired. The powder dissolves quickly in any liquid. See Sources.

Cardamom (Kardemomme)

Cardamom is an Asiatic plant of the ginger family, and a favorite spice in Norwegian baking. Very expensive and worth every penny!

The small cardamom pods (break away and discard) house the black seeds used in the baking. The cardamom pods are either, brown, white or green depending on which method is used to dry them.

Grind only enough cardamom seeds (using a mortar and pestle) as needed for your recipe, their flavor dissipates rather quickly. They are highly aromatic and *an absolute "must spice"* in Norwegian baking. You will find ground cardamom in the spice section of supermarkets, but if cardamom pods are available, choose them first. See Sources.

Orange and Lemon Rind (Appelsin og sitronskall)

Instead of throwing out all those orange and lemon peels, grate some of them. Wash the fruit well. Grate only the orange and yellow peel, the white part though rich in bioflavonoids (an important part of the vitamin C complex) it will leave a bitter taste. Use a dry brush to easily remove all the rind from the grater. If this is too much trouble for you some gourmet shops now have Citrus oils, squeezed from the rind of the fresh fruits; no oil is added. About ½ teaspoon citrus oil equals 1 tablespoon of rind. They can be ordered by mail from The King Arthur Flour Baker's Catalogue. See Sources.

Sources (Kilder)

Braun Food Preparation Center: There are many good food processors on the market, but if you do not have one, or are considering acquiring one, I can highly recommend Braun, a German made 5 in 1 Food Preparation Center. I became interested in Braun on one of my trips to Norway, since several of the people I visited, used and were extremely pleased with Braun.

Five classical appliances in one, it efficiently does the kneading, stirring, mixing, beating, grating, shredding, slicing, chopping and ice crushing, both simply and quickly. It has a mixing/kneading bowl, a universal bowl, and a glass blending, chopping and ice crushing jug. It saves effort and hours. Though I have explained the traditional way of preparing the recipes in this book, I have used Braun whenever a food processor could be used. It is easy to adapt the recipes to using the Braun Food Preparation Center by using their easy to follow booklets. For information write or call: **Braun International, 66 Broadway, Rt. 1, Lynnfield, MA 01940 1-800-272-8611.**

For Scandinavian foods and tools used in this book, call or write for flyers and catalogs:

Glada Grisen, Svenska Stuga Butik, 905 Main Street, Lake Geneva, WI. 53147 1-800-688-0905
Gloria's Scandinavian Gifts, 11915 S. Park Avenue, Tacoma, Wa. 9844-5237 (206) 537-8502
Jacobs of Wilmar, Inc., 5250 Hwy. 71, N.E., Wilmar, MN 56201 (612) 235-5058
Nordic Delicacies, Inc., 6909 3rd Avenue, Brooklyn, N.Y. 11209
Olsen's Scandinavian Foods, 2248 N.W. Market St. Seattle, Wa. 98107 (206) 783-8288
Scandinavian Gift Shop, 2016 N.W. Market Street, Seattle, Wa. 98107 (206) 784-1970
Scandinavian Specialty Prod., Inc., 8539-15th Ave. N.W., Seattle, Wa. 98117 (206) 784-7020
Sweet Celebrations, 7009 Washington Ave. South Edina, Mn. 55439 1-800-328-6722.
Rogaland Fruit Spreads: So undescribably delicious, their flavors are reminiscent of the fresh wild berries we picked during the Norwegian summers. All types, including lingonberries and cloudberry spreads. Rogaland also carries classic juices. Free catalog: **Rogaland Imports,** 2208 15th Street, San Francisco, CA 94114
(415) 255-2700 Fax (415) 487-9026

King Arthur Flour Baker's Catalog: All types of kitchen equipment and bread baking supplies. They sell the digital electronic Add 'n' Weigh Scale by Terraillon. It weighs in both grams and ounces. And the Kitchen Whiz (and it is), a calculator, clock and timer, but most important it instantly converts the metric weight and measures to US measures. For free catalog write to: P.O. Box 876, Norwich, Vermont 05055-0856 1-800-343-3002

Kefir Granules; J. Vee. Health and Diet Foods, 3720 Pacific Ave. S.E. Olympia, WA. 98501 (206) 491-1930.

Pero: An instant natural hot beverage from Germany, which my grandmother used to drink in Norway! Many of my coffee drinking friends have changed to Pero. No caffeine and delicious, it is made from malted barley, barley, chicory and rye. If your market does not carry it yet, write:
Alpursa, P.O. Box 25846, Salt Lake City, UT 84125.

Scandinavian books and/or other products.

Bergquist Imports, Inc., 1412 Highway 33 South, Cloquet, Mn. 55720 1-800-328-0853
Norse Imports, 2116 N.W. Market St. Seattle, Wa. 98107 (206) 784-9420
Penfield Press, 215 Brown St. Iowa City, Iowa 52245 (319) 337-9998
Scandisc, 7616 Lyndale Ave.S., Minneapolis, Mn. 55423 1-800-468-2424

Norwegian Newspapers

Norway Times, 481-81st St. Brooklyn, N.Y. 11209 (718) 238-1100
Western Viking, 2405 N.W. Market St. #201, PO Box 70408, Seattle, Wa. 98107 (206) 784-4617

Credits

Sources of Photographs are:

Ragge Strand in co-operation with Tine, Front cover
Mittet Photo, End sheet

Food Photographs:

Peter Austrud, Else Rønnevig with her award winning breads, Party Table at Snøringsmoen, Lillesand, Norway
Forma's Matforum, Assorted Herring Dishes, Cured and smoked meat is always welcome, Norway's Grand Fruit Pie
A/S Freia, The Freia Boy - *Sjokoladegutten*, Daim Cake
Hjemmet, Lamb Roll
Ideal Wasa, Lutefish
Norwegian Seafood Export Council, Pollack Party Soup, Fishing in Lofoten
Office of Information for Fruit and Vegetables, A holiday spread, Sand Tarts, Strull, and Goro, *Nisser* and fruit for a happy and healthy holiday, A promoter of health, Britt Kåsen
Office of Information for Meat, Lamb and Cabbage
Tine, Marinated cheese, Cheese makes any occasion festive, Nøkkelost Quiche, Dessert Cheese, The Dairy Maid's Wafers and Lefse filled with sour cream
Steve Vento, Almond Tower Cake, Shrovetide buns
Lisa Westgaard, Information office for Eggs and Poultry, A Celebration, Marzipan Wedding Cake
Bengt Wilson, Potato Dumplings with meat

Sources for illustrations:

Ambjørnrud, Olga, *Kokebok*, J.W. Cappelens Forlag
Hårdaskost og Hærdasmat, Hedmark Bondekvinnelag 1980
Marleigh (Martha) Harrison
Steinar Bjarne Karlsen

Bibliography: Permission has been granted and recipes and information have been collected from the following sources:

Alle Tiders Bakebok, A/S Freia
Ambjørnrud, Olga, *Kokebok*, J.W. Cappelens Forlag A/S
Askeland, Gunnar, *Norsk Mat*, A/S Husmorforlaget
Daatland, Ellen, *Familien*
Diesen, Tove, *7x7 Slag*, Chr. Schibsteds Forlag, 1993
Facts about Fish, Norwegian Seafood Export Council
Gammel Norsk Bondekost, No. 2 and 3, Norsk Bondekvinnelag
Hoff Norske Potetindustrier, *Knepene som går i glemmeboken*
Hovig, Ingrid Espelid, *The Best of Norwegian Traditional Cuisine*, Gyldendal Norsk Forlag, *1992*
Innli, Kjell E. *The Norwegian Kitchen*, Kom Forlag A/S 1993
Kielland, Ruth Marcussen, *Ostegleder*,

Kielland, Ruth Marcussen, *Milkshake og Gamalost,* Gyldendal Norsk Forlag A/S, Meierienes Prøvekjøkken
King Oscar, USA, Inc., *A Norwegian Sea Food Saga*
Kongsten, Liv Gregersen, Forma Matforum A/S
Kåsen, Britt, Office of Information for Fruit and Vegetables
Landsverk, Halvor, *Gilde og Gjestebod, Det Norske Samlaget*
Lindstad, Anna-Karin, Tine
Mælseter, Eva, Hjemmet
A/S Nestle, Norway, *Julegotter med Viking Melk*
Nordahl, Evan, Office of Information for Meat
Viking Magazine, Sons of Norway, Minneapolis, MN
Tveit, Guri, Office of Information for Egg and Poultry

English Index

Norwegian Index